# THE CHURCH DIVIDED

## the Holy Spirit
## and a spirit of seduction

Also by Robert Wise:
   *The Pastors' Barracks*
   *How Not to Go Crazy*
   *Your Churning Place*
   *Inner Healing*
   *You Bet Your Life*
   *When There Is No Miracle*

Also by Paul Yonggi Cho:
   *The Fourth Dimension*
   *The Fourth Dimension, Volume 2*
   *The Leap of Faith*
   *Solving Life's Problems*
   *Successful Home Cell Groups*
   *Suffering . . . Why Me?*

Also by Dennis and Rita Bennett:
   *The Holy Spirit & You*
   *The Trinity of Man*

Also by Dennis Bennett:
   *Nine O'Clock in the Morning*
   *How to Pray for the Release of the Holy Spirit*

Also by Trevor Dearing:
   *God and Healing of the Mind*
   *Supernatural Healing Today*

Also by Jim Glennon:
   *Your Healing Is Within You*
   *How Can I Find Healing?*

Also by Mark Virkler:
   *Dialogue With God*
   *Seduction?? A Biblical Response*

Also by Kathryn Kuhlman:
   *A Glimpse Into Glory*

# THE CHURCH DIVIDED

## the Holy Spirit
## and a spirit of seduction

### Robert Wise et al.

Bridge Publishing, Inc.
South Plainfield, NJ

**The Church Divided**
© 1986 Bridge Publishing, Inc.
All rights reserved
Printed in the United States of America
ISBN 0-88270-622-5
Library of Congress catalog number 86-71132
Bridge Publishing, Inc.
2500 Hamilton Blvd.
South Plainfield, NJ 07080

# Contents

# About the Contributors

*Robert Wise*—Pastor of Our Lord's Community Church in Oklahoma City, a fast-growing congregation of the Reformed Church in America, Wise has emphasized meeting people's emotional and spiritual needs through his writing and ministry.

*Paul Yonggi Cho*—Pastor of the Full Gospel Central Church in Seoul, Korea, the world's largest church, now with over 500,000 members. "I discovered in Cho's *The Fourth Dimension* the reality of that dynamic dimension in prayer that comes through visualizing the healing experience"—Robert Schuller.

*Dennis & Rita Bennett*—"When, in 1960, Father Dennis Bennett announced to his congregation that he had experienced a new outpouring of God's Spirit, the recent movement can be said to have begun . . . Before long, 'charismatic renewal' became an issue across the land"—*Encyclopaedia Brittanica*. The Bennetts have been among the foremost leaders of spiritual rewewal during the past twenty-five years.

*John Wesley*—The father of the Methodist Church. His preaching and teaching helped form the foundation of the holiness movement, pentecostalism, and the modern charismatic renewal.

*Jim Glennon*—A canon at St. Andrew's Cathedral in Sydney, Australia, Glennon has been the director of the healing ministry at the church for twenty-five years. Dennis Bennett called *Your Healing Is Within You* "a remarkable book that will help many." Agnes Sanford said Glennon "has become known world-wide as a powerful leader in the healing ministry of the Christian church."

*Trevor Dearing*—An Anglican clergyman with a worldwide healing ministry. The 1969 revival at his church, St. Paul's in Hainault, Essex, England, witnessed the gifts of the Holy Spirit, notably conversions, healing and deliverance.

*Kathryn Kuhlman*—One of the foremost woman evangelists of our century. She was particularly noted for the healings which occurred at her services, and for her television broadcasts.

*Mark Virkler*—Dean of Students and teacher at Buffalo School of the Bible in Buffalo, New York. Has had fifteen years of pastoral experience since graduating from Roberts Wesleyan College. The Reverend Thomas Reid has said that the teaching in Virkler's *Dialogue With God* "is going to change the nation by building a new generation of people that hear God's voice."

*Clare Weakley*—Businessman, author and lecturer with a love of John Wesley that prompted him to produce modern-language paraphrases of Wesley's sermons and writings.

*Bill De Arteaga*—An author and researcher who, with his wife, has an active and blessed ministry of inner healing.

*M.L. Huffman*—A professional librarian working both in a Christian counseling center and in the public library system.

# Introduction

We hope and pray that one day Bridge will have to publish a book called *The Church United*. We will see the answer to Jesus' prayer: "That they may be one" (John 17:13).

Even now the answer is coming, as is partly reflected in this book. While we have felt it necessary to address the division and confusion in the church resulting from publication of *The Seduction of Christianity,* the responses in this book, primarily from people accused of seducing the church, come from Christians of many backgrounds, united in their faith in Jesus Christ and eager for the guidance of His Holy Spirit, and full of love for their brothers and sisters.

We are honored to have material in this book written by born-again members of the Episcopal and Anglican churches, the Reformed Church, the Catholic Church, the Methodist Church and the Yoido Full Gospel Church of Seoul, Korea.

It is their purpose and ours to put forward the truth. There is a great need for caution before accepting any teaching as from God; Christians must be vigilantly on guard against the deceptions of the devil. But the contents of this book will, we hope, better equip you to distinguish the work of the Holy Spirit from that of a spirit of seduction, to measure by God's standards, and to decide for yourself who's seducing whom.

# – 1 –

# Two Spirits at Work in the World

The Christian church today is divided—brother against brother. Christian leaders are denouncing each other, making accusations of deception, seduction, even sorcery. In their zeal to guard against the lies of the devil, they have started a witch hunt, becoming themselves accusers of our brethren.

Indeed, the church is receiving guidance not only from the Holy Spirit: as predicted by St. Paul, some are departing "from the faith, giving heed to seducing spirits, and doctrines of devils" (1 Tim. 4:1 KJV). But rather than "test the spirits, to see whether they are from God" (1 John 4:1 NEB), many have been overpowered by a fear of contamination, creating a climate of mistrust. Serious errors *have* crept into some Christian teaching, and doctrines spawned in hell are leading many astray. But we must remember the admonition to "judge not" (Matt. 7:1), and bear in mind that the Father grants the Holy Spirit to those who ask Him (Luke 11:13).

Let us look at the evidence that two spirits are at work in the world today, and ask the Spirit of Truth to guide us (John 16:13).

### The Holy Spirit at work in the world

The Spirit dwells in the Church and in the hearts of the faithful as in a temple (1 Cor. 3:16, 6:19). In them he prays and bears witness to the fact that they are adopted sons (Gal. 4:6; Rom. 8:15-16, 26). The Spirit guides the Church into the fullness of truth (John 16:13) and gives her a unity of fellowship and service. He furnishes and directs her with various gifts, both hierarchical and charismatic, and adorns

1

her with the fruits of his grace (Eph. 4:11-12; 1 Cor. 12:4; Gal. 5:22). By the power of the gospel, he makes the Church grow, perpetually renews her, and leads her to perfect union with her Spouse. The Spirit and the Bride both say to the Lord Jesus, "Come!" (Rev. 22:17). Thus the Church shines forth as "a people made one with the unity of the Father, the Son and the Holy Spirit."[1]

This concise statement of the Holy Spirit's work comes from the Second Vatican Council of the Catholic Church. It not only describes well the Spirit in the world today; it is a statement that nearly every Christian could agree with, and as such represents an ideal antithesis to the situation described in this book: it represents the church united.

John Wesley also wrote of the Holy Spirit's role, describing in more personal terms His work in individuals[2]:

The Holy Spirit was to give them what is essential for all Christians in all ages. It was to give them the mind which was in Jesus. It was to give them the holy fruit of the Spirit, without which no one is a Christian. The Holy Spirit was to fill them with love, joy, peace, long-suffering, gentleness, and goodness. The Holy Spirit would endue them with faith, fidelity, meekness, and temperance. God's Spirit would enable them to crucify the flesh with its affections and lusts, its passions and desires. As a result of that inward change, they would be able to fulfill all outward righteousness. Through the work of the Holy Spirit, Christians could walk as Jesus also walked in the work of faith, in the patience of hope, and in the labor of love.

The "Life in the Spirit" seminars, an ecumenical teaching series on baptism in the Holy Spirit, further describe the Spirit's work in Christians[3]:

The Lord is working to build His church today in the same way that He worked to build His tabernacle among the people of Israel, or to build the Christian community at Corinth. He has called us to be craftsmen, to be builders in His plan. And the same Holy Spirit that brought ability and understanding to the craftsmen for the tabernacle will work in us to give us the ability and understanding and skill we need to build up the people of God. . . .

Today Christians of all denominations are discovering the power that Jesus gives His people through the Holy Spirit. They are discovering the power to live together in love and peace, to heal the sick and comfort the afflicted, and to worship God with new and abundant praise. Above all, they are discovering a deeper and more personal relationship with Jesus Christ as their very own Lord and Savior.

A salient mark of the Holy Spirit in the church today is the widespread renewal of the gifts of the Holy Spirit that were evidenced in the early church. The fruits of the Spirit (Gal. 5:22) are visibly present in the lives of those blessed with the gifts of the Spirit (1 Cor. 12). Dennis and Rita Bennett wrote of this renewal of the Spirit's gifts[4]:

> . . . the baptism in the Holy Spirit has penetrated the "old-line" churches. Today thousands of ministers and priests of the older denominations have received the Holy Spirit as on the Day of Pentecost, as have millions of lay people. Now, while the testimony goes forward with ever-increasing strength, there is great need for teaching. Someone has pointed out that the return of the appetite to a sick person is one of the first signs of recovery. God's People have been very sick, nigh unto death, but now the Church of God is convalescent, and very hungry!

That hunger has led many Christians to seek the word of life with the anointing of the Spirit outside their home churches. This has resulted in both blessings and problems. Television and radio evangelism, for instance, have brought the gospel message and witness of the Christian way of life to countless people who might never have been reached otherwise. The proliferation of independent ministries, however, has made many vulnerable to straying from the faith because of lack of submission to teaching authority. If believers are to take advantage of the many ministries and programs available, they also must cautiously examine the teachings and practices presented before accepting them as from God.

3

## A spirit of seduction at work in the world

In order "to mislead, if it were possible, even God's own people" (Matt. 24:24 PHILLIPS), the evil one has inspired false prophets to preach error. To be effective, it often is truly seductive: evil will appear harmless or even good. A sugar-coated gospel is much easier to swallow. It is very attractive to accept the blessings without the cross; to choose our own path over "the way, the truth, and the life"; to say, "My will be done."

In *A Crisis of Truth,* Ralph Martin wrote[5]:

> Increasingly a question mark is being placed over God's Word, its reliability questioned, its authority denied, its clarity obscured. Increasingly a relativistic and skeptical attitude to truth is arising even . . . among those who hold positions of responsibility.
>
> Pilate's skeptical and relativistic approach to truth made him vulnerable to the various pressures that were working for Jesus' crucifixion and to undo the plan and purpose of God. As growing numbers of even those dedicated to the Church shrug their shoulders with Pilate and say, "What is truth?" it becomes that much easier for spiritual and temporal forces to undo the work of God in the world and crucify Jesus in his Body, the Church. The satanic intentions and strategy did not cease with the Fall of the first human beings, nor with the crucifixion of Jesus. They continued on into the life of the early Church, and on into the life of the Church today. As St. Paul wrote, "My fear is that, just as the serpent seduced Eve by his cunning, your thoughts may be corrupted and you may fall away from your sincere and complete devotion to Christ" (2 Cor. 11:3).

Martin outlined areas in which some members of the Body of Christ are being led astray:

"Implicit or explicit rejection of the authority of God's Word . . . [is being spread] throughout the Church . . . often, it seems, with the explicit purpose of leading God's people away from His Word, and sometimes to the active encouragement of immorality. . . ."[6]

"Even when the unique and absolute claims of Christ are not clearly rejected on an intellectual level, syncretism often fosters an

4

emotional hostility to such claims. This creates an atmosphere that saps the strength of Christianity as effectively as explicit apostasy. If belief about the unique and absolute claims of Christ is unclear, then faith is corrupted, worship becomes enfeebled and distorted, and evangelism ceases. . . .[7]

"Today the vacuum created by the attack on the authority and sufficiency of Scripture and the tradition of the Church has left the way open for a secular humanist mentality to pervade the life of the Christian people. The secular humanist call to fulfill oneself, to achieve individual happiness, to place one's faith in the inevitability of human progress has a powerful hold on the minds of many Christians today.

For many Christians the desire for worldly happiness and success has become the driving force in their lives. . . .[8]"

Yes, the seduction of Christianity is taking place. But we need to be clear about who the enemy is.

# – 2 –

# Discerning the Spirits

If we accept that the church is not only receiving the guidance of the Holy Spirit but is sometimes being led astray by the evil one, it follows that some Christians and even well-meaning leaders of the church are unable to distinguish the leading of the Holy Spirit, to recognize His work or His fruits, or to recognize the counterfeit when it is presented.

In this sense, that the teachings of demons are counterfeits of the inspiration of the Holy Spirit, the errors in the church truly amount to seduction—they sound attractive, appear deceptively good, but in truth are evil. If we are not to close our hearts to divine guidance, we must be able to determine which spiritual impulses lead us to Jesus and to serve Him and others, and which lead away from that.

James Robison wrote[1]:

> The foremost work of God in the Church today is that of teaching His people to hear Him—and to let their fellow-believers hear Him. Much of the division that has crippled the Church stems from the self-centered tendency to lock onto a doctrine or truth, build a man-made shrine to it, erect a fortress to defend it and then condemn all who don't see it or who disagree with it.
>
> God wants to teach us all—and we all need to be taught. If we believe others are in error, we are probably right. But we must handle the situation with love and patience, because we are also in error. Every believer is, to some extent,

7

mistaken or incomplete in what He believes. If we had all the truth, why would the Father feel it necessary to send the Holy Spirit to guide us into it?

The six essays contained in the rest of this chapter address the need for spiritual discernment and how to go about it properly. Let's turn first, then, to a respected leader of the modern church, John Wesley.

# The Witness of the Holy Spirit
# John Wesley

It is the Spirit himself bearing witness with our spirit that
we are the children of God (Rom. 8:16 RSV).

Many men, confused in their understanding, have misinterpreted
this Scripture to the destruction of their souls. They have mistaken
the voice of their imagination for the witness of the Holy Spirit. The
result was that they idly presumed they were children of God while
they were actually doing the works of the devil.

These are truly and properly fanatics in the worst sense of the word.
It is with great difficulty that they are convinced of their error,
especially if they have been deeply into it. All efforts to bring them to
the knowledge of themselves are considered "fighting against God."
Their contrary spirit, which they term "contending earnestly for the
faith," removes them from all usual methods of conviction. In
observing this situation, we may as well say, "Only God can reach
them."

The general results of such delusions are not surprising.
Reasonable men, seeing the effects of this delusion, attempt to
avoid falling into the same error. Those laboring to keep a distance
from fanaticism often lean toward the other extreme. The result
is that they are not apt to believe any who claim to have this witness
of the Spirit. Because some have been mistaken about inner voices,
they assume all can be mistaken. They are ready to classify as fanatics
all who use this abused expression and spiritual concept. They
question whether the witness or testimony of the Spirit is the privilege
of ordinary Christians. Therefore they are apt to conclude this is one
of the extraordinary gifts which belonged only to the apostolic age.

There is no necessity to fall into either one extreme or the other.
We may steer a middle course. We may keep a sufficient distance
from the spirit of error and fanaticism without denying the gift

9

of God. There is no need to give up this gift and great privilege of His children.

To avoid either of these extremes, we need to consider some questions. First, what is this witness or testimony of our spirit? What is the witness of God's Spirit? How does He bear witness with our spirit that we are the children of God? Next, how is this joint testimony of God's Spirit and our spirit distinguished from the presumptions of a natural mind and the delusions of the devil?

First to be considered is the witness or testimony of our spirit. It must be noted that the biblical text does not speak of the witness of our spirit only. There is a real question if the statement of Paul speaks about our own spirit at all. It is very possible that he was speaking only of the witness of God's Spirit.

In the original text, and in the immediately preceding verse, Paul said, "You have received the spirit of sonship [adoption]. When we cry, 'Abba! Father!' it is the Spirit himself bearing witness with our spirit that we are children of God." This denotes God's witness that we are His children at the same time He enables us to cry, "Abba! Father!"

In saying this about the text at hand, I do not exclude the double witness in the new birth experience. There is both the testimony of God's Spirit and the testimony of the Christian's own spirit that he is a child of God.

With regard to the witness of God's Spirit, numerous texts of Scripture describe the marks of the children of God. Every man who applies those scriptural marks to himself may know whether he is a child of God. Thus, he knows first, "For all who are led by the Spirit of God," into all holy tempers and actions, "are sons of God" (Rom. 8:14 RSV). He can have the infallible assurance of the holy writ. So, he may conclude, "I am thus led by the Spirit of God; therefore, I am a son of God."

John agreed to all this in the plain declarations of his first epistle. "By this we may be sure that we know him, if we keep his commandments. Whoever keeps his word, in him truly love for God is perfected. . . . By this we may be sure that we are in him. . . . If you know that he is righteous, you may be sure that every one who does right is born of him" (1 John 2:3, 5, 29 RSV). "We know that we have passed out of death into life, because we love the brethren. . . . By this we shall know that we are of the truth, and reassure our hearts before him" (1 John 3:14, 19 RSV). This is because we love one another, not in word, neither in tongue, but in deed and truth. "By this we know that we abide in him and he in us, because he has given us of his own spirit" (1 John 4:13 RSV). "By this we know that he abides in us, by the Spirit which he has given us" (1 John 3:24 RSV).

It is highly probable that there never had been any Christian who was further advanced in God's grace than the apostle John when he wrote the words above. Notwithstanding his attainment in grace and the knowledge of our Lord Jesus Christ, he applied these marks to himself. John and all the pillars of the church applied these measures to their own souls for the confirmation of their faith.

Yet all this is no more than rational evidence. It is the witness of our spirit, the witness of our reason and understanding. Those who have these marks are the children of God. We who have these marks are children of God.

How does God's Spirit bear witness with our spirit that we are the children of God? The Spirit directly witnesses to our spirit that we are His children. We are assured that Jesus has loved us and given His life for us. We know that our sins are forgiven and forgotten. Faith becomes personal—I, even I, am reconciled to God.

The testimony of God's Spirit must come before the testimony of our own spirit. This is evident by the fact that we must be holy of heart and holy in life before we can be aware that we are so. We must be inwardly and outwardly holy before we can come to believe that we are holy. It is a fact that we must love God before we can be holy at all. Love of God is the root of all holiness. Now we cannot love God until we know He loves us. "We love, because he first loved us" (1 John 4:19 RSV). We cannot know His pardoning love to us until His Spirit witnesses to it in our spirit. So it is evident the testimony of His Spirit must precede our love of God and all holiness. Consequently, the witness of the Holy Spirit to our spirit precedes our inward consciousness of it and the testimony of our spirit concerning it.

At the moment when the Holy Spirit witnesses to our spirit about these things, we love God because He has loved us. Then for His sake we love our brother also. We know all of these things within ourselves, because we know "the things that are freely given to us of God" (1 Cor. 2:12 KJV). We know that we are of God. This is the testimony of our own spirit. Joined with the testimony of God's Spirit, it affirms that we are children of God. As long as we continue to love God and keep His commandments, we remain His children.

11

This joint testimony of our adoption as sons of God can be distinguished from mistaken hopes. It differs from presumptions of the natural mind and delusions from the devil. It is important for all to understand these differences. An error here results in deception of the soul. Such errors can have fatal consequences. Those making these mistakes seldom discover the mistake until it is too late to correct it.

First, how can presumptions of the natural mind be avoided? It is certain that one who has never been convicted of sin is prone to this error. He is caught in self-flattery, always ready to think more highly of himself than he ought. This is especially so in spiritual things. It is not strange to see a worldly egotist also become a spiritual egotist. When he hears of the privilege Christians have as sons of God, he soon persuades himself that he has the Holy Spirit, too. There are many instances of this around us. This same error has occurred throughout history.

The Scriptures have many marks to help us distinguish truth from presumption. The Scriptures describe and outline the circumstances which go before, which accompany, and which follow the new birth.

The Scriptures describe repentance, or conviction of sin, as constantly going before the witness of pardon. "Repent, for the kingdom of heaven is at hand" (Matt. 3:2 RSV). "Repent, and believe in the gospel" (Mark 1:15 RSV). "Repent, and be baptized every one of you in the name of Jesus Christ for the remission of sins" (Acts 2:38 KJV). "Repent ye therefore, and be converted, that your sins may be blotted out" (Acts 3:19 KJV). In conformity to this, the historical church continually places repentance before pardon, or the witness of it. So the church has confessed, "He pardons and absolves all them that truly repent and absolutely believe His holy gospel." Also, "Almighty God . . . has promised forgiveness of sins to all them who, with heart repentance and true faith, turn unto Him."

Anyone who has never known a broken and contrite heart is a stranger to this true repentance. The "remembrance of his sins" has never been "grievous to him." Their burden has never been intolerable. If the unrepentant person has repeated those words, he never meant what he said. He merely paid a compliment to God. For this reason alone, he can know that he is yet to experience the real knowledge of the Son of God.

Next, the Scriptures describe the experience of being born of God which must precede the witness that we are His children. This new birth is a vast and mighty change from darkness to light. It is a change from the power of Satan unto God. It is a resurrection from the dead—a passing from darkness into light. Thus Paul wrote to the Ephesians, "You he made alive, when you were dead through the trespasses and sins in which you once walked . . . even when we were dead through our trespasses, [God] made us alive together with Christ . . . and raised us up with him, and made us sit with him . . . in the heavenly places in Christ Jesus" (Eph. 2:1, 2, 5, 7 RSV).

Present marks will distinguish a child of God from a self-deceiver. The Scriptures describe that joy in the Lord which accompanies the witness of the Holy Spirit. Such joy is a humble joy, which makes the saved sinner cry out, "Now that my eyes see, I abhor my past life. I am the lowest of all sinners."

Wherever that lowliness is, there is meekness, patience, gentleness, and long-suffering. There is a soft yielding spirit. The forgiven child of God has mildness and sweetness, a tenderness of soul which words cannot express.

Now compare that supposed testimony of the Spirit in the presumptuous man. Just the reverse is in him. The more confident he is of the favor of God, the more he is self-exalting, the more haughty and assuming is his behavior. The stronger witness he imagines himself to have, the more overbearing he is to all around him. Such a person is incapable of receiving any reproof, and more impatient of contradiction. Instead of being meek, gentle, teachable, and "swift to hear, slow to speak," he is the contrary. He is not ready to learn from anyone. He is foul and vehement in his temper and eager in his conversation. There can be a kind of fierceness in his air and manner of speaking. His whole deportment is as if he were going to take matters out of God's hands and devour the adversaries by himself.

The Scriptures teach of one more sign of the witness of the Spirit. "This is the love of God, that we keep his commandments" (1 John 5:2 RSV). Jesus himself said, "He who has my commandments and keeps them, he it is who loves me" (John 14:21 RSV). Love rejoices in obedience, in doing at every point whatever is acceptable to God. A true lover of God hurries to do His will on earth, as it is done in heaven.

Is this the character of the pretender to the love of God? Does this obedience mark his life? No. His "love" gives him a liberty to disobey—to break, not keep the commandments of God. Perhaps when he was in fear of God's punishment, he made an effort to do

His will. Now, looking at himself as not under the law, he thinks that he is no longer required to observe it. He is less zealous of good works. He is less careful about abstaining from evil. He is less careful over his own heart and tongue. He is less concerned about denying himself and taking up his cross daily.

In a word, the whole form of his life is changed since he believes himself to be at liberty. He is no longer directing himself to godliness. He does not wrestle with the world and Satan, enduring hardships while agonizing to enter into the kingdom of God at the straight gate. He believes he has found an easier way to heaven. It is a broad, smooth, flowery path, in which he can say to himself, "Take it easy. Eat, drink, and be merry."

It follows with undeniable evidence that he has not the true testimony of his own spirit. He cannot be aware of having spiritual marks which he does not have. He has no meekness, lowliness, and obedience. Because the Holy Spirit cannot witness to a lie, He does not testify that he is a child of God. Because he does not have this Spirit of adoption, he is manifestly a child of the devil.

Know yourself and do not be a miserable self-deceiver. If you are confident of being a child of God, you say that you have the witness in yourself. Can you defy all your enemies? Are you being weighed in the spiritual scale of God and found wanting? The Word of God tries your soul and finds if it is false. If you are not gentle and meek, your joy is worth nothing. It cannot be the joy of the Lord. If you do not keep the commandments, you do not love Him. If not, you do not have the Holy Spirit. Under those circumstances, it is certain and evident by the Scriptures that the Holy Spirit does not bear witness to your spirit that you are a child of God. If you are not, ask Him to remove the scales from your spiritual eyes. Ask that you may know yourself as you are known by God. Ask to receive the sentence of death so you can experience the forgiveness that raises the dead. Hunger to hear His voice say to your spirit, "Be of good cheer. Your sins are forgiven. Your faith has made you whole."

The immediate fruits of the Spirit, ruling in the heart, are love, joy, peace, mercy, humbleness of mind, meekness, gentleness, and long-suffering. The outward fruits are the doing of good to all men and avoiding the doing of evil to any. It is walking in the light with a zealous, uniform obedience to all the commandments of God.

The same fruits can distinguish the voice of the Holy Spirit from any delusion of the devil. Satan's proud spirit will not allow you to be

14

humble before God. He neither can, nor will, soften your heart toward an earnest mourning for God. He cannot steer you into a child's love for the Father.

It is not Satan that enables you to love your neighbor. He will not allow you to put on meekness, gentleness, patience, temperance, and the whole armor of God. He will never be a destroyer of his own work—sin.

It is only Jesus who comes to destroy the works of the devil. As surely as there is holiness from God, and sin from Satan, surely you have the witness in yourself as to whom you belong—Satan or God.

# Discerning of Spirits
## Dennis & Rita Bennett

Before we talk about spiritual discernment we need to discuss discernment in general. First there is what we may call *"natural discernment"* which Christian and non-Christian alike have. This is the judgment that we pass on people and circumstances, and on our own behavior, and is derived from teachings received in our homes, and the effect of our environment and culture. Our natural "consciences" are composed of this kind of material, and therefore are very unreliable. The mind, and that part of it called the conscience, is a mixture of good and evil, truth and error. Its discernment and moral judgments have no absolute value. It is a truism that standards of human morality vary from culture to culture, and from generation to generation, and all the natural mind can tell is what agrees with or is acceptable or unacceptable to the time and place in which we are living. This is what the world in general uses as a basis for decisions. There is no stability in it.

*True intellectual discernment* comes not from the fallen natural mind but from the mind that is being renewed in Christ. This discernment grows as we meet and receive Christ and get to know Him better, through fellowship and through the study of the Word of God. As the book of Hebrews tells us: "Every one that useth milk is unskilful in the word of righteousness: for he is a babe. But strong meat belongeth to them that are of full age, even those who by reason of use have their senses [Greek: *perceptions, judgment*] exercised to discern both good and evil" (Heb. 5:13-14 KJV). As we grow in the Christian life, the Holy Spirit sorts through our minds and consciences, discarding the wrong and adding what is right. If God is permitted to work in this way, as time goes on, our minds and consciences will become more and more in agreement with the Scriptures and with the Holy Spirit living in us. We will become so imbued with the "flavor" of what Jesus Christ is like, and how God

16

works, that we will immediately recognize *intellectually* something that is different. We receive this knowledge, not through trying to develop some mysterious occult ability, but by living close to God in Jesus Christ, and allowing His Spirit to work in our lives. It is very important for believers to develop this kind of discernment. It is a strong defense against false doctrine. We should be able to say immediately: "That doesn't sound like God! God doesn't *act* that way!" if we hear a strange new teaching that is not in keeping with the truth.

Our own behavior toward God and our fellow man will of course be affected by our growth in intellectual discernment. Before Paul accepted Jesus personally, he thought it a matter of good conscience to persecute Christians. After his conversion, and after many years of walking with the Lord, Paul said:

"I have lived in all good conscience before God until this day" (Acts 23:1 KJV). "I do my utmost always to live my whole life with a clear conscience before God and man" (Acts 24:16 PHILLIPS). We should pray that our minds and consciences will be so renewed by the Spirit that we can say this too.

## Discerning of Spirits

We come now to the spiritual gift. Like all of the gifts this does not come through training but is given in a moment when and as it is needed. Any Christian may manifest this gift, but, like the others, it is intensified after the baptism in the Holy Spirit. Believers who have not been baptized in the Spirit are not likely to be aware enough of the activities of Satan to be concerned about discerning of spirits, although, of course, there are exceptions.

By the gift of discerning of spirits the believer is enabled to know immediately what is motivating a person or situation. A believer may be operating under the inspiration of the Holy Spirit, he may be expressing his own thoughts, feelings, and desires from his soul, it is even possible that he may be allowing an alien spirit to oppress him, and be bringing thoughts from that wrong spirit. An unbeliever, of course, may be completely possessed by the wrong spirit. The gift of discerning of spirits immediately reveals what is taking place.

It may help us to understand the gift of discerning of spirits if we recognize what it is like to discern the Holy Spirit. The gospel song says: "There's a sweet, sweet Spirit in this place and I know that it's the Spirit of the Lord!" Believers know that joyful sense of, or witness

17

to, the presence of the Holy Spirit in another person, or in a meeting. When we say: "I really felt the presence of God," we are speaking of the discerning of the Holy Spirit.

Reports from those who work behind the Iron Curtain reveal that this gift becomes very important as persecution increases. There are many cases of Christian recognizing Christian, each "in the Spirit" without having to use words. In one place, Christian meetings were continuously being interfered with, so the brethren simply stopped announcing any time or place for their fellowship, but depended upon the Holy Spirit to tell those who should be there! Everyone was present and accounted for just the same. This was probably a combination of the gift of knowledge and the gift of discernment.

We may understand the discerning of wrong spirits by seeing it as the opposite of all this. The sense of the presence of the Holy Spirit brings joy and love and peace; the discerning of wrong spirits brings a sense of heaviness and unrest. Please note that "wrong spirits" are not, and cannot be, the spirits of people who have died. Discerning of spirits has nothing to do with spiritism or spiritualism. The spirits of departed human beings are *not* on this earth, and to attempt to contact them is forbidden! The "wrong spirits" we are talking about are spoken of in the Scriptures as "the rulers of the darkness of this world," that is, fallen angels or else demons (Eph. 6:12 KJV; Matt. 10:8 RSV).

The story of Elisha and his servant Gehazi is an Old Testament example of the gifts of discerning of spirits and knowledge. Naaman, a captain in the Syrian army, was a leper. In obedience to the prophet Elisha's instructions he washed in Jordan seven times and was healed. Naaman offered Elisha gifts to show his gratitude but Elisha would not accept them. Elisha's servant Gehazi, however, secretly followed Naaman, and lied to him, telling him that Elisha had just received two unexpected guests, and would Naaman please give two changes of clothing and some money—all of which Gehazi, of course, kept for himself. When Gehazi returned to his master, Elisha discerned his dishonest spirit and then knew by the gift of knowledge exactly what had been done (2 Kings 5).

There are many examples of Jesus' discerning spirits. He had not previously met Nathanael, but discerned immediately that he was "an Israelite indeed, in whom is no guile" (John 1:47 KJV). When Peter made his great confession about Jesus: "Thou art the Christ, the Son of the living God!" Jesus commended him. When Jesus began to tell

His followers, however, that He was to die, Peter would not accept His words. He began to rebuke Jesus, saying, "Be it far from thee, Lord: this shall not be unto thee!" Jesus discerned that Peter was speaking in a wrong spirit, and said, "Get thee behind me, Satan: you are an offence unto me: for thou savourest not the things that be of God, but those that be of men" (Matt. 16:15-23 KJV). When Jesus was not received in the village of the Samaritans, James and John were so angry that they asked Jesus whether they should command fire to come down from heaven and consume the people. But Jesus said: "Ye know not what manner of spirit ye are of" (Luke 9:54-55 KJV). We see by these last two examples that even close followers of Jesus can be temporarily misled.

Fulfilled prophecy and other biblical signs indicate that we may be living in the final part of the Last Days. Scripture teaches that before Jesus Christ returns to earth there will be many more deceiving spirits unleashed, so ability to discern between the counterfeit and true will be increasingly needful (Matt. 24; Rev. 13:11-14).

In "An Important Distinction," Trevor Dearing discussed the difference between divine healing, a work of Jesus Christ, and faith healing, which often is a counterfeit produced by the devil. In the context of discerning the work of the Holy Spirit and a spirit of seduction, his points are applicable to many other areas in which it is necessary to distinguish the holy from the attractive but profane.

# An Important Distinction
# Trevor Dearing

I had not long been involved in ministering healing when I realized that a vital distinction had to be made. I discovered that not all supernatural healing is Christian. "Spiritual healing," "faith healing," and "divine healing" are not interchangeable descriptions of the same phenomenon. The term "faith healing" puts all the emphasis on our trust in anything or anyone. It says nothing at all about God. Christian healing, however, is not merely about a psychological attitude which can produce good results. It affirms the necessity of an openness of spirit and soul to the God and Father of our Lord Jesus Christ.

"Spiritual healing" has even more confusing and dangerous overtones. It is the favorite expression of spiritualistic mediums who lay hands on sick people. They believe that some departed human beings now have spiritual power which they can channel to the sick through psychic men, women, and even children.

By contrast, the ministry of divine healing is based on the person and work of the Lord Jesus Christ. It begins with Him, continues in Him, and ends in Him. It is centered on Jesus of Nazareth, who went about healing all manner of sickness and disease among the people of first-century Palestine (Acts 10:38). Christians believe that this Jesus, now risen from the dead, "is the same yesterday and today and for-ever" (Heb. 13:8 RSV). Divine healing, therefore, emanates from Jesus Christ. It results not only in the well-being of suffering people, but also in glory and honor, praise and thanksgiving, being ascribed to Him by all who experience and witness His mighty works for mankind.

I experienced this divine healing myself when I was only nineteen years of age. At that time I was a mental, physical, and spiritual wreck. I was not then a Christian, having been brought up in a typical, good, middle-class, but nonreligious family. However, when

I heard the gospel of the risen Jesus preached for the first time, I eagerly responded. I began to enter a deep relationship with the Lord and the process of healing began.

Now, twenty-six years later, medical examinations have resulted only in reports of very good health. I have been able to marry a wonderful wife, to be a father of four lovely children, and to undertake a worldwide ministry of evangelism and healing. I have had no recurrence of my former illnesses. Jesus Christ has made me whole.

I was, without a doubt, healed through a deep relationship with Christ and can bear my own testimony to the power of a living God, who heals the sick.

This is divine healing. It is about God's healing power through His Son, our Savior Jesus Christ. It is, therefore, in all its aspects, essentially Christian. It is this exclusive Christocentric emphasis which differentiates it from all other forms of supernatural healing. Christians recognize that the healing miracles of the Old Testament, such as those of Elijah and Elisha were also divine healing, being the activity of the Spirit of God.

These other forms exist in most other world religions, and go back to animism, the religion of primitive, pagan man. Witch doctors have existed from time immemorial and have wielded great power through their definite abilities to make people sick by cursing or well by "blessing." In the massive resurgence of supernaturalism today these practices have been reintroduced to our civilized society. They take the form of black magic if they are for cursing and white magic if they are for blessing. In England, covens of witches and warlocks are rapidly increasing and have attracted the attention of the media. In my ministry I am frequently meeting people who have become involved in these activities. Some have needed exorcism. The Bishop of Truro, Cornwall, recently showed me a collection of sinister charms which have come into his possession, handed over by people who have sought his help.

The most widespread revival of pagan healing, however, is in spiritism or, as its devotees prefer to call it, spiritualism. It is very prevalent in modern society, being a refined form of involving spirits to the aid of men. The *London Times* obituary of Mr. Harry Edwards, the best-known of psychic healers, who died last year, claimed that he made "spiritual healing" respectable. Apparently, he needed sixty secretaries to deal with his vast daily correspondence.

He once wrote to me about people becoming well as "responding to spirit." Certainly, his foundation, The National Federation of Spiritual Healers, is very strong in the United Kingdom, and Spiritist Healing Tabernacles are dotted about all over the country. Sometimes they prominently portray pictures of Jesus as "the Light of the World," which only adds to the confusion between spiritist, occult healing, and the divine healing ministered by the Christian church.

Divine healing is the activity of God in and through the person of Jesus Christ. It is not simply a matter of faith. It is certainly not the result of the activity of spirits whether thought of as human, angelic, or demonic. By such mediumistic activity, people in fact unwittingly open themselves to the supernatural power of the devil who often heals the body in order to ensnare the soul. Divine healing involves the healing of the whole person—spirit, soul, mind, and body through a right relationship with God in Jesus Christ. Faith, for the Christian, is such a trusting and resting in the God revealed to us by Jesus that we open our whole beings to the invasion of His Holy, health-giving Spirit. It is based upon a deep, personal relationship with God. This produces a healing that culminates in heaven, where we shall find ourselves perfectly restored in the whole of our beings.

I have constantly had to speak out in public about this vital distinction and stress the essential difference between divine healing and its many counterfeits. One of my first appearances on television was to refute occult practices which had been given media backing, to declare the exclusiveness of Jesus, the depth of His healing and the glories of His kingdom.

Every meeting I have held has focused on worshipping the glorified Jesus and proclaiming the necessity of responding to His love. An altar call for salvation, followed by careful counseling of converts, has always preceded ministry to the sick. I have always emphasized that I am engaged in *divine healing,* and have expounded its distinctive nature. Often this has brought criticism from commentators who have felt that all men of good will should join together in a ministry like this. Many spiritualists have attended my meetings thinking them to be the same as their own healing activities. However, they have soon been faced with the difference! Praise God, because I have never compromised on the issue, I have had the joy of seeing thousands of people find Jesus Christ as their Lord and Savior—the ultimate in supernatural experience.

In discerning the work of the Holy Spirit in the church, one of the most important criteria is the Scriptures. In measuring ministries and practices against the Scriptures, many people advance an inter-pretation that some practices of the New Testament church are no longer applicable to church life today and that their presence in the Scriptures is not evidence of their propriety in the modern church.

Jim Glennon addresses this contention objectively, offering us a sound basis from which to proceed as we examine the validity of various aspects of twentieth-century church life. As with his other essays in this book, Glennon primarily addresses the issue of healing in the Bible and in the church; his arguments, however, apply to any other practice or gift of the Spirit which detractors might say has passed away.

# Where There Is No Vision . . .
## Jim Glennon

We will now examine as fairly as possible the alternative explanation put forward by those who hold that divine healing is not for today.

This alternative viewpoint begins with the premise that Christ healed to validate His Messiahship and His power to forgive sins. This reason was obviously personal to Him alone, so it follows that healing does not relate to us in the same way. No further validation of Christ's authority is necessary, and in any case we could add nothing to what He has already done. No one has healed people as Christ healed them.

This view goes on to claim that the reason why the apostles and others healed was to validate the church, but once this was done, there was no further need for this sign, and so it was withdrawn. It is maintained that because the references to healing are predominantly in the gospels and Acts, and that there are only two references to healing in the rest of the New Testament, this could imply that healing was already in decline when these later events were recorded. The fact that healing has not been in common evidence since the third century is said to further confirm the probability that it is not intended for the ongoing church. In any case, such healings as do occur today cannot be sufficiently identified with the type of healing recorded in the New Testament to justify the title "divine healing."

Those who expound this position also point out that our Lord's statement that the kingdom of God is among us needs to be balanced by the fact that sin is still a present reality. Perfection of blessing is denied us in this life because we do not have complete and continuous victory over "the world rulers of this present darkness" (Eph. 6:12 RSV). The assurance of God's perfect blessing is something that we can only anticipate in the life to come.

25

It is further affirmed that to conclude a prayer for healing with the words "if it be thy will" is not a prayer of doubt, but one of victorious faith: a faith prepared to leave the ultimate issues with God; a faith ready for death; a faith not stimulated by favorable results, but by complete acceptance of the final outcome—whether in sickness or health, life or death.

These assertions must be looked at critically. For too long they have been accepted without question. That Christ healed to validate His Messiahship is true, but it is not the only reason why He healed; it was *one* reason. The whole truth is that there were many reasons why He healed, and this was one of them. Despite the reasons that were exclusive to Christ, the fact is that He committed the same healing ministry to His followers. This personal factor of validating His Messiahship was therefore not the definitive reason for His healings as some claim it to be.

There is nothing in the New Testament to lend substance to the idea that the disciples healed to validate the Christian church. This is a classic illustration of what is meant by a "tradition of man." When argument is built on that kind of reason, it is as useless as it is misleading. Theological exposition must always be concerned with what is contained in the Scriptures.

Neither is there one word in the New Testament to say or suggest that healing was to be withdrawn. On the contrary, Paul's statement that there are gifts of healing, and James' statement that there is a healing ministry in the church, make it clear and definite that healing was intended to continue. As with Christ's ministry of healing, the only requirement was "the prayer of faith" (James 5:15 KJV).

On the matter of declining references to healing as the New Testament progresses, the same thing can be said about baptism and the Lord's Supper. If it be a guide, the words "baptism" and "to baptize" are used approximately eighty times in the gospels and Acts, and less than twenty in the rest of the New Testament. The Lord's Supper is referred to a dozen times in the gospels and Acts, and once in the epistles. Yet no one deduces from this that the use of the sacraments was already declining as the New Testament period progressed. It is then inconsistent to make that deduction as it concerns healing.

It is agreed that the supernatural gifts of the Spirit, including healing, are not in common evidence today. But what is the real explanation? Dr. Evelyn Frost, in her book *Christian Healing,* said that if we attempt to assess the work of Jesus Christ in history, not merely in regard to the value of each manifestation, but from an overall point of view, we see that:

> The temperature of the spiritual life of the church was the index of her power to heal. As far as the ante-Nicene church is concerned, the history of her spiritual life is one of decline from the higher peaks of the apostolic days to the lower spiritual level at which controversy, apostasy and heresy were formidable weakening factors in her life. Side by side with this growing weakness can be seen a decline in the power of healing.[2]

Once these other factors accounting for the decline in healing are introduced, the whole question is thrown open in a new way. The gifts of the Spirit, including healing, are "the manifestation of the Spirit" (1 Cor. 12:7 KJV). And we have the greatest need, as Bishop John Howe, Secretary-General of the Anglican Consultative Council, has said, "to know what are the factors that will enable the Holy Spirit to be stirred up or released in our contemporary situation."[3] This will involve an historical study, like that of Frost, as well as a scriptural one.

Might it not be that we need a fresh vision of what is available, remembering that God is the same yesterday, today and forever? We also need the repentance, faith and obedience to increasingly draw on these provisions. This may well require a redrawing of our personal and pastoral lives. It is simply not enough for a tiny minority in the church to believe. This is the point made by Frost. It is the whole body of Christ which has to be involved. My own conviction is that the main single reason for the lack of these ministries in the church today, in all their New Testament reality, is that the body of Christ as a whole does not really believe in them.

On the question of identifying what happens now with what happened then, we can only answer that if we were required to measure what happens in our contemporary church life against the experience of the church in the early days of Holy Spirit power, then there would be very little in any area that we could find the same! For example, very few are converted in our western church today— nothing like what we see described in the early church. But no one suggests that what happens today is invalid because of that. Instead we rejoice for what blessing there is, re-examine our position and move in for action. If we are going to be consistent, then what is good for conversion should be good for healing.

The question raised by the present reality of sin, and the qualification this makes to the kingdom of God, is more apparent than real. Sin was just as real in the primitive church when healing was available in response to faith. When it came to the prayer of faith for healing, the reality of sin did not limit the kingdom of God. As with the problem of physical death, the negative did not affect the positive. Again, the disciples did not make a synthesis between them; again, the kingdom of God and the commission of Christ were the operative dimensions. The disciples prayed, and always prayed, in full assurance that healing would eventuate because of their faith. We must of course respect those who believe that it is an affirmation of faith to conclude their prayer for healing with the words "if it be thy will," because they do so with meaningful sincerity. We can all think of devout Christians who have faced sickness, and who have faced death, with that affirmation in their heart and on their lips. But the difficulty with this view, and the reason why it cannot be accepted, is the fact that it was not the way faith was exercised for healing in the New Testament. As we have just noted, the early Christians prayed, and prayed always, with complete conviction that healing would eventuate because of their faith.

If those who speak against the healing ministry still argue that they do not believe in these ministries because they do not see them, one can only reply that they do not see them because they do not believe in them. Faith always precedes sight; and it is faith in the statement of the Scriptures that "the gifts . . . of God are irrevocable" (Rom. 11:29 RSV).

# Rightly Handling the Word of Truth
## Robert Wise

Scripture provides us with the basic direction for understanding which spirits are of God. The general Protestant perspective is that Scripture is the ultimate and only final guide to faith and practice. If a viewpoint is scriptural, it can be accepted; if if is contrary to Scripture, it must be rejected. In this view, the Bible is the ultimate court of appeal for sorting out reality from deception. Unfortunately, a great many people of contrary positions appeal to the same Scriptures to support their positions.

### 1. Get the basic meaning.
The Reformers taught that the Bible should be understood in its basic philological sense. Understanding the original historical and grammatical context is basic to its correct interpretation. Therefore, the only way the Bible can be rightly understood is if it is interpreted in accord with the intention of the original writers. Essentially this is the same approach that one would use in the interpretation of any literature. When reading a book, a poem, or a scientific treatise, we presume that the basic literal sense of the literary form will convey the writer's intention. Failure to recognize the literary and thought forms distorts what the writer was saying.

While this approach might be described as reading the Bible literally, it does not imply a wooden letterism, using the letter of Scripture so literalistically that passages are pushed to take on strange meanings. For example, the book of Revelation speaks about a bear (actually, just the feet of a bear—Rev. 13:2); the Soviet Union's national symbol is a bear. Some writers assume that the Scripture must refer to the Soviet Union. The error is failure to recognize that the original writer was using symbolism to make his point. A true literal interpretation of Scripture acknowledges the symbolic use of language as appropriate.

29

The Bible must be read in its correct context. The Reformers suggested that this could best be done by allowing Scripture to interpret Scripture. A sense of the whole Bible is needed to grasp the meaning of any particular phrase. In addition, the Bible must be interpreted in the cultural context from which the original meaning and definition of words came. When a passage, phrase, or word is lifted out of its first context and given a contemporary redefinition, the result can be disastrous.

Cults often use a method of interpretation that seems to recognize the original historical, grammatical context, but then apply their own esoteric meaning, giving Scripture their particular twist. They make the Bible say what they want to hear and draw completely erroneous conclusions.

Equally ill conceived are attempts to impose a system of thought on the Scripture. While it is difficult to avoid the tendency to let one's doctrines become the eyeglasses through which Scripture is read, there must be a constant vigilance to recognize when this is being done. Devotees of prophecy have a great tendency to use Scripture to support their predetermined positions and, in turn, read Scripture through what their prophetic program for the future suggests it should say. They use the Bible to prove a point rather than allow it to make its unique statement. Correct interpretation goes for the basic meaning, allowing Scripture to speak for itself even if the message is difficult to hear and hard to follow!

## 2. Don't proof-text.

Proof-texters seek to find a chapter and verse for every idea, thought, concern, and position they hold—even if it's not appropriate. Often proof-texters feel that unless they can prove their point by reference to a specific Scripture verse, their whole position is invalidated. As a result, the Bible has been used to prove silly and incredible things. For many centuries various biblical texts were used to prove that the world is actually flat!

Scripture is not an encyclopedia of all knowledge nor does it include the totality of what can be known about God and faith. At no point does Scripture suggest it is a *complete* book of information. In contrast, the great creeds and confessions of the Christian faith have always confirmed that Scripture has all that is necessary for salvation and Christian living. Therefore, we must let Scripture speak its unique message and be cautious to not make it say things it never intended to say. In this sense Martin Luther suggested, "The best teacher is the one who does not bring his meaning into scripture, but gets his meaning from the scripture."[4]

Scripture is violated when we seek passages to either confirm or deny the findings of modern science, psychology, or contemporary forms of investigation. Galileo, Copernicus, and Newton ran into this fallacy when well-meaning people insisted they have a Bible chapter and verse for their findings. When they couldn't produce the documentation, they were declared heretics. Now we can see clearly that the Bible does not contain all the facts of astronomy, geology, chemistry, psychology, etc. Expecting it to do so or using it as a weapon against new discoveries is totally contrary to its intent. If followed to its logical conclusion, this approach would suggest that unless radios, rocketships and cars can be proven valid by Scripture, they should not be used by Christians.

The problem of proof-texting becomes particularly evident when one wades through the enormous volumes of literature on prophecy. Pre-millennialists, post-millennialists, and dispensationalists all use the Bible to substantiate their points of view. The Bible's references to the last days become a field day of excess as people frighten each other with possible fulfillments of the Scriptures in the last moments of history, which of course they consider imminent. Some use the Bible to try to prove everything from future war strategies to identifying contemporary people as the antichrist. The passage of time exposes such claims as nonsense. A.B. Davidson has called this the insanity of literalism.[5] These claims generally violate the historical context of both the prophet and the prophecy, and fail to give careful attention to the grammar of a particular prophetic passage, not recognizing whether the verses are figurative, poetic, symbolic or descriptive in character.

## 3. Seek the Person of Jesus.

While the Reformers saw the Bible primarily as a guide to truth about faith and practice, Scripture also gives direction for personal encounter with the reality of God. While the Scriptures do help us discern correct faith, they also lead us on toward an experience with the risen Christ—eternal life is to know Jesus Christ (John 17:3). For example, in 1 Corinthians 12, Paul directed the church to an effective and balanced use of the Holy Spirit's gifts. Some deny the validity of this passage for contemporary experience, suggesting that the Spirit's gifts were only for the Apostolic age, but the Bible maintains that the experiences of the first Christians should be normative for all following centuries. In fact, the gospels are constructed not as a past accounting, remembering who Jesus was, as much as the unfolding story of the opportunity to encounter Him as He is.

The Bible encourages each person to pursue the most complete encounter possible with Christ. In this way we come to have the witness of the Spirit within us. The Scripture leads to the Spirit and the Spirit brings the Word to life. The Word and the Spirit finally equip us to fully discern the spirits.

The ultimate safeguard we have in our attempt to properly discern the spirits is proper discernment of the Scriptures. We are called to be workers "rightly handling the word of truth" (2 Tim. 2:15 RSV).

# Jesus' Teaching on Discernment
# Bill De Arteaga

Jesus' understanding of spiritual accountability, discernment and evaluation was totally opposite to that of the Pharisees. He completely short-circuited their questions of rabbinical authority, proper origins and pedigrees, and declared that spiritual questions must be evaluated by their fruit (Matt. 7:15-18). John the Baptist had already raised the "fruit" question in regard to the Pharisees who came to him seeking baptism (Matt. 3:8-10). Jesus made fruit central to authentic discernment for His disciples.

> Beware of false prophets, who come to you in sheep's clothing but inwardly are ravenous wolves. You will know them by their fruits. Are grapes gathered from thorns, or figs from thistles? (Matt. 7:15-16 RSV).

The contrast between the Christian view of spiritual accountability and discernment, and the Pharisees' view on the other, is summarized dramatically in the ninth chapter of John, by the healing of a man born blind. When the Pharisees questioned the man and his parents, they were not concerned with the fruit of the incident (that the man had his sight restored), but rather the origins and pedigree of the healer. They wanted to know what rabbinical school Jesus came from that authorized him to do spiritual works. The Pharisees declared, "We are the disciples of Moses. We know that God has spoken to Moses, but as for this man [Jesus], we do not know where he comes from" (John 9:28-29 RSV).

Jesus' injunction to judge the fruit of spiritual phenomena, not their theological origin, was repeated and expanded by the Holy Spirit in Paul's epistles with the concept of *testing* a spiritual phenomenon to see if it is from God or another source.

33

>And this I pray, that your love may abound yet more and more in knowledge and all discernment, that you may approve the things that are excellent, that you may be sincere and without offense till the day of Christ (Phil. 1:9-10 NKJV).

Note that in this passage St. Paul was talking about discernment, but it was not discernment of spirits. Rather, it was associated with knowledge. The purpose of this discernment is to test and accept "what is excellent" (v. 10, RSV). This is repeated in 1 Thessalonians 5:19-22: "Do not quench the Spirit, do not despise prophesying, but test everything; hold fast what is good, abstain from every evil"(RSV). St. Paul thus said that there is a method for testing something new: attending to it fruit, which was Jesus' viewpoint (see also Gal. 5:19-23).

The concept of testing and discernment is a major element of Scripture that has not always been recognized. The church has faced issues and developed procedures not directly mentioned in the Bible but still of God. For example, in the nineteenth century the institution of Sunday school was invented. After much argumentation (and unconscious testing of its fruit), the church approved it as one of the things that are "excellent"(Phil. 1:10 KJV) and adopted it. St. Paul further elaborated the concept of testing fruit by indicating that the spiritual phenomena coming from God have certain characteristics which he named "fruit of the Spirit" in Galatians 5:22-23:

>The fruit of the Spirit is love, joy, peace, patience, kindness, goodness, faithfulness, gentleness, self-control (RSV).

All of this went against the understanding of the Pharisees, who assumed that any phenomenon can be judged by rigorous attention to its theological origins.

## The meaning of faith

Jesus' ministry attacked and challenged the Pharisees' distorted definition of faith. Jesus, in word and deed, reminded all who would listen that the primary meaning of faith is a relationship with God involving trust and expectancy. God provides for believers' needs, delivers the afflicted from the kingdom of Satan, and does great and mighty works. Jesus did not totally disdain theological knowledge and doctrine. Rather, He taught that faith, expectancy and trust in

God are more important than doctrinal beliefs. He demonstrated this in two incidents, the exorcism of the Canaanite woman's daughter (Matt. 15:21-28) and the healing of the centurion's servant (Matt. 8:5-13). In each instance the healing or exorcism was done through the proxy faith of the seekers and at long distance. Neither seeker had "right theology." They were both pagan to some degree, but both had tremendous faith and expectancy which God used to heal them through Jesus. By silence on the matter, Jesus was not affirming their pagan doctrines. Rather He praised and affirmed their faith as a spiritual virtue and example for others. The right theology would come later.

The Pharisees' self-evaluation was that they were on the forefront of what God was doing for Israel; Jesus' judgment of them was considerably different:

> Woe to you, scribes and Pharisees, hypocrites! for you build the tombs of the prophets and adorn the monuments of the righteous, saying, "If we had lived in the days of our fathers, we would not have taken part with them in shedding the blood of the prophets." Thus you witness against yourselves, that you are sons of those who murdered the prophets. Fill up, then, the measure of your fathers. You serpents, you brood of vipers, how are you to escape being sentenced to hell? (Matt. 23:29-33 RSV).

Jesus' argument needs some clarification. He was talking about spiritual inheritance: because the Pharisees opposed the Holy Spirit (in the person of Jesus and His teachings) they had allied themselves with those who had opposed the prophets (and the Holy Spirit in the prophets) in former generations. Although they believed themselves protectors of orthodoxy, they were really the opponents of the Holy Spirit.

# — 3 —

# The Seduction of Christianity

"A compelling look at the times we live in. A clear call to every believer to choose between the Original and the counterfeit." These words were written about *The Seduction to Christianity*, but not by a book reviewer—they appear on the cover, where Harvest House touts their controversial release by Dave Hunt and T.A. McMahon.

The book has had tremendous influence among Christians since its debut in 1985, partly because it gives a surface impression of thorough research. "That is a misimpression which results from a hasty reading and blanket acceptance of scores of footnotes," wrote Alan Langstaff of Kairos Ministries, reviewing the book for *Charisma* magazine.[1] "A careful analysis raises serious questions about the book's scholarly integrity, as well as the validity and accuracy of the authors' conclusions."

Elsewhere in his review, Langstaff summarized the thrust of the book: "They claim that Christianity is being infiltrated by the latest 'fashionable philosophies including the danger in the growing acceptance and practice of positive and possibility thinking, healing of memories, self philosophies, holistic medicine.' "

Hunt and McMahon attacked Rita Bennett, Paul Yonggi Cho, Agnes Sanford, Robert Wise, Kenneth Copeland, James Dobson, Francis MacNutt, Morton Kelsey, Dennis and Matthew Linn, John and Paula Sandford, Robert Schuller, Ruth Carter Stapleton, Robert Tilton, John Wimber, Zig Ziglar and a host of others.

Hunt and McMahon cited practices such as inner healing, positive confession and Christian use of psychology as examples of seduction of the church, branding them as sorcery and shamanism. The authors did include a statement in the introduction expressing their regret at having to write the book and emphasizing that they were not judging the deluded sorcerers they named in the book.

We do not mean to say that the book is without merit. *"The Seduction of Christianity* contains many timely admonitions," wrote Peter Davids, a professor of Regent College, in another *Charisma* review.[2]

Mark Virkler identified some of its strengths[3]:

> David Hunt is obviously a scholar *concerning the beliefs of modern-day cults.* . . . This book will cause all Christians to be *more aware of the possibility of deception* in the age in which we live, and therefore will inspire all Christians to take a deeper look at the biblical foundation for their beliefs. . . .This book will *help Christians clarify and deepen the messages* in the areas in which he [Hunt] attacks. [The emphasis is Virkler's.]

Virkler also pointed out some weaknesses:

> Because Dave Hunt has spent so much time studying cults, *he focuses on the beliefs of cults, rather than on Scripture.* He compares the teachings of outstanding Christian leaders, such as Paul Yonggi Cho, Robert Schuller, Kenneth Hagin and Earl Paulk against what cults believe, rather than against what the Bible teaches. This is a *backward approach* for testing for error and a fundamental flaw in his book.
>
> *Mr. Hunt is not a "Berean,"* in that a Berean "examines the Scriptures daily, to see whether these things are *SO."* Whenever Dave Hunt does go to Scripture, he seeks to prove that these things are *NOT SO,* rather than examine the truth in them. For example, when coming against the belief in a positive mental attitude, David Hunt never once examines [in his book] Philippians 4:8 or any of the hundreds of verses that speak of the scriptural command to have a positive mental attitude. This then becomes *another fundamental flaw of this book,* in that he is seeking to prove error rather than seeking to prove truth, as did the Bereans.
>
> David Hunt accuses leader after leader in the Church of today, and *appears more as "the accuser of the brethren" than the comforter.* . . .

> Dave Hunt . . . slants and alters the intent of what the author was saying. . . .
>
> Dave Hunt fails to see that *the presence of a counterfeit proves that there is also a real, and that this real thing has value.*

Robert Wise cited an example of Hunt and McMahon's faulty logic on the subject of psychology:

> The authors indicate that they do not believe that psychology is a science.[4] Offering no support, they draw the absurd conclusion that psychology is implicitly a religion and that the practice of psychotherapy is demonic. In addition, the authors do not believe there is such a thing as an unconscious mind because they cannot find a biblical basis for the idea. Their thinking is like looking for a biblical text for cars or electric lights.

Peter Davids, in his review of *The Seduction of Christianity,* stated:

> The criticism of psychology . . . is much too sweeping, leaving the reader to doubt whether Christians should use any form of it. Many of Hunt and McMahon's citations attack humanistic psychology, which is only one small branch of the whole. Even that is a varied branch. Many of the non-Christian psychologists they shun would also be derailed by other psychologists.

These comments on *The Seduction of Christianity* use some strong words, and it is worth taking a close look at the logic and approach of the book as well as examining some of the errors and slant in the writing.

# Could This Be Occult?
# Robert Wise

Making up their own definition of key words, Hunt and McMahon define truth in a way peculiar unto themselves. We are never told who Hunt and McMahon are nor what credentials they have. Apparently Hunt is a self-certified authority on cults. While their book appears to be scholarly and researched, much of the material is taken out of context and in some instances material is used in a deceptive manner. Such distortion is particularly evident in the way these authors categorize the use of visualization in prayer.

Using their own idiosyncratic interpretation, they define ancient sorcery as any attempt to manipulate reality by the use of mind over matter.[5] By this definition, the biblical condemnation of the occult appears to condemn psychology. The same logic allows these cult busters to equate Norman Vincent Peale and Robert Schuller with Jean Dixon's astrology or Ernest Holme's science of the mind. Unfortunately, this is an unbiblical and incorrect definition of words as well as an uncharitable way to treat people.

In contrast, Webster defines the word sorcery as "the supposed use of an evil, supernatural power over people and their affairs, i.e. black magic, seemingly magical power or charm."[6] Even by the standards of common usage, Hunt and McMahon's definition is from another world and unique to themselves. The concerned believer will want to know exactly what the Bible really says. To correctly grasp this concept, we need to turn to the original Hebrew and understand what sorcery means in Scripture.

Deuteronomy 18:9ff prohibits sorcery and witchcraft, prescibing the most severe penalties for such practices. Child sacrificers, sorcerers, magicians and snake charmers are all of the same order with necromancers, who seek conversations with the dead. In general, Israel was warned about false prophets who distort God's direction for His people.[7] In this and similar passages (such as

Daniel 2:2) the *mekhashefm* (sorcerers) are people who practice adjurations and magical ceremonies. Often they cast spells, creating havoc by uttering injurious incantations intended to hurt people (Ps. 5:10, 52:4). Primarily the sorcerer is one who actually engages in magic and puts hexes on people.[8] The practices of sorcery include inquiring of and using the dead for magic purposes. As strange as it sounds, sorcery included using the bones of the dead in an attempt to cause spirits of the dead to speak through the sorcerer's armpit or mouth.[9]

Sorcery and witchcraft reflect the ancient view of a world surrounded by mysterious and miraculous forces. These evil practices were an attempt to use such spiritual realities for one's own purposes. While most of these practices sound almost incomprehensibly superstitious to the modern mind, they were seen as frightening ways to manipulate unseen spiritual forces that were opposed to the God of Israel.[10]

In effect, Hunt and McMahon have equated magic with modern science and redefined the practice of attempting to manipulate spirits as being one with using ability to think or be creative. Their whole book is built on this bizarre premise. Magic and meditation are not the same thing; neither are spiritualism and psychology.

To fully lay this problem to rest, we need to dissect a key paragraph in *The Seduction of Christianity:*

"Visualization" and "guided imagery" have long been recognized by sorcerers of all kinds as the most powerful and effective methodology for contacting the spirit world in order to acquire supernatural power, knowledge, and healing. Such methods are neither taught nor practiced in the Bible as helps to faith or prayer. Those who attempt to do so are not following the leading of the Holy Spirit or the Word of God, but are practicing an ancient occultic technique. Legitimate uses of the imagination would involve such things as seeing mental images of something being described in a book; designing, planning, or rehearsing something in our minds; or remembering a place or event. Such mental processes are normal aids to everyday activities and do not involve an attempt to create or control reality through mind-powers."[11]

The authors make the illogical leap that *some* refers to *all*. Without considering that sorcerers could be counterfeits, they assume that because some occultists have used a practice that is like visualization prayer then anyone who uses a similar form is guilty of the same error or motivation. Such logic would conclude that because some witch doctors used knives in their ritual, modern doctors who use scalpels are also guided by the same ideas, beliefs and motivations. The illegitimate use of a practice by the misguided is not the same as the correct application of truth by the informed. Most importantly, the authors offer no documentation whatsoever for their claim that the sorcerer's practice is the same as visualization. From the previous paragraphs we can see it is not.

It's important to recognize that in their suggestion there is a principle of interpretation at work that violates the correct use of Scripture. Hunt and McMahon pursue the error that unless there is a chapter and verse for any practice, then God forbids the method. There are no chapter and verse for modern surgery, air conditioning, cars, or aspirin. The Bible never says clearly that women *can* participate in the Lord's Supper. Should they be disallowed because the practice does not have a supporting text? Equally erroneous is the assumption that the Bible must make a pronouncement on every possible area of concern and practice in Christian spiritual life. Hymnals are not mentioned in the Bible nor is listening to cassettes.

The claim that those who attempt to use guided imagery could not be following the leading of the Holy Spirit or the Word of God is the kind of definitive pronouncement so often found among heretic hunters who declare the truth without documenting it. The authors give no grounds to support their contention that people cannot be led by the Holy Spirit nor use Scripture to develop new forms of prayer. That the church has used images and symbols through the centuries was either not known or not recognized by these authors.

In fact, there are groups who use meditation, visualization, and prayer techniques in ways the Christian community cannot agree with or advocate. In addition, there are teachers and preachers who use motivational techniques to pander selfishness and greed. Certainly self-serving people will go beyond the appropriate boundaries as they seek power with evil intent. Abuses must be recognized and rejected; but to jump from some to all is the shoddiest kind of thinking.

Simply put, *The Seduction of Christianity* has defined the wrong target. Hunt and McMahon's quarrel is not with the occult, but with secular humanism. The real problem lies with those who use the potential of the mind and spirit apart from a relationship to the Creator. Far from being occult, the current problem lies with those who only use the inner world as further opportunity to develop life apart from God's sovereign rule.

Similarities between some Christian teaching and occult activities can also be explained by recognizing that the demonic does counterfeit the real manifestations of the Spirit. These coincidences are not an indictment of the Christian teaching, but demonstrate duplication by the demonic. Paul encountered this phenomenon with a slave girl who had a spirit of divination (Acts 16). When there is a recovery of signs and wonders, we can also expect an occult counterpart. Such similarities actually validate the authentic work God is producing today. Therefore, when we attempt to discern spirits, we must avoid leaping to the conclusion that similarities imply Christian error.

# Errors in
## *The Seduction of Christianity*
# Bill De Arteaga

The Pharisees accused Jesus of sorcery. The accusation had a certain logic to it, given their assumptions. Jesus worked miracles (magic?), yet neither He nor His disciples came from the established rabbinical schools. They accused Jesus of casting out demons by the power of Beelzebul (Matt. 12:24). Jesus answered that the demonic kingdom cannot cast itself out, and that the good fruit of His exorcisms was a sign that His ministry was from God (Matt. 12:25-29). In this incident, and in the context of that false accusation of sorcery, Jesus defined the unforgivable sin against the Holy Spirit: "Whoever says a word against the Son of man will be forgiven; but whoever speaks against the Holy Spirit will not be forgiven, either in this age or in the age to come" (Matt. 12:32 RSV).

Certainly witchcraft and sorcery are serious sins, and when identified they must be denounced. One can define certain acts of sorcery as confusing the spiritual activities of lesser spirits with the work of the Holy Spirit, as in, for example, spiritualism. In this sense spiritualism is a sin of faulty discernment, and it is a serious sin which must be confessed, but it can be forgiven. However, the opposite sin of discernment, claiming that the works of the Holy Spirit are really the product of demonic activity, calling something sorcery when it is in fact from God, is not only a serious sin, it is unforgivable. A Christian should make the accusation of sorcery in the case of an unknown or unusual spiritual phenomenon reluctantly and only after much study and prayer. Caution is especially warranted when judging any form of healing or exorcism. The situation is different if the spiritual activity is what is biblically defined as sorcery: worshiping other gods, acts of obeisance to lesser spirits, fortune telling, or mediumistic communications.

44

Jesus did warn us to be wary of counterfeits of the work of the Spirit:

> False Christs and false prophets will appear and perform great signs and miracles to deceive even the elect—if that were possible (Matt. 24:24 NIV).

He also told us, however, that we can recognize them by their fruits (Matt. 7:15). Christians must also remember, while avoiding evil, not to judge others (Matt. 7:1).

Discerning from fruits is more demanding than discerning from reference to theological orthodoxy, and can be especially difficult in situations were spiritualism is involved. For example, spiritualist healers can and do heal physical ailments. Yet their fruits are superficial and often temporary, leaving the patient in spiritual bondage to demonic entities. Spiritualist healing never gives glory to Jesus as healer, whereas Christian healing always does so. Christian healing brings a new, deeper experience of freedom, and an ability to develop the fruits of the Spirit, such as joy, peace, and longsuffering (Gal. 5:23).

One of the primary errors in *The Seduction of Christianity* is an attitude of spiritual arrogance and failure to properly measure the works and people it examines—that is, by their fruits. The book carries this tone throughout, and amounts to a witch hunt, rather than "spiritual discernment."[12]

An example is the misrepresentation of a case ministered by Mrs. Ruth Carter Stapleton and described in her book *The Experience of Inner Healing*. It involved a severely depressed young woman named Jane who had been an illegitimate and unwanted child. As cited on page 183 of *The Seduction of Christianity:*

> Ruth Carter Stapleton, who, like most of the other leaders in the movement, learned her inner healing from Agnes Sanford, tells of a young woman who became involved in drugs and crime because of the "self-loathing" she felt at being "an illegitimate child." Ruth's solution was to take the young woman back in "a guided meditation" in which Christ was visualized as "present" during the act of fornication that caused her conception and making it "holy and pure, an act of God . . . ordained by her heavenly Father."

The quotations and summary (given in full, the ellipsis ". . ." is in *The Seduction of Christianity*) suggest that Mrs. Stapleton believed that the act of fornication could be made holy. Let us go to her book *The Experience of Inner Healing* to see what Mrs. Stapleton really said:

> I explained to Jane why she was no accident, that God knew her before she was conceived in her mother's womb, and that there may be unholy sex acts but that conception is holy and pure, an act of God, and that her birth had been ordained by her heavenly Father, God. The sense of disgrace related to her conception and birth began to fade as she accepted the truth that her life was a divine intention rather than a biological accident.

By the use of a cut-and-paste method of quotation, the meaning was changed from an affirmation of Jane's conception, in spite of its sinful circumstances, to an affirmation of fornication.

## The assault on Agnes Sanford

The modern use of inner healing began with the healing ministry of Mrs. Agnes Sanford in the decade after World War II as a result of Mrs. Sanford's experiences with a wounded Jewish-American soldier, Harry Goldsmith.[13]

Harry had suffered an artillery wound in the war, and had a severe bone infection when Agnes first met him. The doctors were intending to amputate his leg to the thigh socket. Agnes, like Corrie Ten Boom, had a special love for the Jews, and laid hands on Harry's wound. She also taught him how to pray for his own healing. In a few weeks, he experienced a miraculous recovery, three inches of missing bone were regrown, and he soon walked out of the hospital. Harry converted to Christianity, was baptized by Mrs. Sanford's husband, an Episcopal priest, and went off to New York City for a degree in psychology.

He found that although he was a "new creature" in Christ, his old nature would assert itself in irrational fits of rage and temper. He asked for Agnes' help on this; she prayed for him for several weeks without effect. She then asked God for direction, and the Lord revealed to her that the source of Harry's rage was his childhood in Nazi-occupied Europe. His Jewish neighbors hated him because he was part German, and the Germans brutalized him and his family because he was part Jewish. As a small boy he could not fight back, nor even express his rage, against either. With this revelation Mrs. Sanford went into a period of fasting and intercessory prayer for Harry. She was guided to pray that the Lord comfort and heal the "little boy" within Harry that had been so abused, and to pray for the forgiveness of the many sins of his tormentors. The intercessory prayer culminated in her offering her Sunday communion for the healing of that little boy. The prayer technique of interceding for another through the sacrament of the Lord's Supper is something Agnes had learned from the Episcopal Church. Harry was hundreds of miles away from Agnes the week she prayed for him, but when she completed her intercessory prayers for him he was totally relieved of his depression and fits of temper.

The next inner healing cases were similar. Prayers for the sin-afflicted "inner child" were done by intercession at the communion table. Mrs. Sanford then discovered that the prayer of inner healing worked just as well if she laid hands on the person's head and prayed. She soon included in her prayer ministry of "the healing of memories," as she termed it, an invitation for the person to forgive those who had injured him or her in the past. Mrs. Sanford would often say the words of forgiveness over the person. Sometimes when she prayed for the healing of memories Mrs. Sanford visualized the person at the time of emotional injury, with Jesus present, healing the incident. She discovered that this visualization added force to her spoken prayers of intercession and forgiveness. By the early 1960's her "healing of memories" ministry was essentially established. Her technique was in fact quite simple, and she consciously kept it so. She generally asked three simple questions: Were you happy as a child? if not, why not? and, when did you first become unhappy? This normally triggered a memory of the situation that had produced the inner hurts.

Besides laying on of hands and communion-intercessions, she used "parable prayers" for the healing of memories. For example, when she prayed for the healing of homosexuality (for which she had a specially anointed ministry) she laid hands on the head of the person and prayed that God would redirect the "sexual flow" back to its "proper banks." The important thing about Mrs. Sanford's ministry of healing memories is that it was primarily a ministry of the forgiveness of sins. Her ministry treated sin as biblically defined, that is, as the evil that happens *to* a person, as well as the evil a person

47

does. Visualization was only one type of prayer used for the healing of memories.

*The Seduction of Christianity* claims that Mrs. Sanford's use of visualization was magical and manipulative, and, in a description of Mrs. Sanford's domestic life from *The Healing Light*, claims that she manipulated her children with visualization.[14] Let us go to the original passage[15]:

> I learned this method [of prayer-visualization] by experimenting with my own children. When one of them came in cross and unhappy, instead of flying into a temper, I would quiet myself and by faith make in my mind the picture of the child as he was at his best. "Heavenly Father, that's your little child as you want him to be," I would say. "Please send your Holy Spirit through me now and make him be that way, happy and peaceful and kind. Thank you, because I believe you are doing so. Amen."

This is principally a form of intercessory prayer. She lifted to God a picture of the goal, and simultaneously prayed the prayer of faith expecting that this picture would become reality. The difference between this and praying verbally, "Lord, send your Holy Spirit to calm and quiet my children and make them happy!" is that the imaginative faculty of the mind is added to the mental prayer.

### The issue of Jungian vocabulary

As Mrs. Sanford developed the healing of memories, she began to describe it in conferences and lectures. By the late 1950's she had developed an understanding of the memory-healing process that utilized some vocabulary from Swiss psychologist Carl Jung. It was almost by default, for in the 1950's psychology was dominated by either materialists such as Watson, who avoided mental and spiritual processes, or Freudians, who reduced the spiritual to suppressed sexuality. Jung did at least recognize the critical importance of spiritual processes in man's normal (and abnormal) life. He also developed a rich vocabulary, such as "archetype" and "collective unconscious," to describe the spiritual factors in mental processes.

Mrs. Sanford, who was kept well informed on psychology by the troops of educated guests who showed up in her home to consult with her, incorporated in her own vocabulary several Jungian terms to explain the process of memory healing. Part of the reason for this is that biblical revelation is particularly silent in describing mental states or spiritual processes—a peculiarity of both the Old and the New Testaments. A dramatic example of this is found in 2 Samuel 17:23, where the wise counselor Ahithophel decided to commit suicide because his advice was rejected. Scripture records only his placing his house in order; there is not a word to describe his sense of rejection, anger, anguish, or fear. The same can be said of Abraham's obedience in preparing to sacrifice his son Isaac in Genesis 22. Similarly, Jesus used the word "heart" to describe the levels of mind deeper than the "public" level of consciousness, and from which our true motivations flow, but the terminology is certainly imprecise (Matt. 15:18-19). Christianity has always had to borrow terms from extra-biblical sources to define and separate these deeper levels of the "heart," or simply to categorize different personality types.

*The Seduction of Christianity* asserts that "Christianity and psychotherapy are actually two rival and irreconcilable religious systems."[16] They further make a series of pious-sounding assertions to the effect that a born-again believer does not need counseling, that the experience of "salvation" is all that is needed for mental health.[17] Christian ministers, including evangelical ministers, in positions of responsibility for the emotional and spiritual health of others know differently (Jer. 8:11). The experience of salvation is indeed a wonderful gift that often brings emotional stability and purpose-fulness. But to claim that born-again believers need no other counseling is a cruel parody of the real pastoral situation faced by the churches. In fact, later in the *The Seduction of Christianity* is an admission that some born-again Christians need "professional counsel."[18]

What is the fruit of Agnes Sanford's use of Jungian vocabulary? Apparently it helped her develop new understanding of the passion and atonement of Jesus Christ and their role in the eternal forgiveness of sins and in healing. She related the scourging to our physical healing (Isa. 53:5), and Jesus' sweating blood at Gethsemane as entering all of human history, with all our sins of mental anguish, meanness, rejection, hatred, and lies, and taking upon himself all those sins (cf. 2 Cor. 5:21).

There is a legitimate cause for concern about wholesale association of Jungian psychology with Christian theology and ministry—there are indeed dangerous elements in the Jungian system which, if adopted uncritically, could do serious harm. But Agnes Sanford never took part in Jungian-Christian extremism. She saw the dangers of too close an association with Jungian psychology and made others in the inner healing ministry aware of that. But to assert that there is an intimate and destructive association between Jungian psychology and inner healing is flatly untrue. True, inner healing is *like* psychoanalysis in that it understands that many adult emotional and spiritual problems have origins in early life. But the effectiveness of inner healing depends upon prayer, not upon secular understanding and catharsis. These latter elements of psychoanalysis are often ineffective as therapeutic tools. But to attempt to prove guilt by comparison is a technique of propaganda rather than reason. The same false logic was applied again in an attempt to associate inner healing with Primal Scream therapy, a violent form of therapy that attempts to recreate the birthing experience and allows the counselees to scream in agony. "Primal Scream is so outrageous that most inner healers would denouce it," wrote Hunt and McMahon. "Nevertheless it is true to the basic deterministic theories that underlie psycho-therapies and most forms of healing of the memories."[19] The latter sentence is a bit of convoluted reasoning that tries to obscure the admission of the first sentence by a string of unproven statements: that Primal Scream therapy is true to deterministic theory; that deterministic theories underlie psychotherapies; that deterministic theories underlie most forms of healing of the memories. After that attempt to mislead the reader, Hunt and McMahon went on to describe Primal Scream therapy, having said only that Primal Scream theory is "true" to some theories that allegedly underlie "most" forms of healing of the memories. Is inner healing really rooted in determinism? That's the impression conveyed. Determinism is "the doctrine that everything, esp. one's choice of action, is determined by a sequence of causes independent of one's will."[20] Inner healing acknowledges that people are hurt by others, even that behavior may be governed by compulsions due to emotional wounds, but its focus is action by the individual to allow God to heal the wounds and overcome the compulsions. The forgiveness and prayer encouraged by inner healers involve anything but a negation of free will; rather, they represent an opportunity, through the power of Jesus Christ, to break the cycle of compulsive or sinful behavior.

*The Seduction of Christianity* discredits Agnes Sanford as a far-out cult figure who was essentially a witch, and then points out how most of the major figures in the current inner healing movement were directly influenced by Mrs. Sanford and her writings. This leads the reader to conclude that the entire inner healing movement is hopelessly corrupted with witchcraft. *The Seduction of Christianity* attacks Agnes Sanford as a pantheist:

> After discussing the healing of the subconscious, she calls God "the very life-force existing in a radiation of an energy . . . from which all things evolved," and declares that "God is actually *in* the flowers and all the little chirping, singing things. He made everything out of Himself and somehow He put a part of Himself into everything."

Mrs. Sanford was never a pantheist, never defined God as energy, light or radiation, and never confused energies with God. Her theological insights into the energies of God, as the biblically described light of God, were elaborated in her book *The Healing Power of the Bible*—there she discussed the many biblical passages that relate God with light, or Jesus with light.[21] Mrs. Sanford's theology of the light of God attempted to honor the Genesis account of light coming into existence before the physical sun was created (Gen. 1:1-16) and coordinate it with discoveries in astronomy. She speculated that at the moment of creation the light of God, as a form of primal, nonphysical light, was broadcast throughout the universe, and continues to fill all of creation to this day. That speculation parallels the theory held by many physicists that cosmic rays are the leftover radiation dating to the origin of the universe. It was an interesting theory, well ahead of its time. The theory maintained a clear distinction between Creator and created energy and did not have the slightest connotation of pantheism.

The accusation of pantheism reveals confusion as to what pantheism really is. Pantheism is not merely the belief that God exists in nature, but that God exists *only* in nature and not as a Person. The difference is subtle but profound.

Agnes Sanford believed that God as revealed in the Bible both fills the universe with His presence and being (immanence) and stands above and outside of nature as sovereign God to be worshiped (transcendence). In *The Healing Light,* she wrote:

> God is both within us and without us. He is the source
> of all life; the creator of universe behind universe; and

51

of unimaginable depths of inter-stellar space and of light-years without end. But He is also the indwelling life of our own little selves.[22]

Besides the charge of pantheism, *The Seduction of Christianity* paints Mrs. Sanford as a shaman. A shaman is a form of witch doctor who enters into trance states and pleads or battles with the gods and spirits of the after life. The list of Agnes Sanford's alleged shamanist activities is both tragic and laughable, again betraying an ignorance of the charge being made. Hunt and McMahon accused her of belief in healing by suggestion[23] (contrast this with psychosomatic illness: shamanism?), "apparent belief in an eternal preexistence"[24] "Universalist belief,"[25] "Jungian/occult teaching,"[26] and "syncretistic teachings."[27]

As an example of her "pagan beliefs," they quoted her out of context to give a distorted view of her teaching[28]:

> Wise men of India for many centuries have trod the lofty peaks of spiritual powers and given birth to their oversouls.

Hunt and McMahon then continued to quote Agnes Sanford without any indication that they were jumping ahead to another chapter, proceeding to quote Mrs. Sanford on the communion of saints. The quote above, as it appeared in *The Healing Light,* with the following sentence included and with the six words they dropped from the middle of the sentence they did quote, is[29]:

> Wise men of India for many centuries have trod the lofty peaks of spiritual meditation, developing their psycho-spiritual powers and giving birth to their oversouls. And of all people upon earth their countrymen are the most miserable.

What Hunt and McMahon made to appear an endorsement of Eastern meditation turns out instead to be an expression of the futility of personal spirituality apart from Jesus and His Spirit, as she made clear in the two subsequent paragraphs.

After showing their ignorance of the meaning of pantheism and shamanism, they continued to build a shaky house on the same shifting sands:

> We have already pointed out that Agnes Sanford was a pantheist. This shamanistic philosophy colors all of her

basic ideas and teaching, such as her statement that "every cell in the body has a rudimentary mind and will hear your words."

As a matter of fact, Mrs. Sanford *did* believe in addressing the cells and organs of the body, and believed that lower forms of life have consciousness. Does this belief make a person a shaman, or their belief structure shamanistic? Jesus rebuked the fever of Peter's mother-in-law (Luke 4:39). Was he addressing the virus or bacteria? He cursed the fig tree in direct address, and it withered and died (Mark 11:13-14). When aroused by His frightened disciples who feared for their lives in the midst of a storm, "He rebuked the wind, said to the sea, 'Peace! Be still!' " (Mark 4:39 RSV) and the storm abated immediately. He claimed that if the crowds of Jerusalem would not praise Him, the rocks would (Luke 19:40). Whether or not inanimate objects and lower life forms have any "consciousness," they obey at the name of Jesus. Suggesting that they hear and understand is not contrary to Scripture, nor is it witchcraft.

Hunt and McMahon also painted Agnes Sanford as a spiritualist. This is especially cruel and untrue. Very early in her search for healing knowledge (about 1935), Mrs. Sanford attended two seances. She quickly discerned that all forms of spiritualism were demonic, and was one of the first Christians healers to take such an unequivocal stand. She strongly advised her readers never to pray *with* spiritualists under any circumstances. Further, in the institution she founded, The School of Pastoral Care, she specified that those attending must not have contact with any form of spiritualism.

Hunt and McMahon also tried to relate Mrs. Sanford's supposed shamanism and pantheism to her Baptism in the Holy Spirit:

> Consistent with her shamanistic beliefs, Mrs. Sanford tells of her "baptism of the Holy Ghost" that came "through the sun and the waters in the lake and the wind in the pine trees."[30]

The original quote comes from Mrs. Sanford's *The Healing Gifts of the Spirit,* and refers to an intense prayer experience Mrs. Sanford had while in the woods.[31] Many Christians have felt particularly close to God while in the midst of nature, and the type of prayer experience described by Mrs. Sanford is not uncommon in Christian literature. It is important to understand that the original description made it crystal clear that the spiritual experience was *from* God, through nature. Nature acted *sacramentally* to channel God's graces on her. Mrs. Sanford described the experience as being baptized by the Holy Ghost, but she also explained that, since at the time she did not understand the gifts of the Spirit (1 Cor. 12), she did not know how to accept them. Agnes Sanford described her later baptism in the Holy Spirit, when she received the gifts, in her autobiography, *Sealed Orders.*[32]

The attack on Agnes Sanford is little more than malicious fiction that is given the veneer of scholarship by the use of cut-and-paste quotations and footnotes, a grave injustice to her and her writings.

### Admonishing fellow Christians

John Sanford, in *Elijah House Newsletter,* wrote:

> David Hunt is an apologist, attempting to follow the urging of Jude in verses 3 and 4. We shall always need good apologists. We who teach and write especially need their corrections and rebukes. However, all apologists need to be most circumspectly honest, fair and objective. It pains me to have to report that, in our judgment, David Hunt has been none of these.
>
> He states in a tape of a teaching given in Spokane that he does not need to have followed Matthew 18 to have spoken privately with any of the leaders he attacks because their works are now public domain. But Matthew 18 does not say one does not have to speak to a brother privately if his works are public. Precisely because their works affect the public, David should have consulted with each speaker privately to make certain he was understanding properly what they were saying, and that he was quoting properly.[33]

Opposition to movements of the Holy Spirit has been a repeating phenomenon throughout Church history. In the American experience it has been only in recent decades that mainline denominations have accepted the Pentecostal and charismatic churches as legitimate, non-cult denominations within Christendom. Perhaps the most important anti-Pentecostal and anti-healing book ever written was a volume by Benjamin B. Warfield, *Counterfeit Miracles,* which appeared in 1918.[34]

Warfield was a noted and respected evangelical scholar, and his book took aim at a healing revival then in progress among several evangelical congregations. He brilliantly reasserted traditional Calvinist theology and claimed that the apparent healing miracles produced by the ongoing revival were nothing more than the product of mass suggestion and subconscious delusion. He took special critical aim at A.J. Gordon's book *The Ministry of Healing*. Warfield's arguments against Gordon, judged from the perspective of over half a century later, were deeply mistaken. Warfield was right that *some* healing cases can be attributed to the suggestive powers of the mind, and Gordon was indeed wrong about denying a place to medical science in the total scheme of Christian healing. Yet, for all practical purposes, all Christians now agree that healing prayer for physical illness can be effective and is a proper ministry for the contemporary Christian.

Yet the literature produced by evangelical and mainline scholars against healing and the Pentecostal experience was moderate and fair-minded in comparison with *The Seduction of Christianity*. Warfield's arguments were well structured, did not recourse to logical tricks to gain a point, and were based on an understanding of the original position of Gordon and other Christian healers. At no time did Warfield resort to cut-and-paste quotations to distort his opponents' positions. The scholarship, footnoting, understanding essential arguments involved, and avoidance of exaggerated rhetoric were impeccable. More recently, in 1980, the very fine evangelical anti-occult organization, the Spiritual Counterfeits Project, based in Berkeley, California, did a major study on inner healing. The study started from a viewpoint of reserved suspicion (a good starting point for any Christian) and examined the many aspects of the inner-healing movement. Its conclusion, published in an edition of its journal given over entirely to inner healing, was that the theology and practices of Ruth Carter Stapleton (who at the time was synonymous with inner healing) were not on firm ground. However, they also added that inner healing, as a ministry of "deeper repentance," had great value and potential for all Christians. In other words, this group of experienced, anti-occult evangelicals saw that the fruit of inner healing was proving to be good, and merited more attention.[35] Such a fair-minded and balanced evaluation is what true Christian discernment is all about.

# — 4 —

# Inner Healing

The Spirit of the Lord is upon me,
because he has anointed me to preach good news to the poor.
He has sent me to proclaim release to the captives
and recovering of sight to the blind,
to set at liberty those who are oppressed,
to proclaim the acceptable year of the Lord.

Luke 4:18, 19 RSV

Our ministry as the Church is to do the work of Him who sent us to proclaim the gospel to the ends of the earth. Our ministry as believers in Jesus Christ, in service to the world and to His Body, includes releasing captives, restoring sight to the blind, and freeing the oppressed.

Few would argue that the work of the Church ought to be limited to releasing those physically held captive, healing the literally blind, or freeing those oppressed by their fellow men. In fact, an examination of the earthly ministry of Jesus reveals that He came primarily to release those held captive by sin, that He was as concerned with spiritual blindness as with lack of eyesight, that He freed those oppressed by Satan.

The subtitle of *Inner Healing* by Michael Scanlan provides an apt definition: Ministering to the Human Spirit Through the Power of Prayer. In that book Scanlan stated:[1]

> Inner healing is the healing of the inner man. By inner man
> we mean the intellectual, volitional and affective areas
> commonly referred to as mind, will and heart but including

57

such other areas as related to emotions, psyche, soul and spirit. Inner healing is distinguished from outer healing commonly called physical healing.

We believe that inner healing is clearly found in the ministry of Jesus. This is indicated in the distinction between the "casting out" of evil spirits and the "curing" or "healing" of spirits. There is further contrast between "evil" and "unclean" spirits. Given that all emotional and mental illnesses were attributed to such spirits, the contrast of the terminology indicates more than one ministry.

Scanlan supported his contention by referring to the Greek texts, which he said show the distinction between casting out spirits in cases where the devil or demons were the object of Jesus' action and curing of spirits in cases where people were the object. He identified further consistency in distinguishing unclean (*akathartos*) spirits from evil (*peneros*) spirits.

Jesus healed not only all forms of physical diseases, Scanlan logically maintained, but the very real diseases of the inner man. He cited the healing of a paralytic (Luke 5:17-26) as an example of both inner and physical healing:

First, the Lord restored peace to the inner man by forgiving his sins. This healing gave him the freedom to receive a fullness of physical life, where his paralysis had been both real and symptomatic of his inner bondage.

In Luke 11:33-36 Scanlan found a visual image of inner healing: "So be very careful that your light never becomes darkness. For if your whole body is full of light, with no part of it in shadow, it will all be radiant—it will be like having a bright lamp to give you light" (Luke 11:35, 26 PHILLIPS). Clearly, when Jesus said, "If your whole body is full of light," He did not refer to bodily health alone nor to 20:20 vision; the light is Jesus. "I am the light of the world" (John 8:12 KJV). Jesus exhorted His followers to receive this light and to let it fill every area of their lives.[2]

Being full of the light (Jesus) necessarily involves repentance and acceptance of Jesus' work of atonement; it also involves renewal of the mind and the power of the Spirit at work in the inner man (Eph. 3:16, 4:23, 24). Christians are required not only to abandon the old ways of their sinful nature as they are convicted by the Holy Spirit, they must also be receptive to the gradual renovation of their very souls. Their memories, their attitudes, their fears have all been influenced by the world and by their own sins and those of others. Christians need to be made over in the image of Christ, and this can be effected in part by Christian brothers and sisters "ministering to the human spirit through the power of prayer."

Inner healing, then, is part of the work of bringing the light of Christ into every area of the person. We can expect, therefore, this healing to be a part of the ministry of Christian counseling as well as what is sometimes called "body ministry," the care and prayer of Christians one for another. What needs examination now is the prayer and ministry itself—not whether healing of the inner man has a place, but what methods of ministry are employed today, and their propriety in the Church.

Don Turner, writing in *Fulness*[3] magazine, addressed the controversy over inner healing by interviewing leaders in this ministry and examining in particular the use of visualization, constructive use of imagination, and operation of words of knowledge in prayers for inner healing. He wrote:

> A central technique of almost all inner healing is visualization . . . this varies from creative use of God-given imagination to operation of the gift of a word of knowledge.

He quoted Rita Bennett on the matter of visualizing the healing work of Jesus in relationships with other people or in painful or damaging situations we have encountered:

> The purpose of visualization in prayer is not to create or recreate Jesus. Scripture indicates He is here or was there with us in His omnipresence. Picturing Jesus with us is mainly to assist our faith in what God's word has already declared.
>
> I also do not claim that the past can be recreated through visualization. I teach that our personal past is recorded in our memories and emotion, and that since Jesus is omnipresent, we can recall those memories and know and experience Him there with us. Jesus' healing presence experienced brings healing to our souls.

Mrs. Bennett also pointed out that creative use of our God-given imaginations as Jesus utilized in the parables is an example of visualization. Turner quoted David Seamands on the distinction between Christian visualization and other techniques:

> The occult and perhaps some of the far-out prosperity people do say that if your imagination is strong enough, it will create reality. And this is what inner healers have been accused of doing. What an inner healer might do in counseling a girl raped at the age of six, for example, is suggest to her, "Imagine that Jesus is holding you, washing you, cleansing you. All your guilt and shame is lost." We are not creating Jesus. We are merely using a form of prayer which imagines the reality of the thing.

A word of knowledge is a revelation from the Holy Spirit. This gift is identified by the supernatural character of the revelation—typically it will involve God revealing something the person could not have known otherwise. In prayer for inner healing it is often manifested as an awareness on the part of the counselor of some trouble, need, or incident in the counselee's life that requires healing. Turner quoted Betty Tapscot, a Christian therapist and author of books on inner healing, who emphasized the necessity of reliance on the Holy Spirit:

> The word of knowledge may be in the form of words or revelation, or it may be in the form of a picture in which the Holy Spirit reveals a traumatic experience that occurred in the counselee's past.
>
> We must open ourselves completely to the Lord and His Spirit and ask His guidance. We can't rely on our own intellectual training. I have a master's degree, but that will not heal anybody. No person can heal. Only the Lord can heal.

The Acts of the Apostles contain a classic example of the Holy Spirit granting a disciple a word of knowledge in the story of Peter and Ananias.

> Now a man named Ananias, together with his wife Sapphira, also sold a piece of property. With his wife's full knowledge he kept back part of the money for himself, but brought the rest and put it at the apostles' feet.
>
> Then Peter said, "Ananias, how is it that Satan has so

filled your heart that you have lied to the Holy Spirit and have kept for yourself some of the money you received for the land? Didn't it belong to you before it was sold? And after it was sold, wasn't the money at your disposal? What made you think of doing such a thing? You have not lied to men but to God" (Acts 5:1-4 NIV).

Of course we know that at these words Ananias dropped dead at the feet of Peter, and when Sapphira later came and repeated the lie she suffered the same fate. Yet we also know that God is patient with sinners and wills all to come to repentance (2 Pet. 3:9). Had Satan not filled the hearts of Ananias and Sapphira, the rebuke from Peter might well have provided an opportunity for them to repent instead of being an occurrence of God's judgment.

Jesus, filled with the Holy Spirit, frequently had supernatural knowledge of peoples' lives and used the knowledge to bring them into the kingdom of God. His calling of Nathaniel (John 1:48-50) and His conversaion with the woman at the well (John 4:4-42) demonstrate this. Jesus told the woman at the well all she ever did—He knew every detail of her life and used this knowledge to demonstrate His divinity. As a result of her conversation with Jesus, she became an evangelist, leading many of her neighbors to faith in the Messiah (v. 39).

As disciples of Jesus, we should expect to see every area of our lives transformed. Indeed, He demands that once we put our hand to the plow we not look back. Once we enter the race, we must press on to the finish line. "The One who started the good work in you will bring it to completion" (Phil. 1:6 NEB). By the power of the Holy Spirit and through His Body, the Church, He proclaims release to captives, brings sight to the blind, and sets free those who are oppressed. "He heals the brokenhearted and binds up their wounds" (Ps. 147:3 NIV). If we are seeking the Lord's work and have renounced Satan and his works, we can confidently expect the Lord's touch in our lives. Rita Bennett said, "If during prayer the Holy Spirit shows us Jesus and we experience His healing love, we know it is the Lord and not a counterfeit. When you walk the way Jesus said to walk and you ask Him for bread, He will not give you a stone to break your teeth on."

In *Your Healing Is Within You*[4] (the title, by the way, does not refer to any human ability to heal, but to the kingdom of God within us—see Luke 17:21), Jim Glennon related several instances of inner healing in the ministry at St. Andrew's Episcopal Cathedral in Sydney, Australia. In one case, the relationship between two elderly sisters was healed as a result of prayer.

Mrs. Johnson said, "Canon, will you pray for the healing of the memories for me and for my sister as well?"

I said to her, "Would you like to tell us something of what you want us to pray about? Then we will be able to pray more intelligently and effectively."

"Well," Hilda replied, "this is my story. When I was a little girl there were only three of us—my mother, my sister and myself. And our mother preferred me over my sister. I was always the favored one. My sister felt left out; she felt lonely; and she felt resentful. She couldn't 'take it out' on our mother, because she wanted mother's affection. So she 'took it out' on me. There was constant quarreling and none of the happy relationship which girls growing up should have shared. But it isn't just that. Time has made the difficulties worse. And here we are now, in the last years of our lives, still without the closeness that we should have. Would you pray that our memories be healed—both hers and mine?"

So we laid hands on her and I prayed for her myself. In brief if was something like this: "Our loving Father, we thank you that one of your great and precious promises is that those who are joined to Christ are made so completely new that old things have passed away. By faith, we believe that we are drawing on that blessing for Hilda who all her life has been lonely, and also for her sister who all her life has been resentful. We believe that you are now healing their memories by your love and power. Thank you that you are enabling them to enter into the *full* reality of being new creations in Christ. We praise you for this by faith, and through Christ our Lord. Amen."

Hilda went back to her home in Queensland. She had no opportunity to be in touch with her sister, who lived 900 kilometers away in a country town. But during the following week, she telephoned me in excitement to say: "Canon Glennon, my sister has invited me to go and stay with her for a holiday. She sounded so friendly! I'm going next week!

So off she went, and there followed a most natural, and continuing reconciliation between the two of them. When Hilda came back from her holiday, she wrote to me: "I never told my sister about our prayer, but, do you know, we were sisters for the first time in our lives. And we really loved each other."

Do you see now how we can be in bondage to the events of the past? It could be a lifetime ago. In this case it was seventy years. This simple and beautiful story is all the more valuable because it finds an echo in many a heart. Not that the circumstances would be identical, or even similar to those of Hilda Johnson, but the principle of the story could have a poignant relevance to many. We all need the healing of past experiences that have us in bondage, and will have us in bondage forever, unless we can be set free. And the only person who can really do this is God, for His wonderful provision is that the old passes away and the new comes.

In another case, a gift of the word of knowledge led to healing not only of memories but lack of memories, in this case for a victim of amnesia.

Steven and Elsa Davis had with them a young woman who was staying in their home.

This attractive young woman, Sue, had been involved in a car accident. Before it happened, she had been a happy, healthy, normal young adult. She had not been injured physically in the accident, but as a result of it she suffered total amnesia, a complete forgetfulness of all that had happened. She could not remember one thing about it, but instead of returning to a normal life, she had gradually become what can only be described as a mental vegetable. She had been to psychiatrists who had done their best for her, but there had been no improvement in her condition. So Steven and Elsa brought her to our meeting and asked that we have special prayer for whatever was causing this trouble. I knew nothing more of the problem than this.

As it happened, for some reason I needed to pray for her right away—I think Steven had only a little time available. So I excused myself from the group I was leading and went out of the room to pray for the girl. Len Harris, who had taken over the meeting I'd just left, immediately called on everyone in that group to pray for her too. And I am sure it was their group prayer, with its corporate faith, that brought about what took place.

She could offer no help as to what was troubling her so deeply, because of her total amnesia. So I stood behind her, placed my hands on her head and began to pray, letting the Holy Spirit lead me. After I had been praying quietly in this way for some fifteen minutes, trying, as it were, to let God take over, to my great surprise I "saw" the accident! In my mind's eye it was night time, and I saw two cars. I knew that Sue was the driver of the car on the left, and I could see the other car turned sideways in front of it, but a little distance away. There was a man in the driver's seat of this second car. And as I looked at him, I realized to my horror that he was dead. I did not know it in any other way, but during this time of deep prayer the Spirit of God revealed to me these details of the accident.

Sometimes when I am driving my own car, I think how terrible it would be if I had on my conscience the death of another person in a car accident. This helped me to realize that, because this young women knew she had killed this man, she could not forgive herself. She could not face up to what she had done. She could not carry on with her life. And this was why she had total amnesia, why she needed to forget everything that had happened. She simply could not face the awful reality of it.

I now began gently but plainly to refer, as I prayed, to what I now knew. "Lord, I see there was an accident," I prayed, "and I see that it was a serious accident. . . ."(Come to the point slowly—don't barge in—you can easily make more problems than you solve.) "I see that it had far-reaching consequences, and I can see that someone was injured, and injured so badly that he died . . . Lord, this is why Sue cannot face herself. This is why she cannot forgive herself. . . . As a result of this accident . . . she has killed a man."

I continued to spell out the trouble in this way, carefully, plainly, and with a reliance on God, and taking much more time than I am indicating here. She began to groan within herself. It was not so much with her lips—it seemed rather to come from somewhere deep within her. And then, at last, having spelled out what all the trouble was, without leaving out any detail as she saw it, I began to pray that God would heal her of this memory. Because, you know, when we have done all that we can do, we have to leave behind the things that are past. We have to go on living. God has other things for us to do. If our lives are to be of any further use in the present, we simply cannot go on living in the past.

And so I believed that God was healing her memories— healing all that this traumatic experience had been to her, by the prayer of faith and the prayer of love. I continued to pray and to believe for the healing of her memory, until there wasn't one more word or one more thought that needed to be expressed, after nearly three-quarters of an hour with her. All the people in the next room had been praying for her also, adding their faith to mine. Now I knew there simply wasn't another word, or another ounce of faith, that I could share with her. It was finished! And so I thanked God in the name of Jesus.

Sue was no different when we had finished. But I knew that the prayer of faith had been prayed and by faith I praised God for her healing. Then Steven and Elsa took her home. And from that time on, progressively and quickly, she completely recovered. She could remember everything that had happened, and she could face it. She began to live again, for that is what God wanted her to do.

Of course others had known that Sue had been involved in this fatal accident. Even so, they had not been able to use this information so as to effect any change in her. But I did not know about it at the time. Rather, the Holy Spirit revealed that fact to me through the gift of knowledge, and the prayer of faith enabled it to be used for the healing of her memories.

People need to be made whole. Spirit, mind and body need to be healed, the past as well as the present. God says to us, "If anyone is in Christ, he is a new creation; the old has passed away, behold, the new has come" (2 Cor. 5:17 RSV). Our point has been that so often it is "the old" of our lives that needs healing if that wholeness is to be there.

The old memories . . . sorrows . . . experiences of yesterday and yesteryear—healed so that they have "passed away" and healed so that "the new has come."

David Seamands, in his book *Healing of Memories,*[5] discussed inner healing in terms of putting away childish things (1 Cor. 13:11) while letting Jesus into our hearts, presenting to Him the humility and teachability of a child (Matt. 18:3):

> [Paul] was referring to a combination of emotional and spiritual maturity. . . .
>
> Paul's word for *put away* is the strong Greek word *katergeo,* which means "to render inoperative, inactive or powerless; to remove the meaning and significance from; to free from that which has been keeping one bound or tied up" . . .
>
> This biblical principle forms a fitting foundation for the fact that some people must undergo a healing of memories. Certain problems which prevent maturity we call *hangups.* We say people's hangups keep them *in a bind.* The words are amazingly accurate. When people have never faced their painful memories or been loosened (unbound) from them, they are still *hung up at a certain age and stage of their development.* . . . Many of the hangups come as a result of memories which bind and hold us in a viselike grip.

Seamands also discussed the role of visualization and imagination in prayers for healing of memories:[6]

> Jesus Christ is our eternal contemporary, the Lord of time and our healer; and His Holy Spirit is our present and available helper. The most distinctive part of the healing of memories is the time of prayer. Through the use of imagination, we try to recreate the painful memory and then actually visualize it as it once took place. We pray as if we were actually talking to God on the spot and ask Him to do for us what we would have asked, had we prayed then and there. We ask Him to heal the child or teenager who underwent those experiences—things which really did fixate the child at that place, which made him get stuck at that stage of growth. How can this be possible when the events may have happened many years ago in time? How can our

prayers today possibly affect that inner child or youngster of the long-ago past?

The Scriptures tell us that Christ is the Lord of time—past, present, and future. In a very real sense He is our eternal contemporary, "the same yesterday, today and forever" (Heb. 13:8). When John the Baptist introduced Jesus to the people, he said, "Here is the One I was speaking about when I said that although He would come after me He would always be in front of me; for He existed before I was born!" (John 1:15 PH). In another passage there is a wonderful mix-up of tenses. When the Jews taunted our Lord, "You are not yet fifty years old, and have You seen Abraham?" He answered them with, "Truly, truly, I say to you, before Abraham was, I am" (John 8:57-58 RSV).

If Christ could make these statements during His incarnate earthly existence, how much more can we now make them of the risen, ascended, and glorified Christ! He transcends all time and space, which are, after all, finite concepts of the limitations of our human lives. As Jesus demonstrated on numerous occasions following His resurrection, He was not limited by either time or space, but could appear anywhere and anytime. In a sense, it all is present tense with Him. Because we are bound by time and space, we say Christ "walks back into time" in order to minister to some hurting person. Because of our finite limitations, we do not understand *how* He does this, but we can certainly *visualize Him doing it.* Indeed, on the basis of Scripture, we have every right to picture Him as *here and now.*

But is this all mere autosuggestion? A sort of self-hypnosis where we "psych" ourselves our by the use of mental pictures and strong imagination? No. The promises regarding the work of the Holy Spirit's participating presence and power assure us He really is here . . . the *fact* of His presence pictured by these images is guaranteed by the promises of Scripture.

In another book, *Healing for Damaged Emotions,*[7] Seamands linked the imagination and visualization used in prayers for inner healing to the prophecy of Joel cited in the book of Acts, of the people of God having dreams and visions after the Spirit was poured out on them. He stated that "the Holy Spirit helps us to dream bold dreams, to see visions of what God wants to do for us and in us, and especially through us."

Inner healing must focus on Christ the healer, with prayer guided by the Holy Spirit. Imagination and visualization, in their proper place, do not create the presence of Jesus—He is always present. They merely help us to focus our attention on His presence and become aware of the work He is doing.

Francis MacNutt, in his classic book *Healing,*[8] also related the omnipresence of Jesus to healing the inner man:

> Jesus, who is the same yesterday, today, and forever, can take the memories of our past and
> 1) *Heal* them from the wounds that still remain and affect our present lives;
> 2) *Fill with His love* all these places in us that have been empty for so long, once they have been healed and drained of the poison of past hurts and resentment.

Michael Scanlan, in *Inner Healing*[9], presented what he believes is the Holy Spirit's message to the churches concerning inner healing:

> The Spirit is the Spirit of Jesus who makes Jesus present in power in our midst. This Spirit calls us to expectant faith that reaches to Jesus as our healer. Our faith should not be preoccupied with wonders but with the Lord who is acting in our midst.
>
> The Spirit speaks to the Churches. He calls them to a new fullness of life. . . . But, this Spirit has this against the Churches: they so easily forsake their greatest source of power, the life-giving power that flows from the Lordship of Jesus. The center of the Churches' lives becomes the structure, the activities, the teaching of the professional leadership; good as these things are in perspective, they cannot give life to God's people.
>
> The Spirit says wake up and believe. Get up and work while there is light. Be compassionate as I your God am compassionate; heal my people, my chosen people whom I love and desire to gather under my wing. Heal them!

# Praying With Symbols and Images
# Robert Wise

"You simply can't believe what's happened to me!" Carol's eyes danced and her words sparkled. "I had nearly forgotten how to remember!"

"What do you mean?" I asked in astonishment.

"You've probably forgotten the time last year when you led us in a healing of the memories prayer," she said, smiling.

I had to search my mind to remember that she was talking about the morning that a group had prayed together for release from deeply buried hurts. These people had identified unresolved areas of need and pain. After a time of discussion and inquiry, we had prayed together for the release of this suffering through the power of the Holy Spirit. In the prayer I had asked them to visualize their problem and at the same time to invite the reality of the risen Christ to touch these past needs.

"For the first time I realized how powerful that prayer was!" Carol continued. "Last week when I was talking with my sister, I discovered that the pain had been so completely removed that I was no longer even aware of the old incidents. And, amazingly, I've started to control my weight. I believe I'll be able to quit smoking!"

"That's wonderful!"

"Yes," she exclaimed, "the power of God has released me from those memories of childhood abuse. For the first time I am on my way to freedom!"

God has used forms of visualization and similar methods of prayer to help many people with the burdens they have carried for endless years. These prayers have helped move people into renewal of their minds, fulfilling the scriptural pledge that we become new people in Christ. "If any man be in Christ, he is a new creature: old things are passed away; behold, all things are become new" (2 Cor. 5:17 KJV). But often people are unable to synthesize the biblical promises of regeneration into their lives—the promised renewal of mind has remained a theory instead of a fact. The use of symbols and images in prayer can help people move from possibility to reality; we need to recognize that many people need the help that such prayer can offer.

Prayers for healing of the memories are not a panacea, but neither are they a prayer experiment involving strange or occult practice. They are a valid form of ministry that can be used with great effectiveness by people who are both gifted by the Spirit and professionally trained. To put this ministry in proper perspective, we need to explore the basis for this type of prayer. As we see what happens in this approach to prayer, we can better understand this tool God has given us.

## What does the Bible say?

Let's turn our attention to the scriptural basis for meditational prayers that use symbols, images and visualization. Because references are so extensive, the footnotes include a section listing some of the passages that either allude to, elaborate on, or touch on this practice.[1] Here we will look at several passages that will help us understand how visualization and imagery are a normal part of the devotional practices described in the Bible.

One of the best ways is to study the place of dreams and how they communicated God's truth. Obviously the Bible is filled with these accounts that run from Jacob's great dream at Bethel to the stories surrounding Jesus' birth.

In the Old Testament, the Hebrew word *chalom* refers to a mode of experience in which the content or meaning is conveyed through a visual shape. This can happen while asleep or awake, the former being called a dream and the latter a vision. The New Testament Greek word conveys the same idea. A visual image is one of the means of communication with the divine. Dreams, vision, and images are all of one piece in the Old Testament. While most of the passages describe God speaking *to* humanity in this way, the Psalms

70

particularly use the same metaphors to describe people communicating *with* God.[2]

Even angelic visitations are often of this order. *Malak* (Hebrew for "angel") can describe either a physical entity or a spiritual encounter. Often the biblical writers left no doubt that the angelic visitation was actually of a visionary quality. The story of Jacob's wrestling with the angel strongly suggests an experience of this character.[3]

Communicating with God through both verbal and visual forms was a normal part of the Old Testament experience. The world of the Hebrews abounded with symbols, from the rod of Moses to objects in the Temple. In all of these instances, both truth and the reality of God's presence were communicated through visual forms. We can conclude that one of the reasons the Bible does not stop to give us a "how-to-use" lesson in this kind of communication is that the method was as obvious to them as talking and seeing. Further, we should remember that the "workshop" approach is a Western thought form and relatively foreign to the Hebrew style, which teaches by telling stories in concrete terms. Seldom does the Old Testament editorialize in our Western fashion. Actually, much of the content of the biblical message is conveyed essentially through images in stories without lengthy verbal description or commentary.

The New Testament continues in the same vein. Images, symbols, and visualization all flow together as equal parts of the process by which God and humanity communicate with each other. The three Greek words that are individual aspects of what we mean by "vision" are all related to the verb *horao* which does not distinguish between seeing with the eye and having an inner spiritual vision. In the Scriptures this word is used interchangeably for a dream at night and a vision with the eyes wide open. This usage reflects a rather sophisticated world view in which humanity is understood to be part of both physical and nonphysical reality. Symbols and images are all means by which communication occurs between the spiritual and nonspiritual realms.[4] Visualization put people "in touch" with God.

The nature of Scripture has been hard for many fundamentalists to grasp because they have assumed that words are the ultimate reality or embody final reality. This idea has produced a wooden literalism that is flat and narrow. They do not realize, however, that all words are symbolic and point to a reality beyond themselves. In fact, images are much larger and more powerful symbols than words. John 1:1ff expresses this idea when it speaks of Jesus as the Word or speech of God come in the flesh.

If you want to get the feel of a word taking flesh, think about the word "ring." Just seeing "ring" on the page doesn't do much for you. In fact, you may be confused as to whether we are speaking of a doorbell or an ornament for the finger. On the other hand envision a wedding ring and for a moment consider what values, dreams, and hopes are embodied in that piece of metal. The mental image of the ring has great power to move and touch you. In such a way God has used images to be a vehicle of communication with humanity. Similarily, the Bible illustrates how this process allows us to speak with God.

Here are some examples of God using images to speak to people. In 2 Kings 6:17ff the servant of Elisha opened his eyes and beheld something that obviously cannot be seen by the naked eye under normal circumstances. He saw an ultimate reality beyond physical vision. The text doesn't clearly state how this occurred, but in some way an image was used to convey to him the power of God's presence. The army he saw is a symbol of God's provision. In 1 Chronicles 17:15 we read that Nathan shared with David a prophecy that had come to him "in accordance with all this vision"(RSV). Through visualization he had "seen" the shape of a divine message. First Chronicles 21:16 describes David beholding the angel of the Lord with a sword drawn over Jerusalem. The text is written in a typical Hebrew way that does not reveal whether the experience was an impression on the retina or an image within the mind or soul, but Christian history has generally concluded that David "saw" in the inner sense: the image conveyed the truth. Job 4:16 is a similar illustration of a form that takes shape within the mind of the speaker. These are basic examples of God using visualization to convey His direction, truth, and intention.

Now look at how images are used by individuals in communicating back to God. Psalm 119:18 is a prayer that the believer might "see" more in the Scripture than his physical eyes could encompass. The petition is that the reality locked in the words be opened up. In the same way Psalm 123:1 describes the act of lifting up one's spiritual eyes to see God enthroned in heaven. Obviously this is an attempt to envision something that can't actually be seen with physical eyes. The Psalmist was seeking an image that would convey the deeper realities of God. The Psalmist said further, "Behold, as the eyes of servants look to the hand of their master, as the eyes of a maid to the hand of her mistress, so our eyes look to the Lord our God, till he have mercy upon us" (Ps. 123:2 RSV). This poetic form expresses exactly what happens when people use images in prayer. We shall discuss later how visualization is important in letting the truth penetrate the deepest levels of our being. A similar expression is found in Psalm 141:8 where the prayer is for help against fear. In Isaiah 6:1ff it is not clear from the context whether Isaiah is seeing something entirely impressed upon him from above or arising out of him. Either way, this extraordinary vision of God is like the images used in praying. Isaiah envisioned the majesty of God, which no one can literally see. Further, he wrote in 40:26ff, "Lift up your eyes upon high and see." Such prayers are exactly what imaging and visualization do.

In the New Testament we find similar examples of images working in the believers as they prayed. For example, in Acts 9:12 Ananias saw Paul coming before he ever met him. In Acts 11:15 we have the remarkable vision of Peter seeing a sheet let down. Moreover, in Acts 16:9 Paul received a vision of a man asking for help in Macedonia. Images impressed on and rising from the believers are commonplace in the life of the New Testament. Paul gave us his theological explanation: "Because we look not to the things that are seen but to the things that are unseen; for the things that are seen are transient, but the things that are unseen are eternal" (2 Cor. 4:18 RSV). In this narrative on Christian perspective, Paul was describing what happens in much of inner healing meditation as prayer goes behind the tangible and seeks that intangible aspect of God beyond time itself. In a similar vein, Paul prayed that the eyes of the heart would be enlightened (Eph. 1:18).

Once again, the problem is not form but motivation. Clearly the real issue is not whether Scripture questions using images, but the appropriate use of these forms. Obviously, any attempt to manipulate God or His power is by its very nature idolatrous and blasphemous and ultimately rather silly. However, we are not forbidden to open our minds to allow Him to impress images upon us nor is it wrong for us to present our prayers in similar imagery. Because this approach has so clearly brought people into God's presence, it should not surprise us that it has been copied by people seeking contact with spiritual reality.

### Are imperfect pictures wrong?

Historically there have been those in the Christian community who have declared that any attempt to make an image of the reality of Christ is wrong. Moreover, is it important that my image or symbol of the divine be exactly right? Although the Jewish point of view forbids making images of God, it also doesn't grasp the whole meaning of the Incarnation. Christian artists have always known that the meaning of Word become flesh is that God has presented himself in a comprehensible shape. From the beginning. the Christian community found that the ability to visualize the reality of Jesus was a definite asset in worship. The fidelity of the likeness is beside the point. We cling to a memory, not a photograph. Painting a picture for a church wall does not imply a desire to put Jesus or God on a string; rather, we are illustrating the fact that the "Word became flesh." When people visualize Jesus in prayer, they are doing the same thing.

Occult? Far from it! Symbols and imagery have always had a special place in Christian worship. Because the symbol conveys so many layers of meaning, from the oldest catacombs and the earliest Christian painting onward, visualization has always had an important place in the Christian life. The cross on every church wall undoubtedly looks very different from the actual object of crucifixion, but as a symbol it conveys thousands of messages through its simple structure. Literalists generally fail to grasp how the human mind needs symbols to be confronted in depth by the fullness of God's reality. Symbols have never meant that Christians are bowing down to an idolatrous image of a God they have created. Rather, they are expressing in a limited but human way something of the mystery of God. The incomprehensibility of the total meaning of the Trinity or redemption are expressed concretely in objects such as the cross or triangle, and even in varying pictures of the man Jesus.

## Symbols through the centuries

Because symbols and visualization move us toward encounter, an enormous part of the Christian community has relied heavily on symbolic work through the centuries. The ancient Coptic Church of Egypt, the Orthodox Churches of the Eastern world, the Roman Catholic Church, as well as Anglican and Lutheran communions, have always placed a strong value on symbols and their power to create encounter through images.

One of the classic uses of imaging began in the fifth century with St. Benedict. His three-part method of prayer was defined as *lectio, meditatio,* and *oratio;* or, sacred reading, meditation, and prayer. He taught that after spending time reading the Bible, a passage would be found that attracted the heart. That sentence, phrase, or even word could become the focus of attention. Meditation began when one started saying the passage by using the mouth more than the mind. The phrase or sentence was said over and over again as if the meditator were tasting its very essence. Finally, a prayer would follow that was shaped by the meaning that arose from one's heart. Through repetition, he found that the meaning sank into the soul of the believer, preparing him or her truly to pray as God directed. The images that took shape in prayer touched the person in a powerful and moving way. For centuries Christians have used imagery in Benedict's approach to prayer.[5]

In a similar vein, St. Ignatius of Loyola developed another type of prayer that employed the fantasy of walking around in biblical scenes to help believers consider how they might have interacted with people in the stories. For example, after reading the story of the healing of the lame man at the pool of Bethzatha, one might then relive the story as if lying on the ground, or as one of the sick people who weren't healed. As the improvisation unfolded, one was able to discover new ways in which this story affected them.[6]

Of course, everyone knew that history was not being reconstructed nor the story reshaped to fit personal pleasure. However, the imagination was used to get inside the story and find out how the people really felt. Far from violating the truth, this method recovered the mystery that was latent in history. As symbols on the printed page came to life, wonderful things occurred in the soul. Fantasy led to fulfillment.

Another form of visualization prayer used in the Greek and Russian Orthodox Churches for centuries is the "Jesus Prayer." Using the words "Lord Jesus Christ, have mercy upon me," the faithful begin by practicing an awareness that they are standing in the presence of the risen Christ. As one imagines standing there, these words are prayerfuly repeated again and again, "Lord Jesus Christ, have mercy upon me." The intent is not to communicate requests but to open the heart, mind, and soul to the deepest sense of God's presence. The mind is filled with the reality of the risen Christ. The Psalmist often expressed the same longing of the heart for such divine interaction. As the words are said over and over, the prayer is asking the Holy Spirit to communicate beyond the level even of words. In times when Christians suffered great persecution and pain, this prayer expressed the sighs of the heart when there were no words left to say. By strengthening their resolve to endure, the imagery carried hurting people on to other days.

Meditations for healing of the memories are simply another form of visualization prayer. As in St. Ignatius' prayer, the imagination is used to help God's promises become more real to us. Rather than trying to make God come to us, we are helped to come to the place where God has been waiting for us a long time.

**What shall we conclude?**

The Bible is rich and full in the use of symbols and images as a means to cross from the transient world into the eternal. Far from being legalistic, the Scriptures often demonstrate that the great saints of the past both prayed and were spoken to through metaphors, images, symbols, and visualization. The fact that other religions or secular groups have discovered that these processes will take one beyond what the eye can see only confirms the universality of God's truth.

In addition, through two thousand years of church history, Christians have known that the Bible leads us into new expressions of thought that work especially well for the era in which we are living. Therefore, it is only natural to discover new worship and prayer forms growing out of the Bible. Many times there is no exact chapter or verse to describe the practice, but, after all, Chrsitians are not to use the Bible as Moslems read the Koran.

To attempt to make out some form of meditation or a discovery of modern psychology to be a return to ancient practices of magic and divination is sheer nonsense. In the next chapter, we shall explore how a contemporary understanding of the mind can help us gain deeper insight into why these forms of prayer are able to bring help to so many people.

# – 6 –

# Christians and Psychology

Psychology is so much a part of our everyday lives that we tend to forget that its modern academic application began less than one hundred years ago. Prior to the advent of modern psychology, treatment for the mentally ill typically consisted of imprisonment. At the time Freud began his practice in the 1800's, their treatment had improved—they were merely classified and guarded to protect them from hurting themselves. The mental health field has progressed to immensely more humane treatment and in some cases is able to effect cures of emotional disturbances. In its evolution it has greatly influenced everything in our society. However, in evaluating the use of psychological theories and practices, it is important to remember that the science is young and fallible.

"Much in contemporary psychology is a mixed bag as far as the church is concerned," wrote Robert Wise. "We cannot agree with many of the conclusions of the determinists, the behaviorists, the Freudians and other schools of thought. At the same time, few would deny the significance of discoveries in psychology. Even Freud's attack on religion has helped the Christian church recognize some of its vulnerable points. Most Christian disagreement with psychology does not concern its findings of how human behavior operates; rather, the church must oppose philosophies postulated to define the meaning of humanness or the purpose of life without relationship to God. But the church has benefitted from psychological discoveries: as we better understand the mind, we are better equipped to minister to personal needs. . . .

"Saul and his melancholy are a classic example of being possessed by the shadow side of one's personality. Saul was the victim of his own repressed fears that we would call depression. The story of Nebuchadnezzar's madness is a picture of the unconscious mind unleashed. Many of the stories of demonic possession in the New Testament are expressions of what happens to the ego when evil controls one's mind. The book of James, talking about double-mindedness, gives hints of how the unintegrated personality will subvert the best of intentions. The Scripture writers were highly aware that our behavior is affected by unseen components, none of which denies the reality of free will, but all of which cause behavior to be conditioned by past decisions, actions, and experiences.

"People who try to counsel only by quoting from the Bible have the effect of affronting needy people as if more data will solve the hidden issues rising out of the heart. When depressed people have Scripture verses on "cheering up" quoted to them, they actually have their burden increased. They become more depressed about being depressed! The Bible is better used to bring us to the reality of the healing Christ and to let Him lead us on to wholeness—Scripture is not an end in itself. Like Saul's depression or Jacob's duplicity, many issues of behavior cannot be dealt with successfully until the inner realms of the emotions and mind are penetrated by an encounter with the Holy Spirit. Prayers that imagine the child of the past are not trying to manipulate God; rather, such visualization sets up an experience with God's love."

There can exist a helpful exchange of knowledge between Christian ministry and secular psychology.

"I don't throw out psychology entirely, nor do I accept it indiscriminately," said Rita Bennett. "I accept the study of psychology when it does not work against basic Christian thinking over the centuries, when it is confirmed by God's word, and when it is proven effective in a believer's life.

"Psychology, when it is not against our faith, is an asset to Christianity. However, I understand why some Christians are negative about the subject, especially when it attempts to become a religion. But why do we have to be extremists when we can take the good and leave the rest?"[1]

There is no question, however, that Christ is the answer to illness, whether physical, emotional or mental. While we accept knowledge gleaned from science, there is no substitute for Christian love.

When it is brought to bear on psychological problems, the results can be dramatic. The methods used in integrating the best of psychology with the truths of Christianity are as varied as the individuals applying them.

"The ends of the spectrum range from proponents of Carl Jung to a middle range of integrating the two fields to Jay Adams and his totally biblical 'nouthetic' counseling," wrote Melissa Huffman. "There has historically been an antagonism between the fields of psychology and Christianity—there is also some heat being generated between the ends of the spectrum within Christian counseling.

"There are generally four perspectives with which to view this field:

*"The non-Christian view.* While biblical concepts may occasionally be of some value in the therapeutic process, they must never interfere with its basic course.

*"The 'parallel' view.* The counselor believes in the principles of psychology and is skilled in their application. He knows Christ in a real way and understands the Bible well, yet his Christianity and psychology function independently of the other. Data is stressed from both areas, but is not integrated.

*"The 'integrated' view.* Like the parallel counselor, yet this counselor has an ability to put together truths of psychology and the Bible in a harmonious way, and shows how psychological understanding can often enlighten biblical truth.

*"The 'spiritualized' view.* This counselor views all emotional disturbances as spiritual problems, and sees that obeying God's word is the answer to all mental problems."

A listing of books on the relationship between psychology and Christianity is in Appendix B.

One counseling method that has provided much emotional healing is prayer using imagery. "We can use it to touch the very depths of our personality," wrote Robert Wise, "and essentially fulfill the responsibilities of partnership with God that Genesis calls 'taking dominion over creation.' "

In using imagery Wise has found it extremely important to allow our past to surface in as full and complete a way as possible. One way this can begin is by remembering in detail an emotional situation.

Wise has learned to use the imagination of the people in his pastoral care to invite Christ into the depths of their lives.

He believes that God has ordained us to do His work in this world in cooperation with Him. Because inner transformation demands that we do our part, much of Wise's counseling consists in nurturing an awareness of God's power and providing tools to release that power for wholeness.

# Inspiration Through Imagination
## Robert Wise

I recently prayed with a woman who had been traumatized by her parents' continual fighting. We began praying by having her recall one of the days when they were screaming at each other. Her general recollections were more than adequate to begin the prayer time.

In allowing the Lord to heal this painful memory, I wanted her to not only remember the past but to reexperience it, and to see the experience with the new awareness that Christ, present now in our prayer, was also present during those painful experiences. The Holy Spirit can change us; as we trust in the power of Christ to heal, we move from faith as theory to faith as practicing our conviction.

I asked her to get more fully in touch with how the past felt, and told her to remember her bedroom—how the walls looked, how the pictures were hung, the colors, clothes, and so on, to feel herself back in the same situation. All this was a prelude to prayer. We were walking around in her past, as it were, bringing the trauma to the surface where it could be dealt with and prayed over. Often a person will become very emotional as this sort of exercise is done—a sign that something significant is unfolding. Once she was in touch with the experiences she had stored in her unconscious, we were ready to pray for healing.

As one is aware of Christ being present, it is possible to invite Him to be present to what has been in our mind for a long time. I asked the lady to invite Jesus Christ into this time of active imagination so that He became one of the components in her thinking. Consequently, by faith she was allowing Him to stand in front of all this pain of the past. In that wonderful moment, I instructed her to invite Him to reach out, touch and heal those old wounds. The result was powerful, real, and the fulfillment of becoming a new person in Christ.

Such moments are often times of absolute personal transformation.

We can help people visualize and use their imagination, but only God gives inspiration. The energy and light of God remains His sole property to comprehend and to dispense. How a moment of prayer actually brings the touch of Christ to bear on a problem is still a matter of faith. Mental and emotional healing always remains a matter of trusting Jesus Christ enough to let Him have our fears, as the living Christ, standing at the center of all experience, past, present, and future. Can this be evil? Long ago, Jesus observed that if Satan casts out Satan, his house is divided against itself. Obviously, His conclusion applies.

## Yesterday's child

A similar aid in helping us understand why both visualization and healing of the memories prayers work is the writing of Dr. Hugh Missildine. His book *Your Inner Child of the Past*[2] appeared after Agnes Sanford had already begun her work of praying for past hurts. However, his description of how emotions are stored in the mind is strikingly like her spiritual discoveries. As a psychiatrist, he demonstrated that experiences are kept encapsulated in the same perceptions we have in our childhood experiences. Missildine contended that we often remember and perceive events by emotionally returning to the mindset we had at that point in life. For example, when adults become angry and fight, they often behave like five-year-olds again.

Put simply, Dr. Missildine perceived that a little child lives in all of us. The painful difficult experiences of yesterday do not just float detached and abstractly in our unconscious minds. Rather, they are stored with the same perceptions we had when the events happened to us. To help an adult gain freedom from old compulsions and phobias, it is important to deal with that little person who still resides in one's memories. Once we are aware of this dynamic, we can begin to recognize how that little person is still affecting our thinking and feeling. When we are rejected, we can feel ourselves retreating into patterns that are only repeating the responses we learned at a distant time. While we may not really want to react like this, we have a hard time keeping from becoming the child again. The tendency becomes much more acute when the problems are as severe as childhood deprivation, abuse or molestation.

Missildine's theory about the inner child helps us see another side of why visualization prayers can be so powerful. When we are imagining how we were at a past time, we are really making significant contact with the old perceptions of a previous time of serious need. As this little child is called forth, we also bring up the problems that may be too painful and difficult for us to face otherwise. When our little person is brought before the reality of Christ, we are applying His promises of new life to these repressed past fears. Rather than manipulating God's grace, we are learning how to bring its power to the point of need.

Again, there's nothing new about praying for past needs as we become aware of them. Evangelicals have done the same thing by helping people pray for past guilt that they had not previously confessed. Even though a person may have asked for forgiveness of all past sins, once he prays again about a forgotten source of guilt, and surrenders it, he has one less burden to bear. The process is the same in prayers using imagery except the focus is on emotional need.

**Release from pain and the past**

Failure to make a distinction between willful sin and the repressed pain of the past often only reinforces the suffering of others by insisting that the formula for emotional recovery is as simple as loving and forgiving one's enemies. Victims of depression, abuse, molestation, and rejection by parents are told that the answer to their need is only to believe the gospel is true and then everything will be okay. Such simplistic statements about the grace of God blur the difference between forgiveness for conscious transgression and the need for healing in areas that are often too painful to be consciously recognized.

Of course, we need to sort out good therapy from bad. Some psychotherapies are ill conceived, but not all therapies are the same. The question is whether insight, symbol, and imagery are being used correctly. We need some basic guidelines to distinguish proper and improper use of visualization and imagination in prayer.

**Insights for inspiration**
*Jesus is not an "inner guide."*

Some Eastern religions and a few modern psychologies appear to use "inner guides" to help explore the unconscious mind. Is this the same thing as having Jesus go back into our past experiences?

Some Eastern religions are nothing more than people encountering their own inner world. They simply turn psychology into religion.

These groups mistake the creature for the Creator. Their meditational experiences are only people talking to themselves and offer no transcendent redemptive answer.

Inner guides are generally symbolic expressions of the inner self. However, when people dabble with the occult or seek contact with spirits, a demonic presence can take this form. Seeking "inner guides" is at best a dubious pastime; at worst it is a dangerous practice and a path to self-deception. In the inner world, it is not clear what is good, demonic, or redemptive. The only sure guide into our past is the Holy Spirit. Jesus Christ is the Lord of the present and the past, is the perfect One to help us.

In contrast to use of inner guides, prayer involving reconstruction of experiences is not talking to oneself. Jesus Christ is objective reality who comes in from the outside. Rather than making a general foray into the unconscious, He leads us to the specific contents of actual past experience. As we are in touch with our past need, He comes into that situation. We allow Jesus, Lord of history, to walk down the path to where our wounds lie.

### How do I know the voice of Jesus Christ?

Some people try to use the name of Jesus as an "inner guide" in the same way they would use the name of some other historical figure. This is not biblical. When we are instructed to call on the name of Jesus, we are taught that the name is not nomenclature, but the way in which we come into contact with His personality. The name is the key to the very essence of His person.

The biblical usage is the idea behind Moses asking for the name of God at the burning bush. He knew that the name was the key to reaching the heart of God. Jesus' name is of the same order. John gave us some insight into correct use of the name by instructing, "If we ask anything according to his will he hears us" (1 John 5:14 RSV). The name of Jesus literally means "God is with us" or "He shall deliver His people from their sin."

When we pray in the name of Jesus, we are asking for God to be with us and to make us whole. No one who reaches out to the Spirit of God and seeks contact with His holy person will ever be misled. Of course, as humans we are capable of error in our knowledge and judgment about His presence. This is why Jesus promised that He would send the Holy Spirit (John 16:7-11).

84

When we pray in the name of Jesus of Nazareth, we should be aware that we are calling on the fullness of the Trinity. We are looking to the love of the Father who created us and sent His Son for our redemption. As we ask Him by the power of the Holy Spirit to speak healing words to us, we can be assured that the voice of Jesus has integrity.

## Is it wrong to develop your own image of Jesus?

What about the problem of the Ten Commandments forbidding any graven images? Does the visualization of Jesus in a healing meditation violate that law?

The Law forbids trying to locate the presence of God in an object. It condemns any attempt to reduce the size and person of God to some form that is found in the creation. The result would be to mistake the creation for the Creator.

However, the Scriptures tell us that Jesus Christ is the very image of the Father come to us in human form. Colossians 1:15 explains that "He is the image of the invisible God, the first-born of all creation" (RSV). In addition, John's gospel goes to great length to show us that He is God's speech in flesh (John 1:1-8). The coming of Jesus as the Messiah provided an image of God so we could comprehend the meaning of God's love.

An image of Jesus should never be constructed according to one's own preferences or whims, but it is not wrong to form an image of Jesus in line with the dictates of Scripture. His actual appearance is not the important issue; it is, rather, that faithfulness to His true nature and teachings can lead us to discover an image that leads us closer to the Lord. An image such as this is not forbidden.

Also, praying the name of Jesus may sound somewhat like the way Eastern religions use mantras. It is not. Mantras empty the mind and cause the conscious mind to be blank. In sharp contrast, the Jesus prayer is a means by which we fill the mind with the Holy Spirit so the mind is directly attuned to the presence of Christ.

## How is Christian meditation different from Oriental meditation?

Meditation is as old as the Old Testament. Christians who are apprehensive about Eastern forms of meditation are often surprised to discover that many of the biblical characters practiced what we call meditation. Psalm 1 says that the person who meditates day and night on the Word of God will be blessed. The Psalms have many allusions to the practice of meditation. Genesis 24:63 relates how Isaac meditated in a field. The Bible speaks of meditation as a way to come to God and to prepare to love and serve in the world around us.

In the New Testament, John 15 and 16 give us a framework in which to understand the practice of biblical meditation. As in the Old Testament, the primary concern is to let the Word of God dwell in us. Meditation lets the written Word of God roll around in the mind. However, the purpose is even deeper than just letting words sink into our memory. The ultimate focus should be a personal encounter with the very life of God. It was Jesus' high priestly prayer that we would be one with the Trinity just as He is one with the Father (John 17). Therefore, Christian meditation is an attempt to enter the life of God and allow God to enter us with new fullness.

Christian meditation is a time when we tune the world out so we may fully tune in to God the Holy Spirit. It is not as much a matter of talking to as it is dialoguing with Him in His love and healing power. In inner healing meditation, we do our best to imitate first-century people who personally talked with Jesus. We allow the Word to come to life in us so that we discover the same wholeness He gives His people.

The Bible not only approves of such an approach, it encourages us to use the power that is there. Read John 17:20ff, thinking of Jesus as praying this for you personally. That's what He did just before facing the cross.

*Should I be concerned about who leads me in prayer for inner healing?*

Yes!

The very best context is a combination of competent counseling coupled with a quest for the reality of Christ. It can be dangerous to turn to someone who has no training in giving guidance. A professionally trained and qualified counselor is very often necessary for us to get an objective and competent picture of what is troubling us. Often "Bible quoters" mean well, but can be destructive as counselors for deep-seated personal need.

Moreover, healing of the memories is not for the naive enthusiast. Prayers for reconstruction of experiences are best done by people who have gifts in this area and understand what they are working with.

In addition, most often inner healing is not a one-shot experience. Our problems exist with many layers. After one layer is healed, we may discover other aspects of need that we couldn't have known existed before we were helped. Don't be discouraged if it is necessary to pray many times for resolution of a need. We may want to have a problem solved; God is interested in healing our total person, and that takes a little longer. Some problems vanish only as the total person recovers wholeness.

Set out on a journey in which your goal is to become conformed to the image of Christ. If you truly want to become like Him, He will change and transform anything that stands in the way. Pilgrims make the best candidates for healing.

## Guidelines for growth

How can inspiration be found through the imagination without varying from the course the Scriptures have set for us?

1. An image of Jesus is not to be constructed according to one's whims, but in compliance with the direction of the Scriptures. The issue is not His appearance, but fidelity to His personhood and teachings. Healing of the memories must not try to manipulate the divine, but seek to apply what the Scriptures have promised. We rely on the Holy Spirit to guide and direct us.
2. All results must be tested by Scripture. Whatever is done or prayed must be in harmony with the Bible. Anyone who ministers should also be in complete accord with biblical teaching. For example, if a person has any problem in affirming the totality of the Apostles' Creed, I would quickly back off. Anyone not related to a local congregation nor under the authority of a church, pastor, or priest is questionable.
3. One of the best preparations for ministry or for receiving ministry is participation in the life of the church. Each day both the intercessor and the petitioner should pray to be filled with the light of Christ and kept safe through the blood of Christ.
4. Any form of active imagination is a quest to experience the inner world. You are talking to a part of yourself that has been cut off or suppressed. However, if people go into this world seeking the evil one, he can be found. Therefore, Scripture forbids all such quests. Shamanistic religions have emerged from the perverted use of the spirit world. In addition, occult practices—seances,

witchcraft, etc.—have a reality often expressed in the depths of the inner world. We must sort out what is us, what is evil, and what is the Holy Spirit. This can only be done by the power of the Holy Spirit and through the name of Jesus Christ. Nevertheless, we need not fear past intrusions of evil. In the name of Jesus of Nazareth, all bondage can be broken. Often simply praying the Lord's Prayer with understanding is sufficient to break these bonds and set us free. Remember, the evil one is not alive and well on the planet— he is wounded and dying.

The bottom line is simply this: "God has not given us a spirit of fear, but a spirit of power and love and a sound mind" (2 Tim. 1:7 PHILLIPS). We do not have to retreat from the fears of yesterday, the apprehensions of today, or the uncertainties of tomorrow, nor from the phobias of reactionaries. In every realm, the authority of the risen Christ stands supreme. With boldness and confidence, we can pray our way into the newness and wholeness that the Scriptures promise to the people of God.

# — 7 —

# Positive Speaking

Death and life are in the power of the tongue (Prov. 18:21 KJV).

If anyone says to this mountain, "Go, throw yourself into the sea," and does not doubt in his heart but believes that what he says will happen, it will be done for him (Mark 11:23 NIV).

What you say is what you get. —Don Gossett[1]

The Scriptures indicate that there is tremendous potential for good or evil in the words we say. Does it follow that, as Don Gossett said, "Your own words can tap in on spiritual power that will bring you love, joy, peace, happiness, success and prosperity"[2]? Or is "insistence that God Himself must work even His own miracles within a framework of laws that enables us to tap into and dispense spiritual power by what we think, speak, or do . . . the basis for all ritualism and occultism,"[3] as Hunt and McMahon maintained in *The Seduction of Christianity*?

Let's briefly take a closer look at these two statements about positive speaking—we can fairly say that each represents its school of thought.

In his book *What You Say Is What You Get,* Gossett told his readers that "Can't is a four-letter word"[4] and that all things are "Himpossible."[5] Gossett did emphasize the importance of being in a right relationship with God, and used many Scriptures to make his point that if we are right with God we can ask anything and get it.

However, he seemed to say that blessings of love, joy, peace, happiness, success and prosperity are contingent not just on the Father's will and our relationship to Him as sons and daughters, but on our "claiming" or "confessing" the receipt of those blessings.

The statement from Hunt and McMahon is rather more abstruse. It says that *insistence* that God must work within laws is the basis for all ritualism and occultism. This betrays either a very limited, personal definition of ritual, or else implies that all ritual—set forms for partaking of the Lord's supper, for example—are founded on an insistence that God follow certain laws.

This is a distinct concept from that of God keeping His promises. The more relevant part of their statement describes the framework of laws into which some people try to limit God's work. The framework sounds very like Gossett's postulation of spiritual power we can tap into.

Having taken a glance at two extreme teachings on the power of the spoken word, we now present four essays that provide some more food for thought on the subject.

# The All-Powerful Word
# Trevor Dearing

In the Bible tremendous emphasis is placed upon the power of God's voice. He only has to speak for things to happen. In the beginning, "God *said* 'Let there be light'; and there was light" (Gen. 1:3 RSV, italics mine).

God has promised that the power of His word will accomplish His purposes.

> So shall my word be that goes forth from my mouth; it shall not return to me empty, but it shall accomplish that which I purpose, and prosper in the thing for which I send it (Isa. 55:11 RSV).

In the New Testament, we are told that in Jesus, "The Word became flesh and dwelt among us" (John 1:14 RSV).

There was, therefore, no limit to what Jesus could accomplish, simply by speaking. As we have seen, He spoke forgiveness to the penitent, deliverance to the captives, health to the sick, and life to the dead.

Even our *human* words, once they have been uttered, have power either to hurt or to help people. Sometimes they are still doing damage to the hearers or, most positively, encouraging them, years after they were actually spoken. How much more then do our words have power when He actually speaks through us! He has promised to give our words *His* power by placing *His* Word upon human lips.

> The word is nigh thee, even in thy mouth, and in thy heart: that is, the word of faith, which we preach (Rom. 10:8 KJV).

Paul once said that he was pleased his hearers did not receive his message simply as the words of men, but as it truly was: the word of God (see 1 Cor. 2).

Words, therefore, like the laying on of hands, are of fundamental importance in the healing ministry. It is noticeable that, following the example of Jesus, the apostles not only laid hands upon people, they also spoke God's healing word to them. We must do the same today.

In the power of Jesus, and with His word upon my lips, I have often addressed organs of the body and commanded them to respond to the healing power of Jesus. Healing has often resulted.

"Prostate gland, be healed!" I once cried. The patient, who had been passing blood, later wrote:

> I went into the hospital for an exploration of my bladder. This was two months ago. Today I had to go to the hospital and was told I had a clean bill of health. Praise the Lord!

Sometimes, in the same spirit, I have rebuked sicknesses and commanded them to depart. Frequently the result has been remarkable. Arthritis, in particular, has yielded to this treatment. One lady wrote gratefully:

> I was taken ill with severe arthritis of the spine in June of last year and, in spite of various hospital treatments, my position got worse, culminating in the Royal Free Hospital in London sending me here unable to help me in any way. I came to your mission at Wisbech. I am now greatly relieved. My family thinks a miracle has happened and I am greatly blessed.

Even cancers have shriveled up under the power of this ministry. Frequently I have treated depression and fears in the same way. One testimony:

> My mother, who was suffering from depression, was taking many drugs, tranquilizers, sleeping pills, etc. She stopped them due to your words and has been completely healed.

On that occasion my words had been: "You need to step out into the glorious liberty God has given you through His love." She did— and was delivered.

The word which speaks forgiveness still has great power for the remaking of the whole person. This has been a ministry particularly to those responding to the altar call which always follows the gospel message at my meetings. After each person has expressed penitence for their sins and publicly taken Christ as Savior, I have been able joyously to say: "On the authority of the Word of God, I am able confidently to declare to each one of you that your sins have been forgiven. You stand there in garments as white as snow for 'If we confess our sins, he is faithful and just to forgive us our sins and to cleanse us from all unrighteousness' " (1 John 1:9 KJV).

This was so in the case of young Jacky, who was the first person to come forward in response to the appeal at a rally in Southend, Essex. She was known throughout the school for her terrible temper, which eventually resulted in the headmaster actually expelling her. After my words to her the change in her was truly wonderful. Even unbelievers said, "My, you *have* changed, Jacky!" She was so thrilled that people were noticing the difference. Eventually the school took this transformed young person back again.

Family relationships have frequently been healed as this ministry of forgiveness has put all the past behind and given people the possibility of a new start together. When all parties have themselves received new wholeness of personality, they have been in a far better position to relate to the others.

In my experience of ministering, the word of forgiveness has often been able even to lift depression. The peace of God has flooded the oppressed mind, binding up the broken heart and soothing all the bruises. Even physical sicknesses have been affected by forgiveness.

God still has power today both to heal and to forgive. Further, it is in fact *the only way* that today's captives can be set free from Satan's grip.

In my own ministry, like that of the Lord, I have not searched out demon-possessed people, but have run into them as I have traveled.

In Ongar, Essex, I had hardly begun to minister to the sick when a young woman fell screaming at my feet. She began to knock her head on the floor and writhe about in terrible torment.

"Come out of her, and leave her alone, you unclean spirit," I commanded, "in the name of Jesus."

In a few moments she was free. The spiritual and emotional troubles which assailed her were over.

"It was like streams of clear, fresh water running through my being," she told an inquisitive newspaper reporter.

She was a Roman Catholic by denomination and, after reporting the incident to my bishop, I commended her to her priest for care. She has rejoiced in the Lord ever since.

In another town, by arrangement with the vicar, and by permission of the bishop, we actually held a special deliverance service for a young woman. She had been so involved in occultism and the drug scene that she had a black cross tatooed upside down upon her back. A sympathetic doctor had gone to great trouble to have it removed when she became a Christian. Still, however, she reacted violently to the name of Jesus and especially to the elements of bread and wine at Holy Communion. After the ministry of the delivering word she was able to praise the Lord and partake of the sacrament for the first time.

Later, a mission meeting in a large church in the Midlands was interrupted by the terrible noise of furniture being smashed at the rear of the church. A young man was, in fact, picking up chairs and crashing them one against the other. The minister and stewards tried to restrain him by pinning him to the floor. He shook them off with supernatural strength and ran from the buiding. Immediately I urged the congregation to pray.

"Destructive spirit, I bind you," I declared across the distance. "You shall not hurt him any more. In the name of Jesus, I loose him from your control."

We then prayed that the Spirit of God would direct his feet back to the church.

Surely enough, he returned. I discovered that he had been involved deeply in the meditational exercises of yoga. This had obviously been the point of the spirit's entry.

"I felt my body was going one way, despite all my mind wanted to do. I was taken over by something which used my body," he nervously explained.

It was all over in two minutes. He renounced the practice from the heart and, at the word of command, yet another spirit was dispatched to the pit to await the judgment of Christ.

In these days of the comeback of the supernatural, occultism is rampant. Innocent people, who do not appreciate the dangers, are getting involved in increasing numbers. Exorcism ministry is, therefore, increasingly vital. It is an essential part of divine healing ministry today. The power to deliver lies in the spoken word.

Through this ministry also, alcoholics have been set free, suicidals saved from death, drug addicts delivered, homes and families saved, depressives received new joy, spiritualists converted, and even smokers have been able to discard their last packet of cigarettes.

Letters have just about burst their envelopes with joy. One woman wrote:

> After you had ministered to me, I could have skipped and danced back to my seat (after all, for forty years these dreadful demons have had me in their power). I felt so light and free that I could hardly control my feet from dancing. Then came the acid test: coming home to the house where so much hate has been. I lifted my heart to God and went indoors believing He had done it. And He had, Brother Trevor, healed.

Perhaps one of the most unusual cases I ever had, which proved the power of the inspired spoken word, concerned a young married man classified as schizophrenic. He had lapsed into this state after losing his job and feeling unable to support his pretty wife and two young children. He had entered so deeply into a world of his own that he could not be reached by normal conversation. It was the wife who first sought my help, and I persuaded her to bring him along to my meeting in Hadleigh, Essex, whatever his condition.

The situation did not look very promising because, at the beginning of the service, he was just wandering about the church mumbling incoherently to himself. I went up to him, but could obtain no rational replies to my questions.

Suddenly, however, I felt that I had to begin to prophesy. Promise after promise from God poured from my lips; all of them were especially for that young husband. I found I was declaring God's love for him and the certainty of His forgiveness. Eventually, I began to pray over him in other tongues which I did not even myself understand. Suddenly he looked up. Rationality had returned.

"I'm okay," he said. "Where am I? Where have I been?"

So his children had their father restored to them for Christmas and the family have since emigrated to the U.S.A. The word of God had reached a broken and bruised man where no human words could possibly have touched him.

All these incidents support my contention that liturgical structures and forms of service must leave a great deal of room for spontaneity. This ministry, to be effective, must be far from mechanical. The supernatural gift of discernment has to be sought, to really penetrate the area of need and minister accordingly, with hands and words. The correct verbal ministry is of very great importance for healing.

The words, however, must not be regarded as magical mumbo jumbo, but as the very words of God upon human lips. Once again, this is an extension of the ministry of Jesus in the world today. Words express personality. Jesus himself is met through the words of the preacher and healer, when they are, in fact, in harmony with the Bible's own message. Ultimately, however, it is Jesus who must be trusted to accomplish that which He has promised. It is *He* who must be obeyed as He speaks through His inspired servants. Now, however, He has no voice but that which comes through "anointed" human mouths. Therefore we pray, "Take my lips and let them be filled with messages from *Thee*."

God is still speaking supernatural healing and deliverance in the world today. "To day if ye will hear his voice, harden not your heart . . ." (Ps. 95:7-8 KJV).

# Supernaturally Endowed
## Trevor Dearing

The gospels record that even Jesus had to receive "power from on high" before He could begin His divine healing mission.

"Now, when all the people were baptized, it came to pass, that Jesus also being baptized, and praying, the heaven was opened, And the Holy Ghost descended in a bodily shape like a dove . . ." (Luke 3:21-22 KJV).

"And Jesus being full of the Holy Ghost returned from Jordan" (Luke 4:1 KJV).

The disciples had to receive a similar endowment before they could begin their supernatural ministry (Acts 1:5, 24).

The same is obviously true for ministers of healing today. Yet, at the time of my ordination to Holy Orders, the Church of England taught me nothing at all about moving powerfully in the realm of the supernatural. It had, for centuries, stood for dignified, respectable, safe Christianity. Although both its "Catholic" and "Evangelical" wings had a definite spirituality and sought, in their different ways, to communicate the grace of God to the faithful, supernatural phenomena were not really in evidence and the concept of the miraculous was regarded as a matter of early church history.

Consequently, until 1969 my own ministry was very ordinary. Although I had worked hard as a pastor, I eventually became so disillusioned and frustrated that I forsook full-time parish ministry for a post in religious education.

It was, in fact, the pentecostal branch of the Christian Church, whose supernatural emphasis had for so long been rejected by major denominations, which awakened stirrings in my soul for an endowment of supernatural power. It was what I witnessed in their full gospel meetings that first made me realize the possibilities of ministering God's power today. Hadn't the natural life of mankind been completely revolutionized by new discoveries of physical power? I reasoned, "How much more could happen to our spiritual lives through the rediscovery of spiritual power?"

Coal, gas, electricity, oil and, more recently, nuclear power have transformed our lives. Yet these vast resources of physical energy had existed for countless generations, while human beings had labored in their own strength to achieve their objectives. It had been the *realization* of these resources of power which had been the first step towards the accomplishments of modern technology.

The trouble with the Church, I decided, was that it had labored on without realizing the vast resources of spiritual power God had placed at its disposal since the first Pentecost. The pentecostal churches had helped me to realize that this endowment of the Spirit had not simply been for Peter, James, John, Mary, and the others, but a gift for the whole *Church,* for all time. It had dawned upon me that all the power of heaven was available to us today.

I remembered that although the first apostles had been very ordinary people like ourselves, the Acts of the Apostles told the thrilling story of what they had accomplished when the Spirit of God had come upon them. It was, I decided, my intensive schooling in rationalism which had caused me to lose my expectancy of what God could do today. Like myself, the few people who still attended church went expecting only the same unexciting routines week by week. The service would always take the same form and last approximately the same time. Before going to worship they could even put meat in the oven and set it ready for lunchtime. Everything was so mundane and so predictable.

We were so accustomed to the ordinary and so used to plodding on in our own strength that we had become conditioned to God's activity being a non-event. We were like the Arabs who, years ago, regularly struggled across the desert without realizing that under their feet were oceans of oil that could drive tons of metal across those same deserts at tremendous speed. Similarly, we Christians had had incredible spiritual power 'above' us for nearly two thousand years, but had never realized its potential. The full meaning of Paul's words, "Now unto him that is able to do exceeding abundantly above all that we ask or think, according to the power that worketh in us" (Eph. 3:20 KJV), had never really been grasped by the church of my generation.

I can hardly exaggerate the effect this realization had upon me. It caused me to enter into a new dimension of spiritual power. I am sure that since that time one of the beneficial results of services like my Power, Praise and Healing meetings has been that they awakened the realization that the supernatural power of the Spirit is still available for Christians today.

A second important principle relating to power, however, is that once its possibilities have been released, it still has to be brought within our grasp in order to be useful. Oil, for instance, is no use under the North Sea; it has to be brought ashore in order to be productive. Coal is no use under the earth; miners have to bring it to the surface before it can be used. Similarly, once we have realized the resource of power we have today in the Holy Spirit we must lay hold of it—receive it—in order to use it for a spiritual revolution. Paul asked some men of Ephesus, "have ye received the Holy Ghost since ye believed?" (Acts 19:2 KJV). And this is still a pertinent question for Christians today. Before 1969, I, like those Ephesians, would have had to answer, "I do not know the Holy Spirit is given."

Providentially, receiving the power of the Holy Spirit is a great deal easier than getting oil from the North Sea, for God is more ready to give than we are to receive (Matt. 21:22). Jesus said, "How much more shall your heavenly Father give the Holy Spirit to them that ask Him?" (Luke 11:13 KJV).

Receiving the power of the Holy Spirit is not so much, therefore, a matter of intensive effort, but of getting our lives into the right relationship with God. It is more like refueling a car or plane than digging for coal. To put more gas into a car, we have to bring it into right alignment with the pump at the service station. Similarly, a small fighter plane has to be brought into exactly the right "relationship" with the "parent" plane in order to refuel in midair. When receiving the Holy Spirit, *a right personal relationship with God* is essential.

Occultists look in all directions for sources of supernatural power. Sometimes, without realizing it, they refuel at a service station provided by the devil. The gift of the *Holy* Spirit, however, is for children of the kingdom whose lives have been brought into a right relationship with God through repentance and acceptance of Christ as Savior. Then the gift of the power of the Spirit is available by an act of simple faith. The biblical prescription is, "Repent, and be baptized every one of you in the name of Jesus Christ for the remission of sins, and ye shall receive the gift of the Holy Ghost. For the promise is unto you, and to your children, and to all that are afar off, even as many as the Lord our God shall call" (Acts 2:38-39 KJV).

Christians, in fact, belong to two kingdoms at once—the earthly and the heavenly. They respect and obey their earthly rulers (though not always without question), and also (definitely without question) subscribe to the ultimate authority of their Lord, Jesus Christ. Christians have often been martyred because of this undeniable allegiance to the ultimate authority of the Lord Jesus Christ over their lives.

Jesus, in fact, first portrayed His unique authority during His ministry in first-century Palestine. It was His remarkable authority in teaching, dealing with demons, sickness, circumstances, the forces of nature, and even death, which drew gasps of astonishment from the crowds. Ultimately, His authority was gloriously demonstrated when He rose from the dead. After this remarkable event, He declared to His disciples, "All authority in heaven and on earth has been given to me" (Matt. 28:18).

Christians are those who have submitted to the authority and lordship of Jesus, the "King of kings."

Authority, however, is often delegated to subordinates. By this means, rulers trust and enable others to implement their wishes. So, an "officer of the Crown" may be a very insignificant and unimportant man in normal life, but he is conscious of a very important role indeed when carrying out the instructions of his government. The power he yields has been delegated to him from above. It is effective as long as he remains obedient and faithful in his tasks.

It is wonderfully true also that Jesus, the King of kings, has delegated to *His* subordinates, the children of the kingdom, His unique and wonderful spiritual authority. He has done this by giving us the right to use *His name* as we obey His commission to preach the gospel, heal the sick and cast out demons. We Christians can receive the *energy*-power of heaven and exercise the *authority*-power of the King of kings. What immense, incalculable resources we have at our disposal for the transformation of human life! A power emanates from Jesus and by an authority vested in the use of *His* name. His name guarantees His personals presence, power, authority, and effectiveness, for all who know Him, trust Him, acknowledge His position, and obey His commands.

Apathy, complacency, and spiritual self-satisfaction are the main enemies of revival. We need both a dynamic concept of *mission* and also a dynamic concept of *life in the power of the Holy Spirit* in order to move effectively in God's will. More and more power is ours as we seek Him at greater and greater depths, increasingly submitting to His promptings, and courageously launching out in obedience to His commands. Our resolution should increasingly be (in Hudson Taylor's words) to "Expect great things *from* God and attempt great things *for* God."

Many of the gifts received and ministries granted have been manifested. Other results we shall, perhaps, never hear about this side of eternity. But I receive constant testimony that God has visited His people, revitalizing and equipping them for supernatural ministry by the bestowal of power and authority.

# You Have What You Affirm
## Jim Glennon

"Then it happened, and it was almost a relief to know it was over," Maudie told me.

Five months prior to this conversation the bedside phone had rung just before midnight. Paul reached for it, but before he could speak, a calm but urgent voice came in. "Is that the Beckett's? It's the Cottage Hospital here, Sister Carrington speaking. It's Max—he's had an accident. We don't know how serious it is. The doctor has just arrived. You had better come."

They were out of bed at once, changed clothes quickly, and hurried to the car. Maudie felt in the grip of a cold fear and could only repeat, "I knew it . . . I knew it. . . ." Paul was silent as they drove the three kilometers to the local hospital on the outskirts of the town. Max had been out on his motorbike visiting friends. It must have happened on his way home.

They stopped behind the doctor's car in the drive; the ambulance was further up. At first they walked quickly along the verandah and then more slowly as they came to the ward that served as an emergency room; up ahead they could see light and movement.

Max was lying very still, hardly able to speak, his body in shock from the accident. There was a good deal of blood from the cuts and abrasions where he had hit the road. They waited grimly, hardly daring to speak. Fifteen minutes later the doctor said, "It's not good, we can't keep him here. I'll get the ambulance to take him to the district hospital. It's his arm and his leg, and there may be internal injuries. I think you should go with him."

Maudie paused as she related her story to me. She and her husband Paul were visiting Sydney during the holiday season and, as many visitors do, had come to the Healing Service. They had introduced themselves to me during the greeting time, and, on hearing something of what had happened to them, I invited them to come and see me. Now we were talking in my room at the cathedral.

"He wanted a bike," Paul broke in. "You know what it's like; some of his mates had bikes and he wanted one too."

"I was the one who didn't want him to have it," Maudie went on. "When I was young I knew someone who was killed on a motorbike, and this shocked me deeply—partly because I knew him well, and also because he was a very good rider. I thought if that could happen to Ted, it could happen to anyone."

"Max was twenty years old," his father continued, "so it had to be his own decision."

"I couldn't get it out of my mind that he might have an accident," Maudie said. "It seemed that the very awfulness of it made it stick in my mind. I kept dwelling on it, and it became more and more a burden and nightmare."

"I tried to tell her not to worry," Paul came in, "but that didn't seem to help."

"I didn't want to be afraid, of course," Maudie continued, "but the more I thought about it the worse it became. It was like that for more than twelve months. Then it happened, and . . ."

I thought how distressed she looked as she recalled this harrowing experience. Then she broke down and began to cry. It was important for her to express her feelings, and I helped her do this. "It must have been a terrible time for you. . . ." After she regained her poise, the conversation continued. We finally reached the point where we could review what had been talked about and face up to the fear she had and the problem it caused. They were both able to face this in a positive way and, although there was more to be said, a beginning had been made.

"We've learned a lot from what we have been through," Maudie said ruefully.

"Yes," I understand. Most of the things I know have been learned the hard way," I said. "Would you like us to pray about it and believe for God's help at this time? We could pray for Max too."

They nodded their agreement as Maudie added, "Max is making progress and we are believing for his full recovery, though it will take time."

*"What I dread befalls me"*
My own experience of fear and its results has been like this as well.

It was just as though I had planned it that way. But, of course, it was the very opposite of what I wanted. What I wanted were things that were good, that made for peace of mind and that enabled me to reach the goals I had for my life. Yet the opposite of what I wanted began to happen—and it wasn't on one occasion only.

To begin with, there was only a slight suggestion that what I was afraid would happen *was* happening in point of fact. I didn't see a connection between them at first. But as time went by, it became more obvious. It had the effect of confirming my fears—there was a basis for them after all.

To be afraid that something would happen and then to find it actually happening (even if only in degree) made me more afraid. Then more things went wrong. It isn't too much to say that as time went by, it was like the print that is developed from a negative; one reflected the other in detail. I need to point out that this was a progressive thing spread over a number of years, and like most things that slowly get worse, you don't realize you are caught until it is too late.

If I couldn't do anything about my fears when they were in an incipient form, I certainly couldn't do anything about them as they grew worse. It reached the point where they would sweep over me and I was powerless to resist. Sometimes it was without warning and without reason. I was becoming paralyzed by this problem and my anguish was mounting. Some of the truest words in the Bible are "fear hath torment" (1 John 4:18 KJV). Only those who have been in the grip of fear can understand the agony of mind it brings.

Some time ago I visited a clergyman who was dying of cancer; he was suffering greatly. I had met him only once before. As I took my place by his bedside he said to me, "The only person who can minister to me is someone who has suffered."

I replied, "I have not suffered in the way you are suffering, but I have suffered in my mind."

He looked at me and said quietly, "I feel I have known you all my life." Deep calls unto deep.

Perhaps I should explain that my fears were about people. From my earliest days I have been apprehensive about meeting people whom I did not know. In the long run I was afraid of everyone—some more than others—but, in general, everyone. This was irrational of course, but it wasn't any easier to control because of that.

It was not until I reached a breaking point that I came to understand the awful truth that fear *brings about* what we fear. Two things brought this home to me. The first was a verse in the Bible: "For the thing that I fear comes upon me, and what I dread befalls me" (Job 3:25). This, incidentally, was the explanation Job gave for his troubles.

The second thing is something well known to all Australians. One of the customs of the Australian Aboriginal people in their tribal life is "pointing the bone." The medicine man can point a bone at a member of the tribe, and it means that man is going to die. As a result of the ritual that has been directed to him, the man has an all-consuming fear that he is going to die. He believes this to the point that there is no doubt in his heart. And so he dies.

I am not saying that every passing fear has this result, or that every experience of sustained fear has this result. That would be too sweeping a generalization. There are, of course, other reasons for accidents and sickness. But, nevertheless, as far as fear is concerned, "what I dread befalls me" is a biblical principle, and this is what I am echoing.

This is disconcerting enough, but there is more to follow that affects everybody.

### *"Faith" for your problem*

Whether or not we are fearful, we all have problems of some kind. And there are two things about problems I would like to mention here. The first is that everyone's situation is unique. No two people are the same, and neither are their circumstances. This is what the psychologist calls "the law of individual differences." In passing, this means that the help or ministry that is given to a troubled person is always personal. There is no such thing as everyone receiving a "No. 9 pill" as we used to say in the army about those who reported sick at the Regimental Aid Post. (I don't think that really happened at the R.A.P., but we liked to say it did!)

The second point is that all troubled people have something in common: *they affirm their problem.* You might say that it is inevitable; after all, it is what they have, it is what they see, it is what they are concerned about. It is often given a name and the person is labeled as such: "I am a depressive"; or "my marriage is on the rocks"; or "I have arthritis"; etc.

Although it may be natural to react in those terms, it doesn't alter the fact that this will *perpetuate the problem*. And because it continues, the effect is cumulative and the situation *worsens*. Irrespective of how it came about, it is now being kept alive because it is being *affirmed* in an ongoing way. You see, your faith is what you affirm, and if you are affirming your problem, that is the kind of "faith" you have. Like the Aboriginal who has had the bone pointed at him, *you have "faith" for your problem*.

A good deal of the difficulty lies in the fact that, to begin with, it may not be our fault at all. We may have inherited characteristics that have given us a bad start in some respects. We may be the innocent victim of circumstances that have come upon us. But, not withstanding this, it is also true that if the way we react is keeping things going, then, ultimately, it is a *self-inflicted wound* and the end responsibility is ours.

I said worse was to come, and I haven't finished with that yet. Just as we can keep our own difficulties going, so too can we keep the difficulties going *in other people,* if that is what we affirm about them.

This may seem to be even more incredible, but it is just as true and just as real. The thing that upsets me, perhaps more than anything else, is the knowledge that I can keep, and have kept, other people in their bondage just by reacting to them in terms of the difficulty I see in them. It isn't that I set out to do this; perhaps they have characteristics that offend or disturb me, and which may be making problems for others. When I see someone being hurt by someone else's faults, I tend to get uptight. It is so easy to justify one's irritations.

The Bible's continued abhorrence of "the pointing of the finger" and "calling your brother a fool" are expressions of its concern that, by so doing, we are locking people into their personal difficulties. And that is what I have actually found. As long as I react in this way, the person in question stays in that condition. But when, at last, I react to what they are like in a positive way, so that I am believing something good for them, they are very often released from their bondage and come into a new experience of wholeness.

We are all making this mistake every day about ourselves and others. And we are so used to it that we take it for granted and almost certainly don't realize the consequences. If we were told about our ways, we would be incredulous, and even if we wanted to alter them it would be difficult. Old habits die hard, and bad habits die harder.

Many would affirm that they are only facing the facts and taking a responsible attitude; to do any differently would be to play the ostrich and be unrealistic. Yet it is because I am as realistic and have as deep a sense of responsibility as anyone else that I want to go on record as saying that to react only in terms of the difficulties, either in oneself or in others, is being as shortsighted and destructive as one can possibly be. It is a negative "faith" and brings about a negative result.

# The Creative Ability of Your Words
## Paul Yonggi Cho

Did you know that your words are creative? They are either creative in a positive or negative way. They can produce life or death. Words have a power much greater than most of us can understand today. Psychologists, medical doctors and philosophers are just starting to understand what the Bible has been telling us for thousands of years: "For we all stumble in many things. If anyone does not stumble in word, he is a perfect man, able also to bridle the whole body" (James 3:2 NKJV). The truth given to us in this verse is very important; it enables us to see the impact our words have upon our whole being. James gives us three basic facts about the power of our words:

*Words can be uncontrollable*

How many times have you said something only to later regret having said it? So often our emotions have more control over our words than our logic. We have a tendency to react to someone who has gotten us upset and we say something back that later we feel terrible about. Therefore, James tells us that we stumble over our words.

Our words also can be motivated by our insecurity. Many ministers are guilty of exaggeration. This is due to the fact that preachers receive their approval not from monetary remuneration, but from crowd acceptance. Therefore, by embellishing a story, fact or event, they stand to gain ever greater approval from the crowd.

Our words can be greatly influenced by our associations. If we associate with negative people, we will find our words becoming more negative than normal.

Our words can be controlled by our imagination. Whatever we dwell upon, we will speak. If we daydream about things that are of the flesh, then out of our mouths we will find words coming that will refer to fleshly things and which will be beyond our control.

*What indicates a perfect, or, more accurately stated, a mature man?*

A mature person is one who is able to control his words. This, of course, does not justify those people who find it easy to say nothing. However, James tells us that if someone is so disciplined that he is able to control his speech, he is then mature. The Greek word *teleos* (perfect) means mature or fully tested. But the word translated man is not the more common *anthropos,* but the word *aner.* Kittel states that in classical Greek, this particular use of the word signifies man as opposed to woman.[6] He also states that in the New Testament the word signifies a husband.[7] Robertson agrees with Kittel and translates the verse as "perfect husband."[8]

Those who have been married understand perfectly what James is implying in this verse. If your words are not going to be cautious, they will be so with your spouse. However, the general principle is also true for all people.

### The way to control your body and to avoid its misuse is to control your words

James likens the proper control of the tongue to the control of a horse. He uses the word "bridle." In a well-trained horse, a bridle can serve to either start, stop or change a horse's direction when it is used to exert a small amount of pressure in the horse's mouth. The part of the bridle that is doing the work is not easily visible, but it can dramatically affect the horse's behavior. So too our words. They seem so insignificantly uttered, but they have such great consequences upon us physically, emotionally and spiritually.

James uses the metaphor of a ship's rudder in the fourth verse. Winds, currents and sails do not ultimately determine the direction that a sailing vessel will go. The direction will be determined by a small rudder which is not seen but nonetheless exercises great influence.

The point that James is making by using these two powerful examples is that whatever is in control of your words will control you. If you do not bring your words under your control, your life will be lived as a stumbling horse, directionless and accomplishing very little. Yet a mature spiritual man will make sure that his words are positive and creative. He will not allow himself to be controlled by circumstances, but will control his circumstances because he knows where he is going. He will use his words wisely.

**What are words?**

Although we accept the importance of our words, we have to have an understanding of what words are. After all, as Christians, we are people who are verbally oriented. We believe in the Word (Jesus Christ) according to John 1:1-3. We also accept that the basic force that keeps everything in the physical world together is a word from the Word, "who being the brightness of His glory and the express image of His person, and [*upholds*] *all things by the word of His power* . . . "(Heb. 1:3 NKJV). Our faith is based on trusting in a God who is revealed to our hearts by the Holy Spirit. We accept the truth of a book (the Bible) which is full of words. Yet these words are more than ink on paper; they are the Word of God. Christ challenged us to go into all the world and preach the good news. Therefore, we are people who believe in propagating our faith through the use of words. No other group of people on earth should be more interested in understanding what words are and how they can be used more effectively.

Within the past hundred years many people have been challenged to understand exactly what words are. One of the fathers of modern linguistics, F. de Saussure (a French-Swiss) stated, "The function of language builds on the complex interplay between objective (physical) and subjective (mental) elements. Sounds, such as physical activities, are employed as symbols of meaning which is what ultimately establishes language as a mental rather than a physical phenomenon."[9] Saussure continues, "Everything in language is basically psychological."[10]

What Saussure is basically saying is that words are more than what we say. They begin in the mind as thoughts. This is why people who are mutes can use words in sign language. Although they cannot speak, they can communicate ideas by using physical actions which signify understandable words.

Psychologists have been interested in this subject ever since Wilhelm Wendt (1832-1920) coined the term "psycholinguistics." Believing that by understanding the psychological aspects of words, they might be able to understand the way man's mind functions, he tried to use methods by which he could understand the relationship between ideas and phonomes (words as physical sounds).

Interest in words is not new. Plato gave his ideas concerning the nature of words in his dialogues. St. Augustine stated that every word had a meaning and that sentences were merely a combination of these meanings. However, the study of the psychological, physical and emotional impact of words is basically new to scientists. Much of the philosophy of the West has concentrated on defining what words mean. Ludwig Wittgenstein, however, became skeptical of this practice and stated that objects could never be defined too specifically because of the nature of change within language. The inability to give exact definitions of words caused him to want to understand what words were in essence. "What really comes before our mind when we understand a word?" he asked. "Isn't it something like a picture? Can't it [the word] be a picture?"[11] What Wittgenstein believed is that our understanding comes in the area of our imagination. When we picture something in our mind we understand it. That, in essence, is the definition of that thing. The word sound which is uttered may not be able to fully communicate that picture, but the purpose of communication is to convey the picture to someone else as completely as possible.

Therefore, we understand that words begin in the mind. We visualize something and we associate a phonome with it. The word exists in our mind before it is ever spoken. When we speak, there is a dynamic added to the concept we visualize, for the sound of the word may also add meaning to the word spoken.

In Chinese the same word can have different meanings, depending on the way the word is spoken. The tone that is used and the inflection of the voice lend an added dimension to what is said.

Children understand this concept very well. I have learned much from being a father. One of my three boys was still getting dressed when we were all ready to leave for a church dinner. The rest of us were dressed and still waiting for him. I went into his room and yelled, "Hurry up!" He, being quite young, began to cry. I could have used exactly the same words with a different tone and his reaction would have been much different. He knew what I was trying to communicate to him. My words stated a command; I wanted him to hurry. But the tone of my voice stated, "Hurry up! You have made me upset and you are going to be spanked!"

Words are described by John William Miller as symbols to grasp understandings. Words therefore reproduce the picture that the speaker is conveying in the mind of the hearer. He states that art is also a symbol in that it too tries to communicate ideas or pictures in the artist's mind by the use of a symbol (a work of art).

**The Word in the New Testament Greek Language**

The word translated "speaking" (*lego*) and the word translated "thinking" (*logismos*) both, according to Kittel, have their roots in the Greek word *logos*.[12] Therefore, what we have previously discussed concerning the psychological aspects of words were already in the minds of the Greeks; the idea of the relationship between thinking, speaking and writing is not new.

The word *logos* in the Greek language has a rich meaning and history. It originally had several nuances which were used by John to describe our Lord.

Some of the developmental meanings of the word *logos* are:

a.  the collecting of information
b.  the counting or reckoning of something
c.  mathematical calculations used in accounting
d.  the evaluation of facts
e.  From the previous meanings the word developed into: the assessment of things in general and their correlation. (This is where we get the word "catalogue" in English.)
f.  During the time of Homer the word had the meaning of the reasonable explanation of something.
g.  After the ancient Greek poets, *logos* takes on the meaning of speaking, replacing the previous word, *epos*.

The reason the word changed was because the people changed. As philosophers took a more important role in the lives of the Greek people, they in turn affected the language. Since reason and logic were important to the Greek people, the word signifying "speaking" was then developed from a word whose previous meanings included "the gathering of information" and "the presenting of facts." This had a different nuance than other words such as *epos* and *rama,* which described speech. These two were concerned more with the phonetic implications rather than the reasoning of the philosopher. "The causing of something to be seen for what it is, and the possibility of being oriented thereby is the meaning of logos," Aristotle stated.

Later on, the word *logos* is used in relation to the mythological god, Hermes. Hermes, in mythology, was the mediator between all the other gods. He was the revealer of truth. Therefore, during the Hellenistic period, *logos* took on a significantly religious connotation. The secular Greek use of *logos* was quite different from the New Testament use of the word, specifically as it refers to Jesus Christ in John's Gospel.

## Words Carry the Weight of the Speaker

H. Meyer, a New Testament scholar, believes that the Greek word *logos* had an implied meaning based on the importance of the person speaking. The more important the person, the weightier his words. The principle which Meyer states is true today. If the president of a country makes a speech, his words will carry more weight in that country than if an ordinary citizen states the same thing.

Jesus Christ, being the Son of God and the Redeemer of the world, spoke with such weight that His words produced life. If what was spoken by Jesus was repeated by anyone else, in another name, then his words would not be as powerful. The implication of the principle is that words not only convey meaning, but they also convey the character and personality of the speaker.

Since our words come from within our heart, they divulge the very intent of our thinking. This is why it is not what goes into a man's mouth that defiles him, but what comes out of his mouth. The person speaking a word, or words in a sentence, has to understand the importance of what he is saying, especially if he is a prominent person. People who are highly regarded are going to be heard.

In Korea, I am well known by almost everyone in the whole nation. When I speak, people listen and take what I say very seriously. Since I have never thought of myself as being better or more important than anyone else, I have had a difficult time adjusting to the fact that people are closely listening to my words, especially those words which I speak casually. I have learned that I cannot jest openly. I have to watch what I say. If I were to say something casually in jest, people would take me seriously and spread it all over the country. So I have learned to watch my words for I know that other people are listening to me intently.

The speaker's importance is an additional factor in his word because of the dimension of the speaker's authority. The masses in Israel listened to Christ by the hillside and by the lake and they also listened to the priests in the temple. The comparison that they made was that Christ's words were different, for He spoke as one having authority.

When someone says something, the authority of the individual will determine the degree to which what he says will be obeyed and remembered. The Roman centurion was not worthy that Christ should come under his roof, but he said that he was under authority and that he exercised authority. Taking for granted that the spiritual kingdom of Christ functioned under the same principles as Rome, he then told Christ to simply speak the word and his servant would be healed (Matt. 8:8). Jesus marvelled at the Roman's understanding of spiritual reality, for He had offered to go to his home and had promised the healing. What greater honor could be bestowed on anyone? Yet the centurion knew that only a word (*logos*) was needed for the miracle to take place. He recognized the authority with which Jesus spoke. This does not mean that Jesus spoke in an overly loud voice. At times, those with the least authority speak loudly because of their insecurity. But when someone has authority, that authority is transmitted by the way in which he speaks. Those who hear one who is speaking in such a manner will comprehend the weight of what is spoken, although additional language may not be added.

**The Word of God**

In Acts 6, we learn that the apostles realized that they were not to be involved in the daily administration of the needs of the saints, but their job was to study and teach the Word (*logos*) of God. This truth seems to be lost to much of the ministry today. So many preachers spend more time in their offices doing administrative work than in the Word of God. The fact is that the Word of God has many dimensions which cannot be comprehended by only a single reading. The Bible (God's Word) is not just a piece of literature. It cannot be read once, understood and then taught to others. The Word of God is many-sided and must be studied over and over again.

The Spirit of Truth has come to lead and guide us into all truth. How does He guide us? He, the Holy Spirit, knows the mind of God. He is, therefore, able to explain what was in God's mind when God spoke, both in the Old Testament (through the prophets) and in the New Testament (through the apostles). If we understand that words do not fully and exhaustively explain the mental picture, then it is helpful to have someone who knows the inner working of the mind of the person who spoke. Therefore, it is imperative that we have the Holy Spirit leading and guiding us through the study of the Scriptures.

If the word which is spoken carries the weight of the speaker, then the *logos* of God has a spiritual as well as an intellectual dynamic which makes that word special. If God has told us (in James) that we should be careful in our use of words, then it is certain that God has been careful in the use of every word which has been written in the Scriptures. If words are to convey a mental picture, then we should learn how to visualize the Word of God and try to understand what He sees. We most assuredly need the Holy Spirit in order to do this. Since the Holy Spirit was the one who caused the prophets to speak ("For prophecy never came by the will of man, but holy men of God spoke as they were moved [borne gently] by the Holy Spirit" —2 Pet. 1:21 NKJV), He then is able to interpret best what they said.

Jesus said that the Holy Spirit came upon the prophets as they spoke in the Old Testament. These prophecies were spoken as the Holy Spirit moved the prophets to speak. And these very words are called the Word of God or Scripture (Mark 12:10; 15:28; Luke 4:21; John 7:38; Acts 8:32, etc.). Yet the Word of God found in the Old Testament and the Word of God spoken by our Lord are not only the words called Scripture; the New Testament also is the Word of God:

> Therefore, beloved, looking forward to these things, be diligent to be found by Him in peace, without spot and blameless; and account that the longsuffering of our Lord is salvation—as also our beloved brother Paul, according to the wisdom given to him, has written to you, as also in all his epistles, speaking in them of these things, in which are some things hard to understand, which those who are untaught and unstable twist to their own destruction, as they do also the *rest of the Scriptures* (2 Pet. 3:14-16 NKJV).

Therefore, the same Holy Spirit that came upon the prophets and moved them to speak also moved the writers in the New Testament, but from a different location. Jesus promised that the Holy Spirit would be inside the believer.

As the Holy Spirit has invaded human beings who believe in the Lord Jesus Christ, He is not just occasionally coming upon us, but He lives in the life of Christ in us. This Holy Spirit can cause us to see what was not seen, even by the prophets who heard God speak and faithfully spoke for God, as recounted in the Old Testament. Therefore it was imperative that Christ depart so He could send another Comforter, the Holy Spirit. This is why it is so important for us to depend upon the Holy Spirit as we endeavor in a deeper way to understand God's Word. Paul said,

> But we speak the wisdom of God in a mystery, the hidden wisdom which God ordained before the ages for our glory, which none of the rulers of this age knew; for had they known, they would not have crucified the Lord of glory. But as it is written: "Eye has not seen, nor ear heard, nor have entered into the heart of man the things which God has prepared for those who love Him." But God has revealed them to us through His Spirit. For the Spirit searches all things, yes, the deep things of God (1 Cor. 2:7-10 NKJV).

Although the Old Testament is full of the Word of God coming to the prophets, there are only two instances in the New Testament that the Holy Spirit came in the same way: to Simeon and John the Baptist. We are told that the Holy Spirit directed Simeon to the temple at the same time that Jesus was to be presented before the Lord God (see Luke 2:25-30). As he saw the Christ child, he was moved by the Holy Spirit and began to prophesy. John the Baptist was also moved by the Holy Spirit in the wilderness to begin his prophetic ministry. The term used in the Greek is *rema Theon*. The Word of God came upon him. These are the last two times in the New Testament that God spoke to man in this way. Kittel says, "The phrases *logos tou Theou, logos tou kuriou* and *rema kuriou* (Greek for 'the Word of God' and 'the Word of the Lord') are very common in the New Testament, but, except in the case of these introductory figures (Simeon and John), they are never used of special divine directions. It is not that these do not occur in the New Testament. On the contrary, the apostolic age is full of them. But they are described in many other different ways." The conclusion can therefore be drawn that since the coming of the Lord, who is the Word of God, the Word of God would never come again in the same way. Jesus never received the Word of God because He was the Word of God. Everything that had ever been said by God through the prophets in the past represented only a partial revelation of truth; with the coming of Christ, however, the whole of truth was revealed in a Person. The only times God spoke from heaven (at the Mount of Transfiguration and at Christ's water baptism), the audience was not Christ, but those who were watching God bear witness of Him.

It is not that God would not speak prophetically through His servants in the New Testament, but that there would be a difference in their prophetic ministry. Therefore, Jesus spoke the Word of God as the Word of God. The prophetic realm is a limited one: "For we know in part and we prophesy in part. But when that which is perfect has come, then that which is in part will be done away" (1 Cor. 13:9, 10 NKJV).

How can we speak the Word of God in a complete way? Peter gives us the answer:

> For we did not follow cunningly devised fables when we made known to you the power and coming of our Lord Jesus Christ, but were eyewitnesses of His majesty. For He received from God the Father honor and glory when such a voice came to Him from the Excellent Glory: "This is My beloved Son, in whom I am well pleased." And we heard this voice which came from heaven when we were with Him on the holy mountain. We also have the prophetic word made more sure, which you do well to heed as a light that shines in a dark place, until the day dawns and the morning star rises in your hearts; knowing this first, that no prophecy of Scripture is of any private interpretation (2 Pet. 1:16-20 NKJV).

Written words have a more permanent nature than those that are spoken. My people have learned that misunderstandings can arise when they communicate by phone only, but when they write a letter, which can be answered by a letter, then there is a permanent record of the communicated information. Our faith does not depend on an oral tradition, as many other religions have. God spoke in the Old Testament and what God wanted us to know was written down. God speaks to us today through the Scriptures, both Old and New Testaments. Peter stated that this record is more reliable than actually hearing the voice of God personally. He compared the voice he heard at the Mount of Transfiguration with the record in Scripture and says that the record is a more sure Word of prophecy. This does not mean that man cannot prophesy today. But it does mean that when we speak the Word of God from Scripture, that Word is complete and not partial.

**Words have power**

Solomon said: "Death and life are in the power of the tongue" (Prov. 18:21 KJV).

In volume 1 of *The Fourth Dimension,* I wrote about a neurosurgeon who told me about a new discovery in his field. By now, that principle is a well-established fact. The speech center in the brain has direct influence over the entire nervous system. Solomon, thousands of years before the discovery which science has made in recent years, stated the very same fact. In surgery, the will of the patient to pull through his operation will have as much to do with the success of the operation as any other external factor. The will not only gives the body of the patient the ability to stay alive during the operation, but actually aids in the healing process. That will is affected by what the patient confesses. If he confesses death, then death will begin to work in his system. If he confesses life, the body begins to release the natural forces of healing to make that confession true.

This truth is especially important for older people. One of the most debilitating factors in contemporary society is forced retirement at what is frequently the still productive age of sixty-five. This is just when a person begins to learn about life, just when the cumulative experiences of a lifetime can be most useful. To be forced to go out to pasture at such a time can be disastrous. The mind then starts to think of itself as old and will begin to confess, "I'm retired now. I am too old to do anything productive." The body will respond to those words and begin to age more rapidly. This does not mean that all retired people are unproductive or are forced to retire because they are no longer of use. But it does seem like that to many retired people. They miss years of being useful to God and their society because they feel that they are "too old" and ineffectual. Age is more than chronology; it is a state of mind. That mind is influenced by the words which are spoken.

Poverty is a curse from Satan. God desires that all His people prosper and be healthy as their soul prospers (3 John 1:2). Yet much of the world has not really seen poverty as I have seen it. Especially in the Third World, people live their lives in despair, struggling to survive for one more day. I am from the Third World. I know first-hand what it is not to have anything to eat. My country was ravaged by the Japanese for many years; then we suffered through two wars. Korea is just now rising up economically. Why? One of the reasons we are succeeding and prospering materially is because we are changing our self-image as a nation. While under Japanese colonial rule we found it difficult to have a good self-image and national dignity. But, against great odds, we were able to maintain our language, culture and national identity.

When I started my church, we had just seen the end of the Korean conflict. Our people struggled just to eat. I then saw that God wanted to bless us materially as a testimony to His grace and power. This does not mean that economically underprivileged Christians are second-class citizens. But it does mean that we have to believe that the blessing of God is part of His redemptive provision.

I then started to see the importance of teaching my people the power and substance of their confession. If we confessed we were poor and created a poor self-image by our confession, we would always be poor and in need of material help and handouts from the West. But by trusting in God and working very hard, our people were able to lift themselves from the depths of poverty into a place where they could bless the work of God in our country and throughout the world.

Last year, I spoke at our Church Growth Conference in Sri Lanka. Previously called Ceylon, that nation is one of the poorest countries in the world. The bulk of my ministry was spent teaching them how to change their self-image. They had to realize that God is their source, not America and Europe. The main way a group of people can change their self-image is by carefully using words which are positive and which produce dignity within both the speaker and the hearer. Reports are still coming back about the results of that conference which brought together about five hundred Christian leaders from all Christian denominations.

In Mark's gospel, we have a very beautiful and interesting narrative which reveals the potential power of our words as Christians. After Jesus had returned from His triumphal entry into Jerusalem He went directly to the temple. He saw what was going on but said nothing. He left Jerusalem to spend the night at the home of friends in Bethany. The next morning, He was hurrying and approached a fig tree that had large lovely leaves. Looking under the leaves for the fruit He saw nothing. The tree looked productive, but had produced no fruit. Jesus then cursed the tree and went on back into Jerusalem to cleanse the temple.

Since no action taken by Christ in the Scripture is without meaning, the tree, of course, symbolized Israel. Upon the disciples' return to the area where the tree was, however, Peter looked at the tree and said, "Rabbi, look! The fig tree which you cursed has withered away." Rather than dealing with the symbolic significance of the tree withering away, that they could know the principle that that which cannot bear fruit shouldn't make the appearance of health; Jesus dealt with Peter's surprise at His ability to produce a miracle. This should be surprising to us because Peter had seen Christ perform many more spectacular miracles in the past. However, Jesus used this occasion to reveal the potential power of our words as Christians.

"For assuredly, I say to you, whoever says to this mountain. 'Be removed and be cast into the sea,' and does not doubt in his heart, but believes that those things he says will come to pass, he will have whatever he *says*" (Mark 11:23 NKJV). Merely *thinking* our words does not produce the miracle; the miracle is produced by *saying* what you believe. Christ promised that we could only have what we confessed. The story of the mountain being physically removed is only to add emphasis to the ability of the spoken word. If we as Christians only knew what power we can release when we speak in faith, we would be using our words more effectively.

Our words are important. Malachi tells us that God keeps a book of remembrance. Daniel was told by the angel Gabriel that he had come for his words. Paul tells us that God's redemptive word of salvaton climaxes when we confess Jesus Christ as our Savior. The heart believes unto righteousness. You can be righteous in your heart, but words are necessary for you to be saved. Only thinking in faith will not release the power of God; we must learn to speak in faith. Our words are creative either for good or for evil. God has given all the grace necessary for us to learn to use our words creatively for the purpose of seeing His kingdom established in this earth.

### How to develop a creative word

As we look at the Genesis account of the creation, we can understand how God used His words creatively. Before God said, "Let there be . . . ," He had a clear goal and objective. As we understand by looking carefully at the story of the creation in Genesis, everything was created from the earth's perspective. But why should God create from this perspective since the universe is so vast, with many billions of stars larger than our own sun?

120

The reason for choosing the earth was that this planet was the place where man would dwell. If it were not for this goal, that is, creating a perfect place for man, the earth would be like any other planet, incapable of supporting human life.

Paul shows man's central purpose not only in the earth but also in the universe. He says in Romans 8 that the whole of creation was placed in a decaying process by the sin of Adam, but when man finally comes to the place of total victory and redemption, the creation, which has been waiting in hope, will be set free. The physical law, called by science "entropy," will be reversed even as we see our bodies overcome the process at the end of the age.

In the Letter to the Colossians, Paul reinforces the fact that Christ was the means by which everything, either visible or invisible, was created. Yet Paul immediately links Christ to His physical body on earth, the Church. In Ephesians, Paul states that we were in Christ before the worlds were founded. He then closes the first chapter by stating that we are His fullness which fills all in all. In the Greek text, this passage has even more significance than is obvious in the translation we are using. A more literal translation can be, "fills all that is capable of being filled." The obvious inference is that the Church, filled with Christ's glory, then fulfills His ultimate purpose of having the whole of creation filled with His glory. Our ultimate influence, therefore, is not just limited to this earth, but is intended for the whole of God's creation.

Seeing that we were in God's mind before the world was created, we can then understand the purpose of God choosing to create this planet capable of sustaining human life.

In learning to use our creative words, we must take our lesson from God. So often we speak in faith, but we don't have a clear objective. We don't know where we are going because we live from day to day. You may ask, didn't the Lord tell us to live like this? This is true, but He was dealing with those who worry. I am not speaking about worry. I am speaking about having a clear objective and goal for the future which you have received from the Holy Spirit.

When God said, "Let there be . . . ," He already knew the end of the matter. He saw clearly all of us, not as we are, but as we will be in Christ. He then had a clear objective; He would create a planet for the purpose of having a perfect place for man to inhabit.

Yet before God ever spoke, the Holy Spirit was working in the area of His desire. The Holy Spirit was creating the circumstances which

121

would bring about what God would say. This fact must be very clear if we are ever going to learn how to use our creative language. We must learn to walk in the Holy Spirit and have Him direct us in what God desires. Once we get our instructions from the Holy Spirit, we can speak to our chaotic situations and circumstances with authority and we will see things begin to happen.

I was once invited to a church banquet and at this lovely dinner I used this very principle. One of our elders had a son who had an incurable paralysis which was getting progressively worse. As I was sitting at the table, the Lord spoke to me: "Get up and go to your elder and tell him that tonight his son will be completely healed!" I then began to be fearful in my heart. My wife turned to me and said, "What is wrong with you?" When I told her, she put her hand on my arm and said. "Don't you dare do that! You know that he has been prayed for many times. What if nothing happens? You will be ruined in this church." I agreed with her wisdom but got up anyway. (I have learned that it is better to obey the Holy Spirit at the risk of failure than never to try to see the glory of God manifested.) As I approached the elder, I smiled as he asked me, "What can I do for you, pastor?" I then breathed deeply and plunged into my statement: "The Holy Spirit just told me to to tell you that tonight your son will be healed." Once I had obeyed, I felt total and complete relief. He then told his wife and the two of them began to cry out thanksgiving to God. Before long, everyone knew what I had shared with the elder and they too were praising God.

Once I sat down, my heart sank. What would be the consequences if nothing happened? But it was too late.

That night, the couple went directly to the boy's room and told him what I had said. He tried to get out of bed, but could not. They prayed and he tried again, but still his condition remained the same. Finally, the father said to God, "Lord, you told our pastor tonight that our son would be healed. He is a man of God and we believe him. We know that you would not ask him to say that unless you meant to perform a miracle." With that, the father took his son's arm, pulled him out of the bed and said, "In the name of Jesus, rise up and walk!" As the child stood on his legs, his limbs were strengthened. He stood up and began to run all over the room. The news of that miracle spread all over their community; because of that testimony many families were saved.

In our society we are faced with chaos all around us, just as the earth was chaotic (without form and void) before God spoke. As we learn to walk in obedience to the Holy Spirit, we will learn to use the creative ability of our words to bring order out of chaos.

Our words can make the difference if we learn to use them effectively. We can either spend our Christian lives without proper control over our words, or we will see their importance, power and creativity and use them for the purpose that God originally intended. Let your words be positive and productive. Meditate upon positive and creative things. Fill your mind with the Word of God and you will be able to see the Word of God coming forth from your lips naturally. "Let the words of my mouth, and the meditation of my heart, be acceptable in Thy sight, O Lord, my strength, and my redeemer" (Ps. 19:14 KJV).

# — 8 —

# The Prayer of Faith and the Authority of the Believer

A major bone of contention in the church today is the prayer of faith, that is, praying with the authority given to us as believers in Jesus Christ. He told His disciples, "If anyone should say to this hill, 'Get up and throw yourself into the sea,' and without any doubt in his heart believe that what he says will happen, then it *will* happen! That is why I tell you, whatever you pray about and ask for, believe that you have received it and it will be yours" (Mark 11:23, 24 PHILLIPS).

The story goes that one man wanted to exercise his faith in this way, and at night he prayed, "God, as your disciple, I am commanding that hill behind our house to be lifted up and cast into the sea, and I have no doubt in my heart." The next morning he looked out the kitchen window and saw the hill behind the house, right where it had always been. "I knew it would be there!" he exclaimed.

If we contrast our own experience with scriptural accounts, we find that too often we are unable to exercise the kind of faith Jesus seems to expect of us. Jesus rebuked the storm, and the wind and waves became calm (Mark 4:39); now that Jesus has gone to the Father, we ought to be doing greater works than Jesus (John 14:12). "It was this kind of faith that won their reputation for the saints of old" (Heb. 11:2 PHILLIPS). But our authority lies not in any control over God; rather it comes from following Jesus so closely that we pray confident that what we ask is in line with God's will and His written Word.

Although the following essays particularly address prayers of faith for healing, the lessons and conclusions apply to prayers of faith in every circumstance, and to the results we can expect.

125

# The Prayer of Faith
## Jim Glennon

Now faith is the assurance of things hoped for, the conviction of things not seen (Heb. 11:1 RSV).

As they passed by in the morning, they saw the fig tree withered away to its roots. And Peter remembered and said to him, "Master, look! The fig tree which you cursed has withered." And Jesus answered them, "Have faith in God. Truly, I say to you, whoever says to this mountain, 'Be taken up and cast into the sea,' and does not doubt in his heart, but believes that what he says will come to pass, it will be done for him. Therefore I tell you, whatever you ask in prayer, believe that you receive it, and you will" (Mark 11:20-24 RSV).

Let him ask in faith, with no doubting (James 1:6 RSV).

*What is the prayer of faith?*
From the time that the ministry of divine healing first began to be exercised in St. Andrew's Cathedral in 1960, people have been coming and asking, "What is the prayer of faith?" I wonder what you would say in answer to this question? What, indeed, is the prayer of faith? It isn't much good using an expression unless we have a clear understanding of what it means. We will find an explanation from Jesus himself in the passage from Mark.

You may remember that just before this, Jesus had done a most unlikely thing. He had cursed a fig tree. Why He did this need not concern us here; the fact is that He did. And when our Lord and His disciples came by the next day, Peter noticed that the tree was already dead. He commented on it, and Jesus then used the incident to illustrate what is meant by faith in prayer. Turning to His followers, He said, "Have faith in God. . . . whoever says to this mountain,

'Be taken up and cast into the sea,' and does not doubt in his heart, but believes . . . it will be done for him. Therefore I tell you, whatever you ask in prayer, believe that you receive it, and you will."

Jesus was saying here that if prayer is to be answered, then we have to believe our prayer is *being* answered. His original words really mean, "believe that you *have received* it;" not "might receive," or "will receive," or even "are receiving," but "have received." We are to believe the prayer has been answered; it is an accomplished fact. To make it abundantly clear, Jesus said that this belief is to be to the point where *we do not doubt in our heart.* He left no room for uncertainty or compromise on the matter. We are to believe the answer has been received so that we have no doubt or reservation at all.

When we read in the New Testament about faith for healing, either in the ministry of Christ, or of the disciples, or of our need of faith, this is what is meant. And when Jesus said that if we have faith as a grain of mustard seed, He meant that we need only to have this certainty in the most minute form for there to be blessing.

This certainly applies not only to prayer about healing. In fact healing is not even mentioned in this particular passage. Jesus said, rather, *"Whatever* you ask in prayer . . ." It applies to healing, because it is the prayer of faith that will raise up the sick man. It applies to everything else, because that is how we are *always* to pray if our prayers are to be effective.

Let it be crystal clear that if our prayer, whether it be for healing or anything else, is going to be answered by Almighty God, then we have to pray in the way He has revealed to us through Jesus. For with God there is no variableness or shadow of turning. God does not change to suit us; we have to change to suit Him. This is another reason why we need to search the Scriptures: to see how we are to respond to our heavenly Father. Our need and our responsibility is that we understand how we are to pray. It is fundamental and central to us having any and all of God's blessings in our life and ministry.

So the first point for us to note about the prayer of faith is that we must know what God has promised to give us. The second, and present point, is that we are to believe that we receive these promises so that we have no doubt in our hearts.

*What are your prayers like?*

Do your prayers express such belief in God's answering them that you are sure? Do *you* pray the prayer of faith? This is the question that I hope you are asking yourself at this stage. Because it is not enough for your prayers to have other commendable features; it makes no difference who you are or what denomination you belong to; it doesn't matter whether you are a new Christian or you are one who has known the Lord all your life; if your prayers are going to be answered by God, you have to *believe* they are being answered so that you do not doubt. This fact cannot be overemphasized.

We believe this by faith. A Church Army officer once said to me, "Faith means that you're thanking God *before* it happens." This insight is exactly what we must understand at this point. It echoes those words in the epistle to the Hebrews, "Faith is the assurance of things hoped for, the conviction of things not seen." Jesus said the same thing: "Blessed are those who have not seen and yet believe" (John 20:29 RSV).

Faith is not what we see. Faith always goes beyond what we see to what we hope for and to what we believe and receive. That is why we thank God for the answer to our prayer *before* the answer is seen. When it is seen, we thank Him by sight—but then we are no longer thanking Him by faith. And it is the *prayer of faith* that we are concerned about here, not just for healing, but for any promise of God that we are drawing on.

We will understand this better if we relate it to an area of prayer which is already familiar to us, and where we usually get it right. This will give us guidelines as to how to act out faith in prayer in those areas where at present we do *not* get it right. The area to which I refer is to experience of conversion.

*The prayer of faith for conversion*

We can thank God that in the church generally there is some clarity of understanding and effectiveness of practice on the matter of conversion. This is the area of prayer where faith is understood as it should be. If we see how the prayer of faith is exercised in conversion, we will more easily see the point I am seeking to make about the prayer of faith in general.

If a person wants to become a Christian, he must first realize that he is without Christ in his life. We are either in Christ or we are not; we are either lost or we are found; we are either born again or we are "dead" in trespasses and sin (Eph. 2:1 KJV). *The first* requirement is to know that we *need* to be converted.

The second thing to know is that God has made a precious and very great promise—that if we believe on Christ in repentance, faith and obedience, we will be saved. The jailer at Philippi (Acts 16:30, 31 RSV) said to Paul in prison, "What must I do to be saved?" And Paul replied, "Believe in the Lord Jesus, and you will be saved," meaning, "Put your trust in Him as your Savior and Lord."

The third thing is that we must believe in Christ for ourselves. Different people may act on this in different ways, but there is a word that expresses what every convert does at this point: accept Christ. We come to the point where we make up our mind; we make a decision. And so we respond to the promise of God and consciously accept Christ as the one who saves us. The surer we are that we have done this, the more easily we will enter into the reality of conversion.

What happens at this point can be illustrated quite simply. I might say to someone, "If I want to give you my watch as a gift, what do you have to do for it to be yours?" I want him to see that all he has to do is to accept it, so I get him to take it from my hand. And as he holds the watch, he becomes accustomed to the idea that he has accepted it, and that it is now his. We must accept Christ in the same definite way.

When we have done this, we may find our life changed at the time. But if it isn't we must on no account rely on our feelings. If we are not changed at once, it does not mean that nothing has happened. It means that our faith is being tested and that we must continue to affirm that we have accepted Christ—by faith.

Let me illustrate this from my own experience. I first believed in Christ late in my teenage years at an evangelistic mission conducted by the Reverend (now Canon) H.M. Arrowsmith. We were invited to raise our hands as an outward sign that we were accepting Christ, and that is what I did. We were then asked to stay and the missioner shook hands with each of us. I will always remember him asking me, "Are you sure you have accepted Christ?" I told him that I had.

At that time I had no religious or church background that would give an adequate understanding of the commitment I was making. Perhaps that was the explanation for what subsequently happened, or rather what *didn't* happen, because for three years after I had accepted Christ as my Savior, I neither felt nor saw any difference in my life—nothing at all. I just held on by faith to what I believed had happened. Only as those years went by, and very gradually, did I come to experience the Spirit of God at work in my life.

But isn't this what faith is all about? If a person who has accepted Christ does not experience a change in his life right away, we help him to understand, we call on him to affirm, that he has accepted Christ *by faith.* And if he were to say, "Oh! I accepted Christ, but nothing has happened," we would conclude that he had not reached the point where he understood faith and was exercising it. For when we exercise faith, we are thanking God for what we have asked of Him, even though *we do not see it at the time.* It is most important that we understand this clearly.

The point we are making here is that in conversion we are praying the prayer of faith. To use the language of Mark, chapter 11, we believe that we have received Christ, and we believe to the point where we do not doubt in our heart. To use the language that is in more common use, we accept Christ, and we continue to affirm this by faith. The advantage of this second way of expressing it is that it puts into simple and effective words what we need to know and do if the blessing is to be ours. But let us realize that what we are really talking about is the prayer of faith.

*The prayer of faith for healing*

When someone comes to me wishing to draw upon divine healing, I often ask him if he is a Christian. If he is, I remind him of how he prayed the prayer of faith at his conversion and explain that this is the way we are going to pray the prayer of faith for his healing. Of course, we first talk over the particular problem he has, so that ministry can be offered to him in the most relevant way. But sooner or later we reach the point where we want to appropriate God's promise that the prayer of faith will save the sick man and that the Lord will raise him up.

I am thankful that most people are able to accept divine healing for themselves in a way that is real to them, especially if the principles of the prayer of faith have been explained to them carefully. But it is astonishing how difficult it is for some people—and they are usually the habitual, set-in-their-ways type of church people—to make a simple acceptance of God's blessings, so that they are thanking Him by faith. Instead they use a lot of religious language which, when it is all added up, means very little as far as faith is concerned. They are the most difficult to assist.

In effect, they say: "I prayed the prayer of faith, *but* I am not healed." You can see that if we applied this to conversion, the person would never enter into an assurance of salvation. And so with healing; the person concerned must realize that praying the prayer of faith means thanking God and continuing to thank God by faith, believing that He is answering the prayer.

We are to "walk by faith, not by sight" (2 Cor. 5:7 RSV). We saw in our analogy with conversion that when a person consciously accepts Christ as Savior, he is saying in effect, "I know by faith that I am saved." Similarly, when we consciously accept healing, we then say, "I know by faith that I am healed. This is what I accept. Thank you, Father, in Jesus' name."

Let us summarize what we have said:

We must first know what God has promised to give us.

We then appropriate those promises by faith. Faith believes that we have received these things so that we do not doubt.

Our experience of conversion shows how this is followed through in practice—we accept Christ and we affirm it by faith until we experience it in fact.

So too, with healing. We accept it and we continue to thank God by faith until it becomes what we have by sight. But we are only ever able to thank God by sight because we first of all thanked Him by faith.

## A final word of guidance

There is one thing more that perhaps needs to be said to give balance and perspective to praying in faith. As faith is what *we* are responsible for, we need to realize our limitations. If we are beginners, we need to put our faith into action in a *beginning* way and choose subjects for prayer that lie within our limited faith experience. As we become more fluent in having faith, we will be able to pray for the removal of mountains that are bigger. But even when we are completely experienced, we will still need to recognize our limitations and know when we can pray in faith and when we can only relinquish the matter to God. There is no limit to what God can do, but there *is* a limit to what His servants can do—and wisdom is knowing the difference.

We will go as far as our faith will take us. "All things are possible to him who believes," Jesus said (Mark 9:23 RSV). But He also said, "According to your faith be it done to you" (Matt. 9:29 RSV) and this is our present point. Perhaps the only safe and balanced position is for us all to think of ourselves as those who are *learning* how to pray in faith. We might then say: how can my faith grow?

# The Promises of God and the Will of God
## Jim Glennon

There is no need to say to informed Christians that our Lord preeminently destroyed the works of the devil through His crucifixion and resurrection. By the perfect offering of himself on the altar of the cross He took away the sin of the world, so that He was able to say, "It is finished" (John 19:30 RSV). His resurrection was proof that Satan's rule had been broken and that a new order had been introduced, which He referred to as the kingdom of God. This kingdom is a heavenly and spiritual reality that will be experienced in its fullness only when "the kingdom of the world has become the kingdom of our Lord and of his Christ" (Rev. 11:15 RSV).

But this same kingdom also has been established in the hearts and lives of those who accept what Christ has done, and it has a here-and-now reality as well. "The kingdom of God is in the midst of you," Jesus said (Luke 17:21 RSV). The here-and-now kingdom is made up of the "precious and very great promises" that God has made (2 Pet. 1:4 RSV). Put together, they are what we call the New Testament. God's part has been to provide this resource; our part is to search the Scriptures so we know what it is.

The promises *reveal God's will to us in a fallen world.* It is not enough to know God's will as it was revealed in the Garden of Eden when that will has been frustrated by Satan and by man's disobedience. We need a revelation of His will that takes this into account, as it also takes into account the atoning work of Christ. That is exactly what God has done for us in bestowing on us His rich and wonderful promises as set out in the Scriptures. They reveal God's will for us in the here-and-now kingdom.

Let us look at some of these promises so we have an informed idea of what they are and of their relevance to us.

By way of introduction, let me say that I once led a mission in the Parish of Oakey, which is in Queensland, Australia, near

Toowoomba. Good preparations had been made by the rector and other members of the church, and we had a creative and rewarding week together. The church wasn't big enough for the mission services, so we met in the local high school's fine auditorium. After I had been speaking at the meetings for several days, the rector said to me, "I can't help noticing how you have the promises of God at your finger tips." What he said has remained with me—not because it was complimentary, but because that needs to be characteristic of all Christians who would pray effectively.

That is why we read the Bible, for that is where the promises of God are set out. We do not so much look for a text that says this or that, so much as we want to *understand* the Bible, and the New Testament in particular, *in an overall way*. What we need to see are the promises of God as revealed in the broad themes of Scripture.

We are not to understand the promises by a single verse, and we are not to set aside a broad theme of scriptural promise because of an isolated passage, the more so if that passage is open to more than one interpretation.

Well, what are some of the great themes of scriptural promise? The most important, of course, is the remission of sins God offers to those who believe that Christ died so we might be forgiven. When we accept that forgiveness, we no longer affirm that we are without God in our lives, "because, if you confess with your lips that Jesus is Lord and believe in your heart that God raised him from the dead, you will be saved" (Rom. 10:9 RSV).

Another of the great themes in the New Testament, in the ministry and teaching of our Lord, and in His call and commission to His followers (which includes the church today) is that of healing. This is clearly presented in James 5:14, 15 (RSV): "Is any among you sick? Let him call for the elders of the church, and let them pray over him, anointing him with oil in the name of the Lord; and the prayer of faith will save the sick man, and the Lord will raise him up." His great and gracious words, "Truly, truly, I say to you, he who believes in me will also do the works that I do" (John 14:12 RSV), are to be understood in this context.

Another area of provision we need to be concerned and clear about has to do with material things. As with everything, balance is important. On one hand, Jesus expressly warned against being preoccupied with building up material wealth and giving it priority over "treasure in heaven" (Matt. 6:20 NEB). It is so easy to put riches before God and so make a god of riches. On the other hand, and given that we have our priorities right, God has promised to meet our material needs so that we have what we need to eat and drink and wear. (You can't be more materialistic than that.) Jesus said, "If God so clothes the grass of the field, which today is alive and tomorrow is thrown into the oven, will he not much more clothe you, O men of little faith? Therefore do not be anxious, saying, 'What shall we eat?' or 'What shall we drink?' or 'What shall we wear?' . . . But seek first his kingdom and his righteousness, and all these things shall be yours as well" (Matt. 6:30, 31, 33).

The promises of God reveal the will of God, as developed in the broad themes of Scripture; they are God's covenant with us, and it is His will that we be partakers of them. It is not so much that there is any soundly based argument that says differently (though there are some theologians who expressly take that position); it is more that we are so used to a watered-down version of Christianity that we often do not seriously consider God's promises in their range and detail. Often we are brought to consider God's promises only when we are beset by problems.

*What we are to learn from our difficulties*

The clue to understanding the connection between problems and promises is found in the experience of St. Paul. He had more than his share of difficulties, and it is worth reading about them: "Five times I have received at the hands of the Jews the forty lashes less one. Three times I have been beaten with rods; once I was stoned. Three times I have been shipwrecked; a night and a day I have been adrift at sea; on frequent journeys, in danger from rivers, danger from robbers, danger from my own people, danger from Gentiles, danger in the city, danger in the wilderness, danger at sea, danger from false brethren; in toil and hardship, through many a sleepless night, in hunger and thirst, often without food, in cold and exposure" (2 Cor. 11:24-27 RSV).

He summed it up when he referred to his experiences in Asia: "We do not want you to be ignorant, brethren, of the affliction we experienced in Asia; for we were so utterly, unbearably crushed that we despaired of life itself. Why, we felt that we had received the sentence of death . . ." (2 Cor. 1:8, 9).

My first thought on reading this is to be encouraged by the fact that St. Paul had his problems too. They continued on and had

135

a cumulative effect until he "despaired of life itself." He was at a breakdown point.

Up to that stage he had only been reacting in terms of his difficulties, but then he put on his theological thinking cap. He had been given an "abundance of revelations" (2 Cor. 12:7 RSV) and, in a unique way, could see things from God's perspective. When he did this, he realized that there was more to his problems than he first thought. He knew that "all things work together for good to them that love God" (Rom. 8:28 KJV), which must include the very things that were so hurtful to him. That being so, he then asked the crucial question: "What is the good towards which my problems are working?" He knew that, while they came from the devil and the sin of the world, they had also been allowed by God and were therefore serving a purpose of God that was good, because God is good. But what was that good?

Then he gave us the answer: ". . . we believe now that we had this experience of coming to the end of our tether that we might learn to trust, not in ourselves, but in God who can raise the dead" (2 Cor. 1:9 PHILLIPS). To "trust, not in ourselves, but in God" means that we have been brought to faith—faith in God. And faith in God means, for the Christian, faith in what God has promised.

*How to react in every circumstance*

Once we see this, all our thinking about the difficulties that come our way is transformed. Christ has won the victory over Satan through the cross. God's kingdom has been established and is within you. The purpose of difficulties is to bring us to faith—faith in the promises of God. Suddenly everything hangs together. It makes sense of life. It makes sense of Christianity. And it makes sense (if I may say so with great reverence) of God. We have now a cogent structure of thought to which we will be able to relate all that happens and all that we are to do. It can be rightly called a theology of permitted difficulties.

If reacting to a problem in terms of the problem only perpetuates it and it becomes worse, how can we react in a way that will give a different and better result? The answer is to react to the problem by coming to faith in the relevant promise(s) of God. Then our need is met, His kingdom is extended and His will is done.

To avoid any misunderstanding, we would make the following point with the utmost clarity: We are not to *ignore* the problem;

that would be foolish in the extreme. We are to *face* the problem head on, and to *react* by believing for and bringing to bear the relevant resource that God provides. That, we maintain, is the Christian position.

The problems are what we see. The promises are what we hope for, even though we cannot see them at the time. We are not to affirm the problem we see; we are to affirm the relevant promise by faith.

At first, this is both confusing and frustrating. It just does not seem to make sense. The reaction of some might even be one of indignation. I well remember what I thought when this was first said to me in the context of healing. At that time I had iritis, which is a painful and serious eye complaint. "But what about my iritis?" I kept saying. The real point was that I could not see past what I had and the label that had been put on me. The label was right as far as it went and the medical treatment was necessary. And it was also true that as long as that was what I accepted, I had recurring attacks of iritis. But as I increased in my understanding of what faith meant, so that I affirmed what I was believing for rather than what I had, the attacks became less frequent and less severe until they finally disappeared completely and never returned.

Faith is not what is happening at the moment. Faith is being sure about what is going to happen.

# What You Can Expect in Response to Prayers for Healing
## Jim Glennon

**Recovery can be immediate**

The ideal expectation is for perfect healing, there and then. God has promised; we believe; prayer is answered. This, in principle, is the kind of healing the New Testament records. Those who believe that the commission to preach and heal applies today as well as yesterday also believe that healing happens in the same way today as yesterday. Jesus said it will be "according to your faith" (Matt. 9:29 RSV). Whatever we might think, that is the divine criterion against which our response is to be measured.

Here is an illustration of immediate healing, written by the woman concerned.

"Looking back, I guess I hadn't been completely well since the time I had two difficult pregnancies. Both were full term, but both babies died. This had physical repercussions and it was probably this, the doctor explained, that led to the positive result in a smear test in 1980. An initial biopsy confirmed abnormal tissue growth, termed severe dysplasia, one stage before cancer.

"I entered hospital for a hysterectomy. With all the damaged areas removed, and with the bladder repositioned, I was told I would feel like a new woman within a few months. With some ten years of mediocre health behind me, I looked forward to that prospect with relief and expectancy.

"It didn't happen. There were long-term effects from the anesthetic and I was plagued with infection after infection. I just dragged myself through 1981 and fought a battle both physically and psychologically. By the time I entered hospital for a second major operation, I had had a year of disturbed, painful nights, long aching mornings and afternoons in bed to regain strength for the evenings. Still, this operation was to fix everything. The bladder was to be re-shaped and the infected part removed.

"Once again the effects of the anesthetic were devastating and mending was slow and painful. The discomfort, particularly on going to the toilet, remained extreme. The next consultation was three months after the operation and I shall always remember it was Monday, 8th February, 1982. The ligaments which cause the pelvis to contract after childbirth were diagnosed as being severely infected, and I was told I would have to go back into hospital to be bound up and immobilized for six months.

"I reached my breaking point that night, and wept helplessly as I tried to go to sleep. A real sense of worthlessness overcame me. I felt a failure as a wife and mother and a complete waste of space on this earth. I wanted it all to end, and cried out to God to kill me or heal me—it didn't really matter which. Amazingly I came out of that brokenness refreshed and with the absolute conviction that if I went to the Healing Service at St. Andrew's Cathedral I would be healed.

"We had heard that there was a Healing Ministry at the cathedral, but knew nothing about it at all, so we phoned and found that there was a service held every Wednesday at 6:00 P.M. Today was Tuesday; I counted the hours. Wednesday afternoon arrived at last. I had a nap to muster up the energy to travel, and at last the time came to leave.

"We arrived at the Healing Service, and the first thing that impressed us was the incredible atmosphere of the place—so warm and loving. The service began and was so joyful, the people really were praising the Lord. We felt we had come home. I was just beginning to feel the strain of sitting upright when the invitation was given to those who wanted prayer to raise their hands. Up shot mine and a quite ordinary, gentle sort of fellow rose from among those sitting near and laid his hand on my head. He asked my need and when I told him, he prayed a simple prayer of thanks!

"I truly felt that Jesus had passed by and that I had touched the hem of His garment. The rest of the service passed in a warm blur. Then I was anointed with oil.

"I had been completely healed. I felt a warm vibrating feeling in my hips which contracted a whole size. I stood for over an hour chatting with people without feeling the least strain. We went to dinner afterwards to celebrate and drank red wine. What a thrill to someone who had trouble drinking orange juice! There has been no more infection, no more acute discomfort, no more of the debilitating ill health I had for years.

"But the most wonderful thing of all was the realization that God really is our Father and does care about us, that Jesus is our Lord, Savior and Friend and that He heals today just as He did yesterday. This is not the end of my testimony; it is the beginning of a whole new relationship with God for my family and me.

"It is now over a year since I was healed and I feel younger and fitter than ever. Our lives have been further transformed by the fullness of the Holy Spirit and each day has become a fresh adventure with the Lord.

"Thank you, Lord, that you cared even for me. V.C."

## Recovery can be gradual

For reasons we are now going to examine, healing can be gradual. We need to understand the factors that contribute to this, so that where our response is inadequate, we can remedy that defect if it is possible to do so. This will be a more intelligent and productive approach than the common practice of passing off the lack of answer to prayer by attributing it to God's will.

Not that we are in any way unconcerned about God's will. On the contrary, we have been at pains to begin at that point and affirm that the broad themes of scriptural promise *reveal* God's will to us. Because there is a clear promise that "the prayer offered in faith will make the sick person well" (James 5:15 NIV), we should think it possible that where prayer has been unanswered it may not have to do with God's part but with ours.

### *"My healing didn't last"*

When in the United States some years ago, I had contact with a woman who had been ministered to by Kathryn Kuhlman. She had received such remarkable healing of cancer that it had become front-page news with the press, but now the problem was returning. "My healing didn't last," she told me.

And recently, as I was walking through St. Andrew's Cathedral, a young man approached me and said he had come to the Healing Service a fortnight previously because he was a chronic asthma sufferer, and that he had been prayed for with the laying on of hands. He had been much better during the following week, but now his condition was getting back to what it was like before. He was mystified; obviously there had been a response to prayer, but the improvement had not been maintained.

This happens sometimes in my counseling ministry. At the end of an interview I always believe with my visitor(s) for healing or whatever is the relevant provision of God. Then I arrange for him (or her) to come and see me again, so that the matter can be followed through. On the subsequent occasion, he may be full of gratitude for the subsequent improvement that has followed the earlier visit, but within another week or ten days the sickness may begin to assert itself again.

### Some of the reasons

Before we go any further, it is worth saying that healing isn't the only blessing from God that does not always seem to last. The many who go through the solemn rite of Confirmation and who are never seen again, or who quickly fall away, are a well-known and glaring example. The plain fact is that "the pilgrim way" is littered with blessings from God that have quickly come and quickly gone. What Jesus said about the seed sown in shallow or stony ground surely has some application. The fault is not in the seed—be it healing or salvation—but in the ground in which it was planted; there is something inadequate in our appropriation of what God gives. If the truth be told, we all have areas in our Christian experience where we are shallow ground.

At this point, a question needs to be asked of some people: do they really *want* to get well? Might their partial blessing be because of their partial response?

What is more pertinent to the average person is that the improvement drawn on may well come from the faith that has been exercised on his or her *behalf,* either in the Healing Service or in counseling. This is good as far as it goes, but sooner or later (and the sooner the better) the sick person must learn to make his own faith response if healing is to be drawn on in a continuing and complete way.

Faith for others is like a blood transfusion; it may be necessary and have a wonderful result, but it cannot continue indefinitely. It is a boost designed to get the sick man on his own feet. Prayer for others is a faith "transfusion" with the same strengths and limitations. This is worth thinking about.

Another common reason why blessing can decrease is that the

person is asking the question, "I wonder if it will last?" Often he is hoping for the best but fearing the worst. He may be living on a knife-edge, with faith and praise on one side and doubt and fear on the other. That lurking fear may be something he doesn't want to admit or express, but if it is there, that, more than anything else, is why sickness returns. In what the Mary Sisters refer to as "the battle of faith," so often it is fear that wins out—and we know the consequence of having that destructive companion.

### Take more of the medicine

Assuming that the possible explanations above have been worked through, we can now move ahead in a constructive way. If the sick person has shown some improvement, however partial and transitory, it means he has drawn on healing in degree. It shows that healing is available in response to faith, and he should be greatly encouraged.

Secondly, it is obvious he has not drawn on as much healing as he needs. We need to realize there can be a contest, if that is the right word, between sickness and healing. We might think of the sickness as being the seashore and healing coming in like the tide. Sometimes it does not come in far enough or doesn't go deep enough or, for one reason or another, it isn't maintained. There is also a tendency for the tide to go out, because sickness is a living force; unless it is rooted out completely and in permanence, it will reassert itself.

If for any reason healing has not been received in as complete a way as is needed, we will tend to find the sickness taking over again. This can be a see-saw activity. When this happens, we need to react in a positive way and reaffirm our healing. Something of what can happen for good has been seen, and we need "to take more of the medicine." That is, we are to react to what remains of the problem by continuing to draw on the answer. If the lack of perfect healing has meant that we have reverted to being problem-centered in our thinking, we need to become answer-centered again—*by faith.*

As we continue in prayer, it frequently happens that things come into focus which need to be dealt with, and which so far have not been thought of in the context of healing: the need to forgive and be forgiven, the need to face past hurts and receive the healing of the memories, the need to believe for wholeness in other related areas. It is rather like repairing an old house; you fix up one part and that reveals more trouble. Don't be put off by this; there is no reason why it cannot all be brought into good condition, but it will take time and application.

*Faith is a decision of the mind*

To get these things right in a consistent way requires that we get our faith-thinking right every day. I spend time every morning doing this until my mind is working in a positive and believing way. It is so easy to affirm the problem and not the answer, even when one has come to faith on previous occasions. The mind is a very unruly member, and we can never assume that it will react in faith and praise. Left to itself, it is more likely a case of "I do not do the good I want, but the evil I do not want is what I do" (Rom. 7:19 RSV). When I get it wrong so that the problem is being affirmed, I endeavor to learn from the mistake, so that my reactions in similar circumstances later on will be more effective.

Instead of saying, "My healing didn't last," concentrate on thanking God for what blessing there is, or as the Bible puts it so succinctly, "Continue in prayer, and watch in the same with thanksgiving" (Col. 4:2 KJV). This means we are not to react negatively to any remaining or returning symptoms of sickness, but believe for *further* healing. St. Paul gave us the right word of encouragement: "He who began a good work in you will bring it to completion" (Phil. 1:6 RSV).

Assuming time is on our side and we are doing this with others—we with them and they with us—there is no limit to the healing that can be drawn on from God in a cumulative way. With this in mind, I share with you a further text that is my rule of life and ministry: "Let steadfastness [patience] have its full effect, that you may be perfect and complete, lacking in nothing" (James 1:4).

## Moving the bigger mountains

Many people who draw on divine healing have problems that are longstanding and in an advanced state. Sometimes that is why they come; they have tried everything else, and this is their last resort. That is not a criticism, but it is a factor that has to be taken into account. Some have illnesses that, humanly speaking, are terminal.

*Reservations*

When someone approaches me about healing who has what might

be called "a bigger mountain" to move, I talk the matter over with him and his family in a frank and sensitive way.

It is necessary to make the point that, just as the more advanced the illness is, the more difficult it is for medical treatment to be effective, so too it is more difficult for prayer to be effective. I do not "go out on a limb" and speak about the promise of healing in an unqualified way. This is not to say that God cannot heal; but the size of the mountain has to be taken into account, as do the limits of our faith.

Another part of the whole is that the time comes to each of us when we are to depart this life. Then one does not pray for healing, but for grace to leave this world for the next in a way that befits the person who is trusting in Christ for eternal life. But until that point is reached, I believe healing is available in the same way as the medical resource is available, and our approach to both should be the same.

When we have talked the matter through, I say that within the limitations the circumstances impose, I will help the patient in any way possible, and I set no limit to what God is able to do. Sick people are accustomed to their medical advisors discussing their condition and the available options in a balanced and helpful way, and they should have the same kind of experience when they come to the church to inquire about the healing ministry. Assuming that, I find that people understand and accept what is said in a mature and positive way.

Agnes Sanford, who was the leading authority on the Christian healing ministry, strongly affirmed that we do not automatically pray for healing for every sick person who comes across our path. Because faith is what we are responsible to God for and, again, having in mind the extent of the problem many people have, she would wait on God before committing herself to believe for healing in any particular situation. She often commented that many people who followed her guidelines about healing nevertheless did not follow her on this point. As time goes by, I see and appreciate more of what she said, and both advocate and practice the restraint she advised on this important matter.

## Soaking prayer

Given the above, the principles of persevering prayer need to be clearly understood and acted on with a blend of discipline, courage and a reliance on the guidance of the Holy Spirit. When prayer is made for two minutes there can be minimal change; after fifteen

144

minutes it is more obvious; and after an hour the miraculous is fully apparent. And so on.

This is what is meant and accomplished by fasting. There is no virtue in merely doing without food; that only makes one hungry and miserable. But when one uses the sensation of being without food to provide a continuing stimulus or reminder to be believing God for His blessing, its intended purpose is being served. And far from it being distressing, one quickly comes to an elevated level of communion with God and praise of His holy name that is not drawn on in any other way. Time takes on a new dimension, as one wants the experience to last and not to end.

The hair shirt worn by some of the ancients had the same intention. The irritation was deliberately induced to give them a moment-by-moment reminder to be depending on God.

One can also react to sickness and circumstances in the same way. I can vouch for this through my own experience. When, at last, I came to an awareness that, as far as God was concerned, I did not have to be afraid, I then went on to accept the soundness of mind that it was His will for me to have. But this worked only for as long as it took to make the affirmation. When it finished, the fears were waiting to sweep over me again, and they did. Some progress had been made, but much more was needed.

This came in an unexpected way. One day I was so at the end of myself with anxiety that I decided to get away from it all for a while and see a film. For more than two hours my mind was filled with the story and music of *Oliver!* When it had finished and I came out of the cinema, to my great surprise and relief everything was wonderfully different. I didn't have a fear in the world. I remember saying to myself, "This must be what life is like without fear!" But the act of bringing it to mind seemed to resurrect the problem, and within a short time it was the same as before.

### Put healing in place of sickness

But I had had an experience. This time my fears had been left behind, not just for a moment, but for two hours. Why? Because my mind had been filled with something else—a film. I couldn't go on doing that (and didn't want to). So what else would do the same thing? What better than the power and love and soundness of mind that God wanted me to have? It meant that not only did I accept this provision (I had done that already in a beginning way), but it became what I affirmed in a *continuing* way.

As long as my conscious mind was filled with my continuing affirmations, I had relative peace of mind, but if for any reason they stopped, the fear automatically took over. It was as simple as that. It meant that I had to turn my day into one long affirmation of faith. I reached the point where I was doing this for literally every moment without so much as putting in a comma—before I was out of bed in the morning, while brushing my teeth, driving my car and, with a corner of my mind, whatever else I was doing. Not that I was any better at the day's end, but if nothing else I wasn't worse, which was different from what it had been like up till then. At least I was no longer just giving in to the problem because I did not know what else to do; now I was fighting it with the answer given by God.

The next day the problem was still there, as though the previous day's affirmations hadn't existed. I continued to react positively, because I had to; it was no virtue on my part, it was an exercise in survival. Not infrequently I was holding on for dear life. "Thank you, Father, you are healing me now. . . ."

More than in any other way, I expressed my faith by praising God—for what He had done, was doing, and would do.

As I continued to do this—not only day by day, but month after month—it gradually came through to me that the clouds were shifting and blue skies were beginning to peep through. For short times I could stop my prayer of faith and no fear came; when it returned, I would go back to filling my mind with all the fullness of God in the way that has been described. If you like, the positive was being put in place of the negative. But it was much more than positive thinking; I was believing by faith for God's promised blessing so that I did not doubt in my heart.

It was a tremendous encouragement to find that my persevering prayer was gradually being effective. In a word, healing was increasing and sickness was decreasing. Finally and at long last, and directly as a result of what has been set out in this book and especially in this chapter, I came out on to a plateau where my lifelong fears that had brought me to the breakdown had disappeared—and disappeared so completely that they never so much as come to mind, unless by a deliberate act of recall for the purpose of giving testimony to the healing that God gives through prayer and fasting.

## From death to life

In case there are those who feel this can be done for an emotional condition but not for something physical, the following account is included.

A Christian social worker at the Royal Alexandra Hospital for Children in Sydney referred Tom and Marcia Burrows to me, hoping I might be able to help them. Their infant daughter, aged twelve months, was critically ill with leukemia and not expected to live. Tom and Marcia will not mind my saying that they had only a slender involvement in the Christian religion, and no understanding whatsoever of the healing ministry.

I visited them in the hospital, and realized that Angela was very close to death. I do not feel free to pray for healing with no reservation in this kind of situation. But things didn't work out according to my preconceived position. The parents' love for their little girl and the trust they immediately placed in me led them to ask and press me to pray for healing. Short of walking out on them, I could not avoid their plea. Very much against my better judgment I prayed for healing, and because of that felt obliged to follow the matter through. When I subsequently mentioned this to one of our office staff, who is also committed to the healing ministry, she took up the challenge, which again left me with no alternative but to do my part as best I could.

I visited the baby every day for a month to pray over her in faith, and my prayer partner was equally diligent in her support. For some time Angela hovered in the balance, and then very, very slowly began to improve. The gradual improvement continued, and by the end of the month she had gone into remission and subsequently was discharged from the hospital.

Five years have gone by with no recurrence of the disease, and her physicians describe her condition as being in complete remission. With her parents and a baby brother she lives in one of our Sydney suburbs, and it is a joy to hear from them at Christmas with their loving and grateful greeting. And, perhaps not surprisingly, Angela has a very special relationship with God. Her mother says, "She walks with Jesus."

## Reflections

I am not being defensive in saying the pastoral position I take up is intended to be conservative. Perhaps it is for this reason that sometimes the thing that is a "breakthrough" is learned accidentally. When one is pushed through the mind-barrier that has been set according to our present level of understanding and experience, further knowledge is gained.

When I reflect on Angela's story, I ask myself, do we give up too easily? Something else we fail to consider is that one needs time to pray and minister in this sacrificial way. Often I feel my butter is spread too thinly, because of the number of people to whom I am giving pastoral care. There is a good argument for ministering to few people and in more depth.

Three things need to be remembered in moving the bigger mountains: balance, which is essential; sacrificial prayer; and willingness to be taken further forward.

**Healing leads to wholeness**

As we draw on healing, whether it be immediate or gradual, and as we are concerned with moving bigger mountains, we will find that healing leads to wholeness. By healing, we mean the healing of the immediate circumstances about which we are praying; by wholeness, we mean the healing of everything that is relevant to our well-being.

The point I would make, and with considerable emphasis, is that healing cannot be looked at in isolation. If it is, it may well be short-lived, even if it is drawn on. And when healing is short-lived, it is not so easy to draw on the second time round. Perhaps the most important thing in all that we are saying is that we need wholeness *as well as* healing. That is the message of the Christian healing ministry.

*Profit from what has happened*

The first thing to think about is that we must profit from what has happened. In the future we will discipline our mind and feelings to react in terms of the relevant answer God provides, and not in terms of the stress. Subsequent stress can come from an entirely different source, but it can activate the same weak spot in our physical and emotional makeup.

We have to be concerned with wholeness. We cannot divide ourselves up into compartments so that we are practicing healing in one of them and allowing an activity that promotes sickness to run riot in another. Our whole life needs to profit from our experience, so that we believe for wholeness in ourselves, in others and in our environment. This should not come as any surprise to followers of

Christ, because that is what Christianity is all about. God is not concerned only to clear up one room of our house; He will certainly go through every room and every grubby corner until all things are made new.

If we don't have this approach, then healing, whether it be from prayer or medicine, will be like putting plaster over an infection. The illness may well recur at a later time in the same or in a different form.

### Make healing a way of life

Make make healing a way of thought and a way of life.

After reading *The Cross and the Switchblade* by David Wilkerson, I went, at a later time, to visit Teen Challenge in Brooklyn, New York, where he had begun his work of ministering to drug addicts and others for whom no effective community resource was available. In the course of being shown around, I met a number of fellows who were in the Intake Center for men.

Two things struck me. The first was the lurid backgrounds of these young men. You name it, they had done it—drugs, crime, sex, alcohol and other things, some of which I had never heard of before. The second was that these young fellows were like "the boy next door." They were upright in bearing, courteous in manner, and (very noticeably) compassionate to one another. I am not exaggerating; they were like the best products from our church schools.

I was intrigued and nonplussed. How could these two characteristics be reconciled? I talked this over with Dave Wilkerson and found the explanation to be simplicity itself, and something that fitted closely into my own evangelical background.

In brief, Christ was presented to these men as Savior and Healer, and they were called on to accept Him for every need they had. This meant that they accepted Christ as their Savior and they accepted Christ as their Healer. If they were alcoholics, they accepted Christ for the healing of their alcoholism in the same way as they accepted Christ for the forgiveness of their sins. That is, they accepted their healing, they made a decision to that end, and they affirmed what they had done by faith. This is what I have been saying, and this is where I learned it.

Subsequent to this, they would go through the trauma of withdrawal when they had a craving to return to alcohol or whatever the problem was that they had to begin with. At this point, members of the staff and others who were more advanced in the program would stand by the one going through withdrawal, supporting him in his new-found faith, and affirming with him and for him the healing that was being believed for. Even when they were at the end of their tether, they would continue to affirm their blessing by faith.

Because of this persevering, sacrificial and vicarious prayer, the person concerned would finally come through, so that the old cravings no longer had sway over his life. Instead he had the wholeness of Christ in the ways that were needed. Complementing this, he then went into a program of re-education, so that he became rooted and grounded in the Christian faith and life. This full-time program lasted, in all, about nine months.

By their fruits shall they be known. The success rate of those who went through the Teen Challenge program was of the order of eighty-six percent, which is a far, far better result than any other program of rehabilitation for these kinds of problems.

## All or nothing at all

A further and equally important point about their practice of ministry was that their acceptance of healing was affirmed in a *total* kind of way. There were no half measures.

When I had first arrived, Dave Wilkerson could not meet with me because he was in the process of dismissing a man who was on the program but was not fitting into their rules. Believe it or not, all he had been guilty of was continuing to talk to others about his former life. But the problem was really a matter of fundamental importance, because in effect he was keeping his own and other men's problems going, preventing from being fully effective the healing that he and they were, at the same time, professing and needing. He wanted it both ways. But it didn't work both ways. It only worked when he was willing to switch over to his new life with no reservation at all. Given that, he would have become "a new creation" (2 Cor. 5:17), which was the explanation for the extraordinary before-and-after stories of Teen Challenge, New York.

While the problems of men and women at Teen Challenge may well be different from those most of us have, the principle of healing and the principle of discipline required are the same. Three quarters of the reason why the Christian answer doesn't work as it should is that we do not apply it in the thoroughgoing and wholehearted way that it needs to be applied. G.K. Chesterton's famous words have an application: "It is not that Christianity has been weighed in the balance and found wanting. It has been found to be difficult and therefore not tried." It is for good reason that Jesus said that, if we were going to be effective in the new life, the old life had to be put to death. And this concerns healing as well. The problems need to be crucified with Christ, and we need to believe in a complete and total way.

## The most important part of wholeness

An essential requirement, if we are to have wholeness as well as healing, is that we believe on Christ for salvation, and have His presence and power in our lives. Before this happens we are lost; afterwards we are found. Before, we are dead in our sins; afterwards, we are alive unto God. Before, Christ is a figure in history; afterwards, He is our mighty and ever living Savior. It isn't enough to be a churchgoer or to obey the Golden Rule or to have healing or anything else; we must have the living Christ in our lives and trust only in Him if we are to be made right with the Father.

## Is death failure?

A minority of those who are prayed for are healed at once; the majority of those who are healed are healed gradually. There are those who are healed partially; and there are those who are not healed physically, but who have a healing of the spirit.

There are also those who are prayed for and who die. Whether or not this is part of what one expects, it is part of what can happen, and we need to talk about it in an open way from experience.

One comment made by critics is that the spiritual condition of the sick person and their family will be adversely affected if they have faith for a healing and death is the outcome, so that the last stage is worse than the first. Our experience shows that this is not a problem, *provided* the person and the family are members of a soundly based and pastorally active healing ministry congregation.

Let me share with you a story from our pastoral casebook that will bring into focus what we have learned in this connection.

John and Libby Galston called me on the phone to say that their young son Mark was critically ill in the Children's Hospital; they had read my book *Your Healing Is Within You* and could I help in any way with the healing ministry? The matter was obviously urgent, so we arranged a time, and they were in my office within an hour or so of their first telephoning.

151

At an earlier time, their little boy, aged nine, had complained of headaches, and ultimately he was diagnosed as having a brain tumor. This had been removed by a surgical procedure, and he was able to resume his ordinary activity, including going to school. But there had been a reappearance of his symptoms at this later time, and a recurrence of the tumor had been diagnosed. Their medical specialist said that if Mark was his child he would not let him have a further operation and advised against it. He said the only help that could be given was palliative, and they would keep Mark comfortable with sedation. He was unconscious at the present time, and his parents were awaiting the end.

I explained to them sensitively and carefully the reservations I have about exercising the healing ministry in these circumstances, and said that provided they understood this, I would help in any way that was possible. I said I would be prepared to pray in a positive way about healing, provided we were open to any further guidance that God might be pleased to give. They were perfectly happy for us to proceed in this way, and together we went to the hospital to visit their son. He was in a coma. Everything that could be done for him medically had been done. We took our places around his bedside, rested our hands lightly on his arms, and I prayed:

*Our loving Father in heaven, we know that you have a special love for children because Jesus called them to Him, and we know that your love and provision for Mark is perfect in both this life and the next. We lay our hands on him as a sign of our faith and our love, and pray that you will give him all the healing that can be given. We do not know all that you have for him, but we would be channels of your perfect blessing for his life, and we believe you are using our faith so that our Lord Jesus Christ is glorified in Mark and in us. By faith we praise you for answering our prayer in Jesus' name.*

I anointed him with holy oil, and we prayed the Lord's Prayer together and said the Grace.

The next day, to the incredulity of the hospital staff, Mark came out of his coma and was in full possession of his faculties, though still confined to his bed. The transformation of this little boy from what he had been like the previous day could only be described as miraculous. We thanked God for His blessing and continued to believe that He was showing us more of His will and provision for Mark.

We hadn't long to wait. When I subsequently visited him, I found he was rather a demanding little boy and wanted this and that done for him. At first I met his requests, but when I didn't measure up to exactly what he wanted, he began to abuse me and used some very bad language. I put up with this for a while, until one day I walked out on him and could hear him shouting even after I had left the ward. I remember asking him on one occasion at this time whether he loved Jesus, but this only brought forth another outburst.

It was obvious that he was very disturbed, and his behavior was a sign and symptom of someone who was trying to call attention, albeit in an asocial way, to an inner and unresolved need.

I met with his parents, who were delightful people and obviously embarrassed because of what was happening. In reply to my questions, they said he had been a happy and well-adjusted child until a younger sister was born, and then he began to act up. In particular he was hostile toward his mother and would sometimes throw stones at her. I explained to them that the coming of his younger sister had put his nose out of joint, so to speak, and that his aggressive behavior was a way of trying to get the attention he had been used to before his sister came, and which he now *felt* he was being deprived of. The ministry he needed was that of inner healing, and we prayed to that end:

*We believe that you are coming into Mark's life, making up for the love that he* feels *he hasn't got, and enabling him to be healed and made mature in his relationships with his family and with everyone else.*

I disciplined my mind to react to the difficulties by affirming the answer by faith and on his behalf. Two other members of our congregation were visiting him by now, and we believed this together, as did his parents.

As we continued to affirm the inner healing he needed and disciplined ourselves to react to any problem in behavior in this positive way, he began to quiet down, until after several weeks he finally became a normal and charming little fellow.

By now he was calling me "Uncle Jim," and I reached the point of asking him again if he loved the Lord Jesus. He wasn't sure how to go about this, so I said to him that Jesus first loved us and we are just returning His love. He smiled and showed he understood. Shortly after, he was confirmed in his church; I attended the service and was asked to be one of his sponsors. It was a wonderfully happy and uplifting occasion with other members of his family present; an afternoon party of tea and cookies followed, which had been thoughtfully prepared by the hospital staff. After that the religious Sister brought him Holy Communion regularly. He said to me one day (this was not a reference to Holy Communion): "Jesus comes to visit me and He sits over there." He was happy and in perfect harmony with Jesus and the members of his family and with everyone else.

On a Sunday morning, some six weeks after his parents had first approached me, I received an urgent phone call from his father asking me to come as soon as possible. When I was free from my duties at the cathedral, I went to the hospital. The boy was deeply unconscious, and his parents and I knew that God's redemptive work had been done and that the time had come for Mark to go and be with the Lord. We committed him to Jesus who had given such a wonderful experience of healing, and we felt God's presence with us and especially with Mark. At five o'clock that afternoon he moved peacefully into eternal life.

After the funeral, his parents, who had come to the Healing Service throughout the time of his illness, came again with his brothers and sisters and sat in the front row. Their smiling faces were a testimony of God's blessing in the midst of their bereavement. And John now attends Holy Communion regularly in the cathedral at our weekday services. "All this has brought me back to God," he said quietly and meaningfully.

We have found that where prayer is made over someone who subsequently dies, his life span is wonderfully extended, and during that time he is prepared for eternity by the Holy Spirit. As well as his own needs being met, so too are the needs of those who are near and dear to him. When this has been done, he quietly goes to be with Christ. And everyone knows and says there has been a blessing that only God can give.

Far from the healing ministry being destructive when the person concerned subsequently dies, it enables blessing to be there that transforms death into Christian victory. Surely there is healing in that too.

# Four Common Objections
# Jim Glennon

*The value of suffering*

It is often said that there is "value in suffering," that we need to conclude our prayer with the phrase "if it be thy will."

But is this the right understanding of the matter? Obviously, the first requirement is to avoid making any uncritical assumptions. Our only guide is what God has revealed to us in His written Word. What, then, does the Bible reveal to us about suffering?

It was said of Christ, "Although he was a Son, he learned obedience through what he suffered" (Heb. 5:8 RSV). If we ask in what way Christ suffered, we find the answer in Matthew 16:21 (RSV): "Jesus began to show his disciples that he must go to Jerusalem and suffer many things from the elders and chief priests and scribes, and be killed, and on the third day be raised." Luke said the same thing: "Thus it is written, that the Christ should suffer and on the third day rise from the dead" (24:46 RSV).

The suffering of Christ has to do with His atonement. Through His suffering He learned obedience to His Father's will, "and being made perfect he became the source of eternal salvation to all who obey him" (Heb. 5:9 RSV).

When it comes to the suffering experienced by the followers of Christ, "we share abundantly in Christ's sufferings" (2 Cor. 1:5 RSV). This does not mean we share in the suffering of our Lord's atonement, but the meaning becomes clear as we examine and compare other references. The apostles rejoiced "that they were counted worthy to suffer dishonor for the name" (Acts 5:41 RSV). Peter said, "Even if you do suffer for righteousness' sake, you will be blessed. . . . It is better to suffer for doing right, if that should be God's will, than for doing wrong" (1 Pet. 3:14-17 RSV). To the Thessalonians Paul said, "You suffered the same things from your own countrymen as they did from the Jews" (1 Thess. 2:14 RSV).

Of St. Paul and his suffering Jesus said, "He is a chosen instrument of mine . . . I will show him how much he must suffer for the sake of my name" (Acts 9:15, 16 RSV).

The meaning of "suffering" in the New Testament, as far as the Christian is concerned, is the persecution that comes from being a Christian. This is the broad and consistent theme and there are no exceptions.

Suffering for the Christian is intended to be a redemptive experience by which we learn the obedience of trusting not in ourselves, but in God. This is the value of suffering, and its importance cannot be overstressed.

*Paul's thorn*

This is the illustration from the New Testament which is so often used to maintain that it may not be God's will to heal. If God did not heal St. Paul, who prayed three times that his "thorn in the flesh" (2 Cor. 12:8 RSV) be taken from him, and to whom God said, "My grace is sufficient" (v. 8), then He might not will to heal us. If so, we have to pray, "if it be thy will."

If this understanding of Paul's thorn is correct, then we must accept it. But we must be quite certain about it, because, if true, it qualifies our Lord's teaching and practice that only faith is needed for healing. It likewise comprises the teaching and practice of Paul himself, who saw that the cripple "had faith to be made well" (Acts 14:9 RSV). It is no light matter to compromise what Christ himself said and taught. If, on the other hand, our enquiry shows the common understanding of Paul's thorn to be no more than a tradition of man, we have a clear duty to expose that fallacy and to reject it.

In the Old Testament, "thorns" were used as a figure of speech, and always referred to people, never to things or conditions. "The inhabitants of the land . . . shall be as pricks in your eyes and thorns in your sides . . ." (Num. 33:55 RSV). "They shall be a scourge on your sides, and thorns in your eyes" (Jos. 23:13 RSV). Obviously these statements meant that people, described as "thorns in your sides," were going to be very hurtful. "Thorns" in the Scriptures were always people; they were never sicknesses or the spirits of sickness.

When we come to Paul's use of the word, we see, as we might expect from this background of understanding, that it stands for a person. "A thorn was given me in the flesh, *a messenger of Satan*"

156

(2 Cor. 12:7 RSV, emphasis added). In the original Greek, the word "messenger" is *angelos,* which appears 188 times in the New Testament. It is translated 181 times as "angel" and in seven cases as "messenger." It is always translated as a person, never as an object, and has no connection with sickness.

The straightforward interpretation of what Paul wrote is that a messenger (a person) of Satan was a thorn in the flesh to him. The thorn in the flesh was a figurative way of describing a messenger or angel of Satan who continually harassed him—in much the same way as we say that someone is "a pain in the neck." No one would ever think that a person referred to in this way was literally causing a pain in the neck.

To regard the "thorn" as a sickness is to impart to it a meaning which the Old Testament use of the word does not contain, and to ignore the meaning which is plainly employed. For there is a positive identification of the "thorn" with a person, both in the Old Testament, and in Paul's own explanation of what he meant. Among those who have identified the thorn with a person are Chrysostom, who noted it in his commentaries on the Epistles to the Corinthians, and Augustine of Hippo.

At this point we need take into account Paul's statement that the "thorn" and the consequent "weaknesses' were a redemptive experience for him. He rejoiced that he had been made weak in himself, so that he was strong in the Lord. As there is no reason to think the "thorn" was a sickness, this further identifies it with suffering. The context is plainly what we have come to see suffering to be, as distinct from sickness. Paul said, "For the sake of Christ, then, I am content with weaknesses, insults, hardships, persecutions and calamities" (2 Cor. 12:10 RSV). The only logical deduction from this is that the thorn and the resulting weaknesses were part of the suffering that came from his apostleship. This dovetails perfectly with our Lord's prophecy that in the course of carrying Christ's name before the Gentiles and kings and the sons of Israel, Paul would suffer greatly for His name's sake.

But irrespective of what the "thorn" was, the unique circumstances which led to Paul having this visitation make it most difficult to apply his experience in a general way. It is implied that Paul was caught up into the third heaven and heard unspeakable words. Because of that, he goes on to say, "To keep me from being too elated by the abundance of revelations, a thorn was given me in the flesh, a messenger of Satan . . ." (2 Cor. 12:9 RSV). Doubtless it was this "abundance of revelations" that enabled Paul to discharge his responsibilities as the Apostle to the Gentiles, and provided the content of his epistles.

Once Paul's thorn is seen in its full perspective, it cannot rightly be used to weaken the rule of healing as revealed by Christ. To use such an exception to set aside the unequivocal teaching of the Lord Jesus Christ, as well as the otherwise unanimous record of the New Testament, cannot be regarded as sound and reasonable biblical exegesis.

Notwithstanding what has been argued so far, it is possible for a "messenger of Satan," in the shape of sickness, not to be removed by God. But if the person is not to be healed, this fact will be revealed by God. It also means that, up to this point, the prayer of faith will be acted upon in full expectancy of healing. Furthermore, if it is then revealed that healing is not to take place, it means that the sick person will "all the more gladly boast of [his or her] weaknesses," as did St. Paul, and will not continue to seek their removal.

### Trophimus, Timothy and Epaphroditus

Paul left Trophimus "ill at Miletus" (2 Tim. 4:20 RSV), and he referred to Timothy's "frequent ailments" (1 Tim. 5:23 RSV). Epaphroditus had been "ill, near to death" (Phil. 2:27 RSV), but recovered, and Paul sent him to those who had been distressed by his illness, that they might "rejoice at seeing him again" (v. 28). Some argue that if healing were available in response to faith, then surely Paul would have healed his companions.

It is possible that he did heal Epaphroditus; he certainly said that he recovered because "God had mercy on him" (Phil. 2:27 RSV). If Epaphroditus was the only one to be considered, no reasonable person would bring him forward as a reason for maintaining that healing was not available in response to faith. The only case that can be made out is in respect to Trophimus and Timothy, who were sick at the time of Paul's writing. So let us consider these two.

If Paul had said that these two men were not converted at the time he was writing, would we conclude that it may not be God's will for all men to be saved? Of course not! We would make a judgment on the matter in the light of what the Bible otherwise said. And since the Bible says it is God's desire that all men should be saved (1 Tim. 2:4), we would assume that some deficiency on their part, or on the part of their spiritual advisors, had prevented them from appropriating this blessing.

By using the same reasonable approach to make a judgment on the validity of healing in this situation, we would have to say that the Bible makes an express promise that the prayer of faith will save the sick man and that the Lord will raise him up. We would also have to say that the New Testament testimony is wholly consistent on this matter. As a possible explanation of the difficulty, we would refer to another occasion where the disciples had actually attempted to heal someone and failed, and the Lord had stated that the hindrance was their "little faith" (Matt. 17:20 RSV). When this was made good by His own perfect faith, the person concerned was immediately healed. Our Lord then explained that this was a deeper problem needing sacrificial prayer—showing, incidentally, that there is a quantitative aspect to faith.

Healing, like forgiveness, has to be drawn upon by faith and it can be difficult to believe for healing effectively. There is nothing to say that Trophimus and Timothy had been prayed for, and there is nothing to say they were not subsequently healed. (At any one time there are many who are sick and who are later healed, just as there are many unconverted who are later converted.) Thus, to deduce that healing is not available in response to faith, merely because two persons happened to be sick at a particular time, is unreasonable.

*The will of God*

It is frequently said that we do not know the will of God; therefore we cannot pray with undoubting faith that God will answer in the affirmative, so we have to conclude our prayer with the proviso "if it be thy will."

That we have to pray according to God's will if our prayers are to be answered is not in question. Nor is the fact that there are times when we do not know God's will. But there are many matters on which we *can* know God's will, because it is revealed in the Bible. His will for us is contained in "his precious and very great promises" (2 Pet. 1:4 RSV), and we search the Scriptures to see what these promises are. Once we determine what they are, we can appropriate them by the prayer of faith.

Often the phrase, "not my will, but thine, be done" (Luke 22:42 RSV) is used to create a false dichotomy. It is agreed that we must pray

159

according to God's will. But His will is revealed to us in His promises; if we accept His promises by faith, we are praying according to His will.

Two writers said recently, "There are magnificent promises in the scripture to do with prayer. Take James 5:15, where we read, '. . . the prayer of faith will save the sick man, and the Lord will raise him up . . .' These are encouragements to faith in God, for this is a necessity in prayer." Yet they then continued, "But of course we must realise that God does not give us the things which are contrary to his will."

Our whole relationship with God is built on the magnificent promises in the Scriptures. The view that it may not be God's will for us to have them in reality is a contradiction in terms. It runs contrary to the basic concept of a promise-making and promise-keeping God. Without God's promises we have no assurance of God's blessing—for salvation or anything else. We are "partakers of the promise in Christ Jesus through the gospel" (Eph. 3:6 RSV). "All the promises of God find their Yes in him" (2 Cor. 7:20 RSV).

\*      \*      \*

A critical examination of these four common objectives shows them to be weak and misleading. They have been brought out so often and for so long that we assume them to be valid. We adopt them readily because they seem at first sight to be reasonable, and, perhaps without realizing it, because they excuse us from becoming involved in something which would make very great demands on us, and which we are not prepared to face.

# What About Those
# Who Are Not Healed?
# Kathryn Kuhlman

Whether one is healed or not is in the hands of God. At no time is it my responsibility. I am not perfect wisdom, I am not perfect knowledge. I have no healing virtue. I have never healed anyone. I have no power to heal. The whole responsibility rests in the hands of God and the individual. And it's just like that.

But of course I'm human. No one really knows how I hurt inside when a service is over, and I see those who have come in wheelchairs leaving in the same wheelchairs in which they came. You'll never know the ache on the inside—the suffering that I feel. But the answer I must leave with God. And one of these days, when I get home to glory, I'm going to ask Him to give me the answer from His own lips, as to why everyone is not healed.

Something happened while I was in Kansas City. The *Kansas City Star* sent a reporter to the services. I became acquainted with her, a lovely young woman with a keen journalistic mind. She attended all the services, and the last night, following the services, she came back to my dressing room. One of my helpers let her in, and she found me crying. She was embarrassed, but I went ahead and just sort of bared my soul to her, forgetting she was a reporter.

I said, "You know, people would think that after a miracle service like this, when scores and scores have been healed, that I would be the happiest person in the whole world. I am grateful I have seen the manifestation of God's power. But no one knows the hurt and grief I feel for those who were not healed. I wonder if perhaps had I known better how to cooperate with the Holy Spirit, more might have been accomplished for God." I could not hold back the flood of tears, and the reporter finally slipped out.

About three weeks later, I received a letter from this reporter. She said, "I am not writing as a reporter for the *Kansas City Star,* but as someone who had a friend in that last service. He was an attorney. He was dying of cancer. They brought him in on a stretcher. About a week after you left Kansas City, I went to his home and was greeted at the front door by his wife. She told me Tom had died. I started to leave, but she insisted I come in. Her face was radiant. She said, 'That service in the auditorium was the greatest thing that happened to Tom. Obviously he was not healed. We took him back home on the same stretcher on which he was carried in. But it was during that service that Tom prepared for death. Lying on that stretcher, while the power of God was falling, my husband accepted Christ and received forgiveness for his sins. Before then, he was struggling. Afterwards, he was peaceful. Death was easy—victorious. It was glorious to hear him thanking Jesus for the forgiveness of his sins.' "

The reporter finished her letter: "Kathryn Kuhlman, don't weep after a service any more. When you think there should have been greater results than the healing of sick bodies, always remember my friend Tom. The greatest miracle that could have happened to him was the salvation of his soul."

No, I don't understand why not everyone is healed physically. But all can be healed spiritually. That's the greatest miracle any human being can know.

# – 9 –

# The Protection of Church Authority

Blessed and holy are those who have part in the first resurrection. The second death has no power over them, but they will be priests of God and of Christ and will reign with him for a thousand years (Rev. 20:6 NIV).

Let us therefore approach the throne of grace with fullest confidence (Heb. 4:16 PHILLIPS).

Let the elders who rule well be considered worthy of double honor (1 Tim. 5:17 RSV).

An overseer is entrusted with God's work . . . He must hold firmly to the trustworthy message as it has been taught, so that he can encourage others by sound doctrine and refute those who oppose it (Titus 1:7, 9 NIV).

We can boldly approach God as individual believers; we each have His Holy Spirit dwelling within us to guide us, and we are given the mind of Christ. Yet the Lord has ordained that we be subject to the elders or overseers of His church and accept their teaching as protection from error.

Jim Glennon wrote: "To do only what is right in one's own sight will inevitably lead to confusion and division."[1] Expressing his relationship to the Anglican Church, he said: "I am under the authority of my bishop. Far from this being a limitation, it releases me to have my own authority within my membership in the church. It reflects our submission to Christ and 'the glorious liberty of the children of God' (Rom. 8:21) that results from that."[2]

163

In *Living in the Kingdom Here and Now,* Tony Lighterness wrote: "The elders are set in the authority so that the disciples might be blessed by their service of oversight . . . a source of joy if the disciples submit."[3] Lighterness also wrote: "A pastor, elder, evangelist, prophet or apostle will be recognized by his gifts and his ministry."[4]

Besides testing the fruits of ministries and teachers, Christians can look to see whether those whose teaching and ministry they accept are in turn submitting to church authority. This sign of protection, while not a guarantee of orthodoxy, nevertheless indicates that a leader is under pastoral care to be encouraged in sound doctrine and refuted when in error.

"Within the Church there is a great variety of ministries and even among ordained ministers there is a plurality of specific callings and services to be performed. However, since the mission of the Church is one, namely, to spread the Good News so as to bring all men to salvation, it can only be carried out in union with the whole body and especially in communion with [those] who possess authority," wrote Joseph Culliton in *Obedience: Gateway to Freedom.*[5] Later, in the same chapter on clerical obedience, he wrote, "The distinctive quality of the life of the minister of Christ is that he is a loving servant who devotes his life to the service of God and God's people. This service cannot be accomplished without the type of obedience which is a genuine, lasting donation of self. This form of obedience is an assurance that the minister is not serving or seeking his own interests, but is truly ministering to God's people."[6]

Tony Lighterness, again in *Living in the Kingdom Here and Now,* emphasized the difference between license and liberty. True liberty works within the limits of God's law and will, which do not restrict us from doing any good thing. "[God] says that His children are to lead the way into 'the glorious liberty of the sons of God' and that means submission to His will and the harmony, beauty and blessedness that flows from that state. . . . I hope we have been shaken by how very wrong our natural understanding can be. I hope our confidence in an intellectual interpretation of God's Word, without the ministry of the Spirit, has been shattered."[7]

"Not many of you should act as teachers, my brothers, because you know that we who teach will be judged more strictly" (James 3:1 NIV). Just as Christ was subject to His parents and to the Father, we can expect that teachers will likewise be in submission to God-given authority. Those who have learned submission are lifted up by God to positions of authority. The Lord raises up all those who are bowed down (Ps. 145:14).

In the following article, Mark Virkler discusses the need to test our spiritual experiences and what we believe is God's word to us by submitting to authority.

# Authority and Submission
## Mark Virkler

Most Westerners have been taught to live rationally, according to the dictates of our mind. I have tried, however, to dethrone my mind since it is not the organ that receives revelation from God. The heart is the place of Spirit-to-spirit encounter. However, we must never get the idea that as Christians we should throw our minds away. The mind has a very necessary place in the spiritual walk—it is the organ used for testing.

As we try to live out of our spiritual dimension, we will make mistakes. The Bible recognizes that fact and accepts it. First Thessalonians 5:21 tells us to "examine everything carefully; hold fast to that which is good" (NAS). We shouldn't jump on what is not good, and berate ourselves for our mistakes. Instead we should simply test everything we receive, ignore whatever is not of God, and move on with what is good. To make mistakes is human. The important thing is to learn from those mistakes.

Our goal, as always, is to come to a balance. God created both the head and the heart. He ordained the functions of each to complement the other. If we try to live our Christian lives out of either one alone, we will find ourselves going in circles, like a boat with only one oar. We need both the head and the heart, the rational and the spiritual aspects of our communion with the Lord.

I'd like to share two examples that firmly planted within my heart a conviction of the need for testing revelations I receive by submitting them to the authorities God has placed in my life. First, there was a man in a church I pastored whose ability to hear from the Lord and whose gift of prophecy were highly regarded by the fellowship. One day we heard that he had received a "revelation" that his marriage was not of God because neither he nor his wife had been Christians at the time of their marriage. Therefore, he had been told "by the Lord" that he should put away his wife in divorce.

As soon as I heard this rumor, I went to his home to see if it was true. He confirmed his "revelation" and his intentions. I shared with him from Scripture that God hated divorce and that his "leading" violated both the letter and the Spirit of the Word. Therefore, I felt that he was being deceived. He rejected my words, insisting that he knew the Lord's voice and that was that. As directed in the Bible, I returned to him a few days later with the other two elders, who confirmed my position and shared more Scripture contrary to his "leading." He responded by showing us scriptural examples and verses (all out of context) that supported his "revelation." We met with him many times during the next two or three months, seeking to draw him out of his deception. However, he grew increasingly arrogant and self-righteous. Finally we had no choice but to bring the issue before the entire Body. He presented his "revelation" to them and they unanimously assured him that he was in error. But he responded, "I don't care. I'm going to do it anyway." He walked out in his arrogance, bringing destruction into not only his own life, but also the lives of his wife and children and the young woman who believed his "revelation" that she was to be his wife "in the Lord."

Another time, I was in prayer when I received a "revelation" that a certain man in my congregation was having an affair with his secretary. I wasn't too thrilled with the prospect of confronting him with this word. If it were not true, it could cause a lot of problems. In fact, even if it were true, it could cause a lot of problems! But if the Lord had given me this information so that I could help lead him out of his sin, I was willing to risk it. First, however, I submitted my "revelation" to my co-elder Charles, whose ability to hear from the Lord I highly respected. After listening carefully to what I had to say, he went home to pray about it. Later he returned to me with the two words he had sensed from the Lord, "lying spirit." He believed that a lying spirit was seeking to deceive me and cause great destruction of relationships within the fellowship.

I returned to my prayer journal and asked the Lord to take away the leading I felt if Charles were correct and my "revelation" was a lie. Within days the feeling, which had remained very strong for three weeks, began to wane and soon disappeared. I blessed God for leading me into submission before I could make such a big mistake.

## Factors affecting the spirit

One of the primary reasons we need to test all revelations we receive is that our spirits can be affected by factors other than God. According to 1 Corinthians 6:17, the spirit of a Christian is joined together with the Holy Spirit. However, this does not preclude other factors from moving upon our spirits and tainting the revelation we receive. When we are overcome with a great sorrow, our spirits can be affected and the messages received through them can be incorrect. Our physical, bodily conditions can also influence our spirits. In 1 Samuel 30, David's men came upon a man who had been left for dead by a retreating army. He was very ill and had had neither food nor drink for three days. They gave him bread and fruit and water to drink, and "his spirit revived" (v. 12). We have all experienced the effects of sickness upon our spirits. Doubt and discouragement easily find their way into our hearts when our bodies are weak or filled with pain. We must be particularly cautious about acting upon revelation received when we are physically weak or in pain, until it has been submitted to another, or tested when we are physically stronger. This does not, of course, always apply to weakness during a fast. On the other hand, fasting unto the Lord can have a strengthening effect upon our spirits, purifying the flow from them.

Satan is also able to affect our hearts. John 13:2 shows that Satan put the idea into Judas' heart to betray Jesus. Both the man who sought to divorce his wife and I were deceived by lying spirits. Often it is difficult for us alone to recognize that we are being led into deception. We need the help of a brother or sister who loves us to show us the truth. The other kind of response often made to this involves totally rejecting spiritual encounters, because of fear of deception. But spiritual encounter is God's gift to His people. Satan is the great copy-cat and he has attempted to steal away this precious gift. He has introduced a host of counterfeits of the spiritual reality intended for the Church, which has led many of us to reject the real out of fear of the counterfeit.

We forget that the presence of the counterfeit is proof of two things: First, there is a real item that is very similar to the counterfeit. No one would make counterfeit $21 bills. Who would take them? The counterfeit is one proof that the real exists. I believe that communion between my spirit and the Holy Spirit is the reality that "spirit guides" seek to counterfeit. Second, the presence of a counterfeit shows that the real item has value. No one is going to take the time to make counterfeit $1 bills. They are not worth the effort. Similarly, Satan's demonic counterfeit of spiritual encounter makes it clear that he considers true Holy Spirit encounter of great value.

We certainly must use care and not stand alone when we are dealing with spiritual experiences, but we need not run away from them. God provides us with ample safeguards in His Word, and the authorities He has placed over us, His church, if only we will humbly submit to them.

Finally, I myself can influence my spirit. Proverbs 16:21 tells us that "he who rules his spirit, [is better] than he who captures a city" (NAS). Our motives must be pure and our wills aligned with Christ's or the "revelation" we receive will be a dream of our own making.

Since so many factors other than the Holy Spirit can influence our spirits and cause impurities in how we hear God, the first thing we must look for in testing any kind of revelation is evidence of these other influences. We should test the origin, the content and the fruit of spiritual impressions.

Thoughts from my own spirit are born in meditation. They are the result of a progressive building of ideas, based on what I have learned. If I have been feeding on what is worldly or evil, that is what will come out of my heart. If I have been guarding my spirit, allowing only what is good and pure and holy to enter, then the meditations of my spirit will be a reflection of that.

Satan's injected thoughts come as flashing ideas or images into my mind. They do not fit my train of thought and seem like an intrusion. They are destructive and evil. They bring me into fear or bondage. I may feel pressured or compelled to obey their promptings. They are contrary to both the nature and Spirit of God. They will resist being submitted to either the Word or the Church, often by appealing to my ego.

Revelation from the Holy Spirit is encouraging and comforting. If it involves a conviction of sin, it is specific and instructive, not general or condemning. It has no fear of testing and even encourages it. It is completely in harmony with the nature and the Word of God, and quickens my faith and brings peace to my inner man. It is wise. It encourages the development of the fruit of the Spirit in my life.

Every revelation should also be tested against the Logos, the written Word of God. It is absolutely essential that you have a good working knowledge of the Bible if you are going to investigate the spiritual dimension. The Bible is our absolute standard of truth!

Any revelation from God will be in perfect agreement with the letter and the Spirit of the Word. It will be in keeping with the whole counsel of God on that subject, as revealed throughout the entire Bible. A single verse is insufficient grounds for doctrine or belief.

Another vitally important tool for testing revelation is the Body of Christ, the Church. When we become Christians, we become members one of another, united as the visible expression of Christ on the earth. There is safety in our relationship to a Bible-believing church. And the power and ability to grow is dynamically increased when we are covenanted together with others of like goals.

It is especially helpful to be in an accountability relationship when we are trying to change deeply engrained habits. If you've tried to shed some extra pounds alone, you probably have experienced discouragement and failure. But when we join with others who are experiencing the same difficulties in achieving the same goals, and especially others who have successfully achieved those goals, the chances of success are greater. It is even more effective when those others know your goals and will hold you accountable for progress toward them on a regular basis. An alcoholic rarely is able to remain dry alone, but with the help of relationships in Alcoholics Anonymous many are able to succeed.

How often have you read self-help books that promised to reshape your personality and make you a success? You probably tried on your own to apply the teachings, but rarely had long-term success. But if you have studied the same kind of book with a group of others, meeting regularly to share how you've applied it, and the results and your goals for the next week, you likely have experienced a change in your life for the long term. Growth and change rarely come to those who try to make it on their own. Growth and change happen within relationships.

God has ordained that everyone is to have a particular type of relationship with at least one other human being. Ephesians 5:21 tells us to submit ourselves one to another. Protestant Americans have a particularly hard time with this type of relationship. One of the things that Protestants reacted against at the time of the Reformation was the excessive authority exercised by the Roman Church. Along with this reaction, however, the truth of submission was thrown out by many as well. There is a God-ordained need for submission among believers.

The American ideal of rugged individualism also prevents us from embracing the concept of submission. Our American heros tend to be rebels, non-conformists who fight the system. Our idols are the Lone Ranger, John Wayne, Butch and Sundance, and criminals who outsmart the law. We laugh and applaud when the police or other authorities are depicted as bumbling fools. We are the culture of the anti-hero. We don't want to hear about authority or submission or accountability.

God did not give us authorities to make our lives more difficult. Authority is a precious gift from the Lord, given for our protection and benefit. Proverbs 11:14 declares, "In abundance of counselors there is victory." It is so easy to make a mistake or be deceived, and God has gifted us with the counsel of our brothers and sisters. Romans 13:4 reminds us that authority "is a minister of God to you for good." Authority is a good gift from God.

There are some clearly defined authority relationships in the New Testament. Children are to submit to parents (Col. 3:20), wives to husbands (Eph. 5:22-24), husbands to the elders of a local church (1 Pet. 5:1-5; Heb. 13:17) and elders to each other (Eph. 5:21). Employees are under the authority of their employers (Eph. 6:5-8; 1 Pet. 2:18-23) as the employers are under God (Eph. 6:9). Employers who are successful are also submissive to their employees and customers (Mark 10:44-45). All citizens are to be subject to every form of government for the governments are but servants of God (Rom. 13:17; 1 Pet. 2:13-15; see also Dan. 2:20-21; Prov. 21:1). In an age of lawlessness, lawfulness and order should characterize God's people.

Especially for those of us who desire spiritual encounters with God, there is a need for authority relationships. I wouldn't walk this way alone. There is too much possibility for error and deception, too much temptation to pride and self-righteousness. I need a brother who is also walking in the Spirit to help me stay on the right track. When I receive what I believe to be a word from the Lord, I want the confirmation of another who also knows God's voice. I do not make any major commitment of my time or my money, or make any major change in the direction of my life without first submitting it for confirmation by my brother. I am not talking about a life of bondage in which I can do nothing without another's permission. I don't run to my brother every day with what I have received in my journal. I am free to grow and make mistakes on my own. But before I make a major move, one that could have a long-term effect on my life and my family, I want the Lord's confirmation through another.

I have heard people say, "Why should I submit to anyone else? The Lord talks to me just as much as He does to them. Why should I have to listen to anyone else?" That is exactly what Miriam and Aaron said about Moses (Num. 12:1-15). It was true! The Lord did speak to them and through them. But God became very angry when they used that as an excuse for a rebellious attitude. As a result of her words, Miriam became leprous and only Moses' prayers brought her healing.

People often ask me how they can find a spiritual counselor, someone to whom they can submit their impressions and their major decisions. The greatest thing you can do is to pray for God to bring you together. He wants you to walk with another. He is the One who said, "It is not good for the man to be alone"(Gen. 2:18). He will help you.

There are certain characteristics you should look for in a counselor. First and foremost, he or she *must* be a friend. This relationship is built on love and friendship. It must be someone with the time and willingness to spend much time with you. This is especially important at first, when you will have lots of questions that need discussing. Your friend should take this relationship seriously, being willing to really seek the Lord for you, not just offer his own advice.

Your counselor should be a "biblical" man (or woman), with a good knowledge of the Word and a life based on it. Your counselor also should be a spiritual man or woman, able to discern the purposes of God, and should be someone who is under authority—anyone standing alone is susceptible to deception. You do not want to be led astray by the rebellion of another. Finally, your friend does *not* need to be an ordained minister. In a practical sense, not many pastors are able to have the kind of close relationship we are talking about with everyone in his congregation. But more importantly, it is not necessary to be ordained to be able to walk in the Spirit.

There is often no need to look far to find a spiritual counselor. Your spouse is a good place to start. I don't make decisions affecting our family unless Patti and I are in agreement. However, sometimes we are both too close to a situation to completely trust our own discernment. Then we agree to look to another for confirmation. A cell or home Bible study leader may be the right person for you.

As a young youth pastor fresh out of college, I watched as a mature pastor stood alone and unsubmitted and brought a major division in his church. Therefore, when I found myself in a position of senior pastor at the very young age of twenty-four, I knew I could not adequately fulfill the role alone. As a result of our study of New Testament Church structures, our fledgling fellowship wrote the concept of submission among the elders of the body into its constitution. I voluntarily brought my life under the authority of two of my brothers. I began to submit to them not only in matters of the church but in all major decisions of my personal life as well.

Since that time I have remained in submission to two or three men at all times. I do not make any major commitment of my time or money, or any change in the direction of my life, without first submitting the decision to the appropriate people. I cannot express how highly I value these relationships. I honor these men who willingly give of themselves to care for me in such a close, personal way. I am so grateful to the Lord for His protection of me through these authorities. They have guided me in troubled times and prevented me from making mistakes that could have cost me my family, my resources and my ministry.

**Understanding the principle of authority**

I am grateful to Bill Gothard for the teaching on authority he gives in his seminar *Basic Youth Conflicts.* Many of the ideas expressed below are based on what I have learned from him.

In order to properly relate to and respect authority, there are several things we must realize. First and foremost, we must accept the fact that God is responsible for placing all authority over us. Romans 13:1 declares, "There is no authority except from God, and those which exist are established by God." The Psalmist tells us that, "Not from the east, nor from the west, nor from the desert comes exaltation; but God is the Judge; He puts down one and exalts another" (Ps. 75:6, 7). No one can usurp any authority without God's permission. No one has authority over us except the people God wants to have authority over us.

A question that often arises is, what about evil authority? What about people like Hitler? Surely he wasn't God's minister! Surely he was a man out of control. The Israelites had their own version of Hitler—Nebuchadnezzar. He swept down upon Judah, bringing death, destruction and terror upon all the land. The people cried out for deliverance from his hand, but a prophet of God named Jeremiah rose up and said, "Don't resist him. Nebuchadnezzar is God's servant, sent to repay us for our evil ways. He is but God's war-club, a weapon of war in God's hand" (see Jer. 25:8-12; 51:20-23).

But do we really have to obey such evil authorities? The Roman government Paul lived under when he wrote the epistle to the Romans was perverted, sadistic and wicked. Christians were used as torches to light the streets, as bait for hungry lions, and were tormented by the gladiators for the amusement of the people. Yet, to believe living in the very seat of that cruel government, Paul wrote that they were to subject themselves to the government authorities. "He who resists authority has opposed the ordinance of God; and they who have opposed will receive condemnation upon themselves . . . wherefore it is necessary to be in subjection, not only because of wrath, but also for conscience' sake" (Rom. 13:2, 5). Jesus told His disciples to render to Caesar the things that were Caesar's.

Peter exhorted us to submit ourselves

> . . . for the Lord's sake to every human institution . . . For such is the will of God that by doing right you may silence the ignorance of foolish men . . . Servants, be submissive to your masters with all respect, not only to those who are good and gentle, but also to those who are unreasonable. For this finds favor, if for the sake of conscience toward God a man bears up under sorrows when suffering unjustly. For what credit is there if, when you sin and are harshly treated, you endure it with patience? But if when you do what is right and suffer for it you patiently endure it, this finds favor with God. For you have been called for this purpose, since Christ also suffered for you, leaving you an example to follow in His steps (1 Pet. 2:13-21).

The second important principle to remember is that God is bigger than any authority. My confidence is not in a man, but in God's ability to work through the man. Sometimes we are tempted to protest against submitting to another imperfect human. It's easy to say we are submitted to Christ because He is perfect. But why should we open ourselves up to the influence of another person who could be wrong? The simple answer is that my assurance is in God, that He will work through the authorities He has ordained in my life. Proverbs 21:1 says, "The king's heart is like channels of water in the hand of the Lord; He turns it wherever He wishes." As we confidently place ourselves in the hands of those He has placed over us, He will cause their hearts to be turned according to His will. And even if they try to arrogantly resist the Lord's influence upon their hearts, He can cause them to say the opposite of what they planned, so that His will is still accomplished! (Prov. 16:1).

All authority is from God. Anyone who has authority over me does so only because the Lord has allowed Him to exercise it. The authorities in our lives cannot exist except through the power God has given them. Jesus did not answer Pilate when He was being questioned. Finally, in fear and frustration, Pilate cried, "Why won't you answer me? Don't you know that I have the authority to either release you or have you executed?" But Jesus replied, "You would have no authority over me, unless it had been given you from above" (see John 19:8-11). There are not two or three or four authorities in your life. There is but one authority, who is God, exercising His will through men.

When God used nations such as Assyria to chastise His people in the Old Testament, they were allowed to have a certain amount of authority over Israel. But those nations grew arrogant, and soon thought that by their own greatness they had taken Israel captive. So when they had accomplished the purpose for which they had been ordained, God withdrew their power and punished them. He said, "Is the axe to boast itself over the one who chops with it?" (Isa. 10:15). All authority comes from God, and He has authority over all authority. Authorities over us can do only what He allows them to do.

Since God is over all of our authorities, Timothy urged us to make entreaties and prayers, petitions and thanksgivings on behalf of all who are in authority (1 Tim. 2:1, 2). Through our prayers we are able to lead a quiet and tranquil life in all dignity and godliness.

During the sixties and seventies, our nation was in a downward economic and moral spiral. Inflation was out of control. Abortion on demand became the law. Patriotism became a dirty word. Government handouts coupled with government controls crept into almost every aspect of our lives. At some point, Christians finally awakened to the seriousness of the situation and assumed their responsibility to pray. In 1976 organizations such as "Intercessors for America" began to appear, who were dedicated to using their authority through prayer to bring our nation back to the biblical principles upon which it was founded. The eight years since have brought decisive changes. Inflation is finally coming under control. The Christian church has begun to recognize the result of the direction in which we were heading and is speaking up for righteousness. Our nation is once again returning to her Judeo-Christian heritage as a direct result, I believe, of the prayers of her saints. Prayer is altering the authority under which we must live.

If we do believe that God is responsible for the authorities in our lives, we can certainly ask Him why He has placed them over us. He does not act capriciously or unjustly. Nebuchadnezzar was given authority to hold Judah captive for 70 years. Jeremiah told the people the reason why this was allowed. For 490 years, Israel had neglected the celebration of the Year of Jubilee. They had stolen 70 years of rest from the land and from the Lord. So, they were forced to pay back that time. There was a reason, not only for the captivity, but also for the precise length of it.

The hard-to-get-along-with characteristics of the authorities over us represent an underlying purpose of God for our lives. We are being molded into His image: and molding requires pressures. God is perfecting us, and He will use authorities to do so. As Peter reminded us, if we suffer injustice patiently, we are following in the steps of our Lord.

## Disagreeing with authority

There are times when we will be in disagreement with our authorities and counselors. Perhaps it is simply a difference of opinion, in which there is no clear biblical command to determine the issues. Perhaps we believe the Lord has told us to do something, but our spiritual friend disagrees, What do we do then?

We have a few choices. We can reassert our independence and break away from the relationship, confident that we know God's voice and what is best for us. Or, since we are convinced God works through submission, we can lay down and become a nonperson. We can shut off our own minds and lines of communication with the Lord and respond like robots. So often we seem to think that these are our only two choices in an accountability relationship. Personally I don't like either one.

God, as always, has a better idea! If we do it His way, we can have disagreement without destruction. We can be submitted, meek persons without becoming mindless, spiritless doormats. In Daniel 1

176

we find a clear description of the way God guides us in providing creative alternatives which can satisfy both our counselors and ourselves. Daniel was a young man who was taken into captivity by Nebuchadnezzar. He was chosen to be trained at the palace for service in the king's court. As such, he was given rich, unclean foods and wine as his daily ration. Daniel had never eaten such things and didn't intend to start. There was a great potential for trouble in that situation: government versus religion. But Daniel was able to resolve the issue with no exchange of hostilities.

The first thing he did was make sure his own heart was purified with tender love. He made sure his conscience was clear, that there were no critical, resistant or condemning attitudes in him. He knew that if he approached the commander with those kind of feelings the commander would sense them, which would destroy any possibility of relationship. But because Daniel's heart was right, the commander responded with favor and compassion (Dan. 1:9). Though there was disagreement, there was love and honor between them.

If we find that our attitudes have been wrong, if we have felt anger and condemnation toward the authority God has placed over us, we must ask forgiveness of both God and that person. There is no place for *"I think* I might have had a bad attitude toward you." There can be no passing the buck: "I have been angry *because you* did such and such." Nor will generalizations do: *"If I* did anything to hurt you, I'm sorry." We are responsible for our own actions and reactions. Therefore, we need to repent deeply for our wrong thoughts, attitudes or words. We can either rationalize or repent. If we want to be open to the movement of God, repentance is only one choice. A pure heart opens us up for good things to happen.

When Daniel was sure that he had done his part to maintain a good relationship, he sought to discern the basic intention of the one over him. The commander's intention was simple—he wanted to live! If he disobeyed the king's command and the young men suffered as a result, the king would have his head. But why did the king want the boys to each such rich foods? Was he trying to defile their religion? Was he deliberately forcing them to choose between obedience to God and man? No! Nebuchadnezzar wanted the boys to be strong and healthy and intelligent. He was giving them the best he had to offer, food from his own table. His basic intention was their well-being.

177

Often when we disagree with someone we can only see our own point of view. We are blinded by our own wrong attitudes. But when our hearts are pure, we are able to recognize the motives behind their requests. Often we are then able to see that they are really looking out for our best interests.

Daniel was faced with an authority who told him to act in disobedience to God's law. He could have risen up in rebellion and simply said, "No! I will not obey!" and he would no doubt have lost his head on the spot. But by keeping his heart full of love, he was able to come up with an alternative that satisfied both his God and his king. As a result, he rose to a position of authority, where he was able to exercise godly influence in an ungodly land.

The solution Daniel suggested was that he and his friends take a ten-day test. During that time they would abstain from the king's food and eat only vegetables and drink only water. At the end of the trial period, the commander could compare them to the other youths who continued to eat the king's delicacies. Based on what he observed at that time, he could then make his decision.

The commander could accept that. The boys would be in his care for three years. Any damage done in ten days could easily be repaired in three years. So he agreed to the test, and, of course, Daniel and his friends were in better physical condition than the rest of the young men at the end of the test period.

In order to come up with such a creative alternative, we must be in touch with the creative One. We must have moved beyond anger to love, so we can clearly hear God's voice in our hearts. When we are faced with a disagreement with our counselor or other authority, we need to prayerfully ask the Lord for an idea that will bring a satisfactory resolution to the problem.

Several years ago, because of a theological difference, I was asked to leave a community church in which I was serving as associate pastor. A large group of faithful attenders were also asked to leave for the same reason. There was no other church in the area that would welcome us into their fellowship, so I was asked to pastor a brand-new church. Laying out the foundation of a new ministry was quite an experience. There were many joys and many heartaches, but mostly a lot of hard work. After five years, we had our own building and had established policies and traditions we expected to last a long time. I planned to live in that parsonage and pastor those people the rest of my life.

Unfortunately such peace and satisfaction didn't last forever. Theological issues again threatened to bring division. Finally a group of six men presented me with a formal request for my resignation. I was shocked and, of course, very hurt. How could they ask me to leave the fellowship for which I had labored so hard? At the time, I knew that I could not pastor anyone who didn't want me as their shepherd. If it were a consensus of the people, then I would leave.

I needed wisdom, so I went to the Lord. He told me in my journal that I was not to resign. He had placed me as pastor over that flock and I was responsible for it until He told me otherwise. I was there not by the will of man, but by the ordination of God. The men had made no provision for someone to take my place so, if I resigned, I would be guilty of leaving the flock of God unprotected without a shepherd. I couldn't do that!

That still left me with a problem. An outright refusal of the request of those men could have caused such damage that the church might not have recovered. But I couldn't disobey God's commission either. I asked the Lord to show me the underlying reason for the men's request. He showed me that the men were unhappy with some of my beliefs and teachings. They really wanted the problems worked out. They didn't want the church split any more than I did. But as long as I was in the forefront of the church activities, teaching in all the services and fulfilling my other pastoral duties, the problems also remained in the forefront. What the men really wanted was a "time out," a chance for tempers to cool and attitudes to be cleansed. Then we could discuss our problems and our differences could be worked out.

The Lord gave me a creative alternative. I would not resign as pastor, but I would step into the background for a period of six weeks. I would maintain my God-given responsibility for the flock, but all of my pastoral duties would be assumed by those men and the other elders. I submitted this idea to Roger, my co-elder, and he agreed that it was the right action to take. When I presented this alternative plan to the six men, they accepted it and immediately put it into effect.

I had a wonderful six weeks. Essentially I had been given a paid sabbatical in which I could do the thing I loved most—study the Word. During that period, I did an intensive study of the heart and spirit of man, examining every verse in the Bible on the subject. I organized what I found and, as a result of that time away, wrote two courses on *Abiding in Christ* which are used in our Bible school today.

During those six weeks, our congregation also spent time talking about our problems and differences. We brought in the Reverend Tommy Reid, a well-known pastor respected by everyone, to help arbitrate. Understanding was restored. Compromises were made and a major division averted.

Over the next six months, the Lord began working in my heart. He showed me that the deepest gift and calling in my life was teaching rather than pastoring. The desire grew in me to devote myself to full-time study and teaching. Eventually I felt that the Lord had released me from my pastoral responsibilities, freeing me to seek other employement. I again submitted this leading to Roger, who confirmed that the time was right. I announced my resignation, giving thirty days notice, and we separated on friendly terms, because God had given me a creative alternative to division.

When Daniel presented his alternative to the commander, he did so respectfully, emphasizing how it would meet the king's goals (Dan. 1:12, 13). He made it clear that the decision would still be the commander's at the end of the test period. We must also be careful to present our appeals with respect, maintaining our meek spirit and allowing no hint of condemnation to contaminate our hearts or our words.

Once we have presented our alternative, we must then step back and give God time to change the authority's mind. We should be aware that, since God is putting pressure on him, he is likely to put pressure on us also. When God is trying to change our mind, there is often an inner warfare that spills over onto those around us. When this happens, we should allow God to use the pressure being put on us to build godly character into our lives. We must continue to respond in love and righteousness.

On rare occasions, an authority may force us into the position of Peter and John, who found that they had to choose between obeying God and man. Occasionally it is impossible to work out a creative alternative that can satisfy the authority's goals without violating our own conscience. If an authority commands us to do something which is directly contrary to the written Word of God, if no alternative can satisfy both, we must obey God, not man. In such a case we may have to suffer, even though we have done nothing wrong.

Daniel faced that situation when he was in a position of high authority in the Babylonian government. King Darius was tricked into signing a decree that allowed no prayers to be made to anyone other than the king for a period of thirty days. This time there was no room for compromise, and Daniel went to the lion's den. But God was his strength, and through supernatural deliverance the name of the Lord was glorified (Dan. 6).

It is important, however, that we first make very sure that there is no way to obey both God and His ordained authorities before we resist that authority. Our disobedience must be based on a clear command of Scripture, not our fuzzy personal interpretation. We must remember that if we resist our authority when they are not asking us to disobey God's Word, then we are resisting God himself (Rom. 13:2).

**Changing authorities**

There are times throughout our lives when we make changes that disrupt existing authority relationships. When we marry, get a new job, move to a new location, or change churches, our authorities will change. Whenever such a change must occur, we should do our best to make it a smooth and harmonious transition. "If possible, so far as it depends on you, be at peace with all men" (Rom. 12:18). If there has been tension, seek forgiveness. Be sure your heart is filled with only love and acceptance. If at all possible, there should be an agreement between you and your authority concerning the upcoming change. Regrettably, however, this is not always possible.

The important thing is that as we leave one relationship we should enter another. We should always be committed and submitted in a local expression of the body of Christ. Our shepherd acts as an umbrella of protection, providing safety and covering as we walk through life.

**Conclusion**

The principle of authority should never become a source of bondage in a believer's life. It is a principle that must be applied through the revelation of the Spirit. Authority and submission can be a great blessing, or a great source of pain. My goal is not to bring anyone under a new law, but to illustrate the great value submission has had for me. If this teaching seems foreign or burdensome, if it would be a great struggle for you to put it into practice, know that you are not alone. Although I have a great love for submission, there are times when I too struggle and resist it. But when I give in, it has always been a blessing in my life.

Permit me to share one more story. From the time we were in college, Patti and I had a strong interest in Christian communities. We believed that by pooling our resources and sharing expenses with other families, we would be able to give much more financially to the work of the Lord. We even designed a house in which we planned to live with our best friends.

Our college plans didn't work out, but several years later the desire for community again rose within us. We had grown very close to two other couples in our fellowship and began making plans to live together. We were looking for houses that could accomodate three families when I suddenly realized that I was planning to make a major decision without having first submitted it to my brothers. Not expecting any problem, I submitted the idea to Roger. I was shocked when he replied, "I think you had better wait."

I had journaled about this plan and I believed the Lord was calling us to the communal lifestyle. But I also respected Roger and the Lord's ability to speak through him. So instead of growing angry and rebellious, I looked for Roger's basic intention. It was easy to find. He loved us and wanted our well-being, not our hurt. And the Lord gave me a creative alternative that met Roger's desire for us to wait, and my desire for community living. With Roger's blessing, we began visiting communities throughout the northeastern United States and Canada. We lived with various communities for two or three days, working with them, eating with them, and worshiping with them. They represented many theological convictions and many different ways of implementing community life.

When we returned home, I wrote a summary paper of all that we had observed and learned. (I haven't really learned something until I write it down!) One of the biggest things we discovered was the concept of a "ministering household." Rather than complete families coming together in one house, a family unit took in individuals and broken families. Singles, divorced people, single-parent families, and runaways could all find the love and acceptance of family in a ministering household.

We felt drawn to this and asked Roger if he could confirm our moving in that direction. He did, and over the next three years we had thirteen different individuals staying in our home. They ranged from pre-teen runaways to sick elderly men, from seminary students to runaway mothers. Their stays with us lasted from one night to two years. Eventually the Lord led us out of that ministry and into others, but the important thing here is that we have never regretted our obedience to authority. We now realized that for us, at that time, community would have been a disastrous mistake. We will always be grateful to the Lord and to Roger for protecting us from going our own way.

If you don't feel you can accept all that I have said here about authority, just "put it on the back burner and let it simmer awhile." You don't have to wrestle with it. Let the Lord work out the truth of it for you. Let Him teach you how He wants you to apply it in your life. If authority and accountability seem too strong for you now, please at least find a friend with whom you can share. Don't try to explore the spiritual dimension of Christianity alone.

> Two are better than one because they have a good return for their labor. For if either of them falls, the one will lift up his companion. But woe to the one who falls when there is not another to lift him up . . . And if one can overpower him who is alone, two can resist him (Eccl. 4:9-12).

# — 10 —

# Who Was Agnes Sanford?
# Robert Wise

Agnes Sanford was an amazing Epicosopalian lady used by God in a miraculous healing ministry.[1] She is known the world over as the pioneer in rediscovering healing in the mainline churches and healing of the inner man.[2]

Agnes did create controversy.

The spiritual power of her life and ministry was so dramatic that it left results not everyone understood. She was anything but divisive, quarrelsome or heretical. Quite often she instructed people not to tell anyone that her prayers had been part of the extraordinary work God had done. Yet the results spoke for themselves. The consternation of people who did not understand was parallel to the problems of perplexity that erupted in the ministry of Jesus.

The last thing in the world Agnes Sanford would have wanted or approved of was being made to appear a saint. She was a very unpretentious, genuine person, and lived with a basic realism about herself and others. Yet there was a lofty purity in her motivations. Agnes felt that the only reason for being in healing ministry was love and compassion for others; this she had in abundance. She worked hard to learn "to see the Christ" in everyone she met. Agnes believed that healing ministry depends on the capacity to find the best even in the worst of people.[3]

"From the days when heretics were burned at the stake," she wrote, "no one can be more utterly condemnatory toward an aspect of Christianity that they do not believe in than can another Christian."[4]

185

As Jesus was accused of healing by the power of the devil, so now, even after her death, Agnes' ministry on behalf of the Christ has been similarily indicted. Well, that does put her in good company! Only someone who never knew Agnes Sanford personally could think of her as being in any way associated with evil.

In contrast, she and her family always lived a financially modest life, often allowing themselves to be taken advantage of by people who pressed their needs upon them. She was an inspiration to all who knew her. So to answer any questions about her teaching, let's begin by putting her ideas in the context of her life and work.

## A Child of China

Agnes Sanford was born in China to Presbyterian missionary parents; her first recorded words were, "Baby want to see God." That earliest recollection proved to be an amazingly prophetic description of the motivations that would direct her life. The full scope of her own memoirs is recorded in her autobiography, *Sealed Orders*. In reading about Agnes's earliest years, one quickly discovers that she had an acute sense of the transcendence and mystery of God.

Around nine years of age she began to wonder why no one any longer experienced miracles. The missionaries' dispensational explanation that the miraculous belonged to another era never satisfied her. The profound impression left by her sister Virginia's death caused her to wonder if things might have been different had they known how to pray. She felt the painful discrepancy between the promise of the gospels and the practices of her childhood church.

Unquestionably, Agnes Sanford had the mystical bent of the most spiritually gifted. Her extraordinary sensitivity included an unusual ability to experience God in nature. Her overwhelming experiences of the presence of God charged her soul with the very energy of life that she, in turn, prayed for others to receive.[5] Agnes' soul always needed the outdoors and beauty for her to thrive. Such harmony with nature empowered her with a remarkable ability to pray about natural phenomena.[6]

The unusual sensitivity of her mind and spirit made Agnes a natural candidate for problems of depression. Quite early in her life, a nagging, haunting cloud of depression fell upon her. China was a place of great pain. Bombarded by the sights of many tragedies and the fear of oncoming war, Agnes began to experience the ravages of the darkness that depression brings. Only later, after her return to the

United States, did she become aware of how enormous the problem was. To the outward observer, she often seemed shy, stiff and removed. To those who knew her, it was obvious that deep wounds had gouged her soul. Struggling to be true to who she was, Agnes was also feeling the weight of realizing that years of missionary work in China were disintegrating. The wail of dying Chinese babies lodged itself somewhere deep in her soul until she became fearful for her own sanity. The struggle to find emotional health was to be one of the key factors that led to her own remarkable work.

By this time she and Ted, an Episcopal priest, had three children and were very deeply involved in parish life. Even though they were a happy family, depression hung like a millstone around her neck. Eventually she went to Hollis Colwell, an Episcopal priest in their area through whose prayer their son's ears had been healed. He prayed for Agnes by laying on hands and asking that her depression be released in Jesus' name. To her utter amazement, for the first time in years she found relief from her burden of emotional illness. Her astonishment at how the prayer had been answered was the beginning of her own healing ministry.[7]

In the years that followed, Agnes Sanford began experimenting with laying on of hands and praying for people in need. She began to find over and over again that tragic conditions were reversed and that vitality returned to broken people. Some of her most remarkable work was accomplished during World War II when she was a volunteer in a military hospital. As she prayed for people with hopeless conditions, she saw miracle after miracle that often confounded the hospital staff.

As word of these curses spread, so did Agnes' reputation. Although she tried to keep her work as quiet as possible, inevitably there was a degree of controversy. In 1940 few Christians really believed healing was possible. Subsequently, the profound results she had received through prayer became, for many, more a source of consternation than admiration.

Her Episcopal priest husband struggled to know what to do with a wife who was anything but the typical, quiet, hidden manager of the manse. Only after years of ministry did he become comfortable with the astonishing results she had achieved for many a broken person. She was more than cautious to keep her life not only within the proper boundaries for a minister's wife but in accord with Christian social expectations. Proper and sometimes emotionally distant, she quietly went about the business of promoting the recovery of healing ministry. Although Agnes struggled to define her role as wife and mother in the midst of a growing ministry, she was always a feminine, balanced person. Equally apt in needlepoint as she was a marvelous cook, Agnes loved gardening and was well known for her magnificent flower arrangements. Inundated with constant demands for speaking engagements, many, many times Agnes would have been happy to have just stayed at home.

### And to what end?

Running through the cloth from which Agnes' life was cut was a constant thread: a passion for the renewal of the church and a recovery of the ministry of the Holy Spirit. Her life could be described by 2 Corinthians 4:18 (RSV): "We look not to the things that are seen but to the things that are unseen; for the things that are seen are transient, but the things that are unseen are eternal." The potential of unseen things prompted her to believe that healing ministry could be brought back into the mainstream of church life. She sought help wherever it could be found and often turned in directions that would not be appreciated by the whole of the Christian community. While many would condemn Christian Science, she did not share their scorn. She felt that group had recognized healing ministry when the rest of the church had denied it.[8] In the late sixties, she even found "Jesus people" exhilarating because of their life and vitality. Agnes always kept probing for the deeper realities.

When Agnes Sanford's life is put in historic perspective, it is clear that she was one of the key contributors to the recovery of healing ministry in the church. Fighting an atmosphere of denial and distrust, she groped along the edges of this revival ministry, not always sure of the way. In those days there were few guides. Whatever the limitations in her teaching, relatively alone she made a courageous foray into a field that theologians and pastors had ignored for centuries. Considering her conservative background in China and her husband's own very traditional stance, her accomplishments are all the more remarkable.

No estimate can be made of the countless numbers of individuals who came to her in desperation and were brought back from the brink of disaster. With a special compassion for the needs of children, Agnes prayed many a person into renewed health and vitality. However, Agnes is probably best remembered for her work with emotional need through what is now popularly called "healing of the memories."

She was never completely happy with the designation. However, she recognized the potential of the risen Christ to go back through time and touch buried fears and old resentments hidden in memory. In *Sealed Orders* she described how this discovery began. She was trying to minister to a young man, John, who was filled with anger and fear. Agnes knew personally that emotional release was possible for those who let prayer touch their emotional need. What she didn't see was the relationship of John's behavior to how he had been abused as a child in Czechoslovakia. She felt that the Lord was telling her through her prayerful meditation that the problem lay not with John the man but with John the child. Agnes began to pray for the little boy that still lived in the man. In turn, John was amazed that relief from old fears and emotional outburst just "began" to result! A new ministry was begun and now many people are praying for the power of Christ to heal memories and old wounds. Anyone who has found that her type of prayer released the power of Christ remains grateful for Agnes' pioneering work.[9]

While Agnes considered her writing to be one of her most important accomplishments, her work in the realm of spiritual warfare may be her most significant contribution. She demonstrated that the promises Jesus Christ made to His Church can still be realized in any age if His disciples exercise obedient and expectant faith. She dared to go beyond the ecclesiastical pronouncements of her time, and her recoveries of the work of the Holy Spirit made her a modern religious pioneer. In turn, an unusual ability to intercede for natural phenomena emerged from her prayer life. Similar results occurred in the ministry of evangelist Charles E. Fuller when on a number of occasions he prayed that weather would not disturb evangelistic meetings. People were amazed as rain stopped and clouds moved on.

The stories of Agnes praying for sky and earth are truly the stuff from which the stories of the ancient saints spring. Standing on the veranda of her home in Monrovia, I observed the results when she asked God to move the winds against an all-consuming fire and to fulfill His promise to heal the land (2 Chron. 7:13-15).

No small part of the Sanford legacy is the model that she and her husband left for pastoral ministry. Far from lofty dreams of building their own reputations, their minds were fixed on helping people.

Agnes sought pratical, down-to-earth dimensions for ministry. From this concern sprang the School of Pastoral Care. At an advanced age, the Sanfords traveled tirelessly across the United States, counseling, praying for, and instructing clergy in how to continue the work of bringing healing to others. Many a desperate clergyman found renewal and revitalization during these clinics. From the Schools, the word spread about the possibility of healing work. In addition, when Agnes spoke at Camp Farthest Out gatherings all around the world, lay people found themselves excited about the new promise that she embodied. The Schools and Camps became key seedbeds from which the charismatic movement would spring in later years.

Year after year, Agnes maintained a compassionate concern for people, combined with an unusual objective balance for expressing love. Love that is too subjective becomes sentimental; love that is too objective turns to dogmatism. She felt that incarnational love is a disciplined obedience that seeks what is best for people regardless of how it must be expressed.

**Let these things edify**

The ministry and teaching of any person needs to be considered against the background of his or her whole life; no part can be extracted in isolation without distorting this meaning. Any question about Agnes' authenticity and orthodoxy can be answered by simply looking through the full scope of her work, including *The Healing Light, The Healing Gifts of the Spirit, Behold Your God, The Healing Power of the Bible,* and *Sealed Orders.* Deeply concerned about spiritualism and occult practice, she was always horrified to see any literature from Edgar Cayce or other spiritualistic authors mixed with Christian writings. Agnes abhorred this spiritual confusion and would not pray with those who were so deceived.[10]

Actually, Agnes Sanford was always a daughter of the church. Completely obedient to her bishop wherever she resided or ministered, she trusted the Episcopal Church implicitly and turned to its theologians for guidance. She felt it was improper for her to hear confession and would turn such needs toward a pastor or priest. In fact, she did not like to see women officiate in worship services and never interjected herself into formal worship.[11] Agnes maintained the firm conviction that the best way to avoid error to stay resonant with the traditions of one's church.[12] To suggest that Agnes was seduced by evil is to indict the whole tradition of the Episcopal Church.

Although much of what Agnes taught sounds as if it is based on a relatively simple orthodox biblical foundation, her thought conceals a very sophisticated world view with a penetrating grasp of the meaning of time. Eternity was not a continuation of time for her as much as it was the magnificent infusing of the eternal into the present moment. Many of her extraordinary mystical experiences were personal moments when she stood on borderline between time and eternity, allowing her to sense what it is like to stand in the actual presence of God, even if only for a fleeting second. Often her encounters were of such overpowering bliss that they were almost unbearable.[13] While she did not have the theological training to articulate the meaning of these quantum leaps of faith in her spiritual adventures, actually she was decades ahead of the shift that is now taking place in theology: she had recovered the importance of pneumatology.

Agnes demonstrated that the eternal order, which is beyond time, can nevertheless penetrate the present moment in such a way that every day becomes a place where we truly touch eternity. Therefore, because Jesus Christ can redeem the now, He is also able to reach beyond this hour and touch both the past and the future. Because all time is present tense to God, His healing capacity can truly reach in all directions. Rather than an occult attempt to manipulate reality, this biblical view was the primary idea behind the ministry of healing memories. Once one accepts Christ's healing work in this age, it follows that He can also reach back into our past experiences. Agnes Sanford truly saw Jesus as the Lord of time who is not bound by our limited, conventional definitions of reality.

The closed world view that is a product of the Enlightenment must conclude that much of what she experienced is unintelligible. For a dispensationalist, rationalist, fundamentalist or liberal who does not believe that God still does the miraculous, her experiences cannot be grasped or accepted. However, we are only now realizing that the idea of a closed world order is painfully distant from the world view of the New Testament and the teachings of Jesus. In contrast, Agnes had a foot in our time and one in the first century.

In praying for God's penetration of time barriers, Agnes always made a distinction between sin—the willful violation of God's moral law—and the problem of repressed hurts of the past. She did not try in some willy-nilly way to erase the responsibility we each have for our actions. Rather, she grasped the fundamental fact that people also suffer from the undeserved actions of others; multitudes live with fractured minds and emotions. She prayed for healing of wounds such as a childhood experience of a parent's death, or other forms of tragedy beyond resolution by forgiving someone. And reality was truly changed. Not that the facts were altered; healing the person's interpretation and perspective of the old facts freed the adult from the fears and bondages of the child!

Agnes made a careful distinction between forgiveness and healing. She recognized that a wide range of possibilities result when one walks in the healing presence of Christ. When His light is focused on the past, the result is the healing of memories. When we see His illumination in the present, the result is the development of faith and trust. When the splendor of the risen Christ is aimed toward the future, prophecy and the word of hope are produced. On the other hand, forgiveness is concerned with sin. Indiscretions and transgressions have to be brought to the cross to receive God's forgiveness for our burdens. Very few people can help others find both the forgiveness of sin and the recovery of a sound mind with a joyful spirit.

**What shall we conclude?**

Agnes Sanford was concerned for the total person. Because she was a product of orthodox Christian faith, she spent little time debating the basic creeds and affirmations of the historic church; these she accepted as the ground floor from which all practical ministry springs.

When the intervention of God did not come immediately in response to prayer, she sought to understand how to respond to lingering pain and often came up with novel approaches. For example, she asked that the sufferer bless the pain because it demonstrated the body's intention to work at the healing process. Intuitively she found unusual approaches to allow prayer to reach the human vascular or nervous systems.[14] Her concern for results allowed her to receive insight from many sources. Her willingness to accept truth regardless of the source made her vulnerable to criticism. In that sense, Agnes' grasp of truth was often broader than most are capable of embracing—she had confidence in the ability of people to think for themselves.

Some of Agnes' experiences are best understood and expressed in psychological rather than theological terms. While she did not always elaborate on her inner experiences in either of these ways, she was always moved by a theological motivation. One of the weaknesses of her writing was that she often did not explain the theological underpinnings of many of her metaphysical statements. However, if one had the occasion to discuss these with her, the theological insights became clear and precise. Consequently, if her experiences are taken out of context, it is easy to make her sound extreme. Of course, this is true for most of us, but in her case it is exceptionally true because of her mystical bent. Many of her great spiritual breakthroughs find their counterpart in the stories of saints in past centuries. Yet, from Agnes' own point of view, her interest was always very pragmatic. For her the basic issue was whether any experience bore fruit worthy of the Gospel.

Because of her Christ-centered concern, she was not an egocentric person. The healing of her depression caused Agnes to see all need in the light of Calvary. The depth of this healing was so extraordinary that it gave her an unusual grasp of the all-encompassing, all-accepting love of God. Subsequently, she had no need to exploit or promote herself.

I'll always remember sitting in her living room and feeling a deep sense of peace at being in her house. Her presence carried that effect. Having her pray for me will remain an indelible memory.

Her life touched many people. Where there had been despair, she left behind peace; where anguish had gripped people's lives, she introduced hope. Brokenness and helplessness gave way to faith that brought a new day. People who have greatly profited from prayers for healing of memories, and felt the release of their past burdens, know that her work was a singular gift from God.

Perhaps one's life is best measured by those who have directly touched it in some way or another. Anyone who knew Agnes personally considered that knowledge to be one of their life's most precious, treasured gifts.

# Footnotes

**Chapter One**

1 Second Vatican Council, "Dogmatic Constitution on the Church," no. 4.
2 John Wesley, paraphrased by Clare Weakley, *The Holy Spirit and Power* (South Plainfield, NJ: Bridge Publishing, Inc., 1977), p. 148.
3 *The Life in the Spirit Seminars Team Manual* (Ann Arbor, MI: Word of Life, 1973), pp. 12, 13, 15.
4 Dennis and Rita Bennett, *The Holy Spirit and You* (Plainfield, NJ: Logos, 1971), p. 7.
5 Ralph Martin, *A Crisis of Truth* (Ann Arbor, MI: Servant Books, 1982), p. 17.
6 Ibid., p. 21.
7 Ibid., p. 58.
8 Ibid., pp. 102-103.

**Chapter Two**

1 James Robison, "Building God's Holy Temple," *Days of Restoration* March/April 1986.
2 Evelyn Frost, *Healing* (London: Hodder & Stoughton), p. 50.
3 Synod Sermon in Sydney Cathedral, May 1973.
4 Frederic W. Farrar, *History of Interpretation* (Grand Rapids, MI: Baker, 1979), p. 475.
5 A.B. Davidson, *Old Testament Prophecy*, p. 475.

**Chapter Three**

1 *Charisma,* March 1986, p. 32.
2 Ibid, p. 33.

## Chapter Three, Continued

3 Mark Virkler, *Seduction?? A Biblical Response* (Buffalo, NY: Buffalo School of the Bible, 1986), pp. 7, 8.

4 Hunt & McMahon, *The Seduction of Christianity* (Eugene, OR: Harvest House, 1985), p. 191.

5 Ibid., p. 12.

6 *Webster New World Dictionary, 2nd ed.* (New York: Simon & Schuster, 1948).

7 Keil & Delitzsch, *Commentary on the Old Testament,* Vol. 1 (Grand Rapids, MI: Eerdmans), pp. 392-95.

8 *Encyclopedia Judaica,* Vol. 11 (Jerusalem: Keter Publishing, 1972), p. 704.

9 Ibid., Vol. 15, p. 164.

10 Ibid., Vol. 11, p. 706.

11 Hunt & McMahon, op. cit., p. 123.

12 Ibid., front cover.

13 Agnes Sanford, *Sealed Orders* (Plainfield, NJ: Logos, 1972), pp. 193-196. In this account she referred to him as "John."

14 Hunt & McMahon, op. cit., pp. 146-47.

15 Agnes Sanford, *The Healing Light* (Plainfield, NJ: Logos, 1972). p. 61.

16 Hunt & McMahon, op. cit., p. 30.

17 Ibid., pp. 180, 187.

18 Ibid., p. 209.

19 Ibid., p. 180.

20 *Webster's New World Dictionary,* Second College Edition (William Collins + World Publishing, 1978).

21 Agnes Sanford, *The Healing Power of the Bible* (Philadelphia: J.B. Lippincott, 1969).

22 Agnes Sanford, *The Healing Light,* p. 4.

23 Hunt & McMahon, op. cit., p. 127.

24 Ibid., p. 128.

25 Ibid.

26 Ibid.

27 Ibid., p. 129.

28 Ibid., p. 127.

29 Agnes Sanford, *The Healing Light,* p. 109.

30 Hunt & McMahon, op. cit., p. 129.

31 Agnes Sanford, *The Healing Gifts of the Spirit* (Philadelphia: J.B. Lippincott, 1966), pp. 25-26.

**Chapter Three, Continued**

32  Agnes Sanford, *Sealed Orders,* pp. 216ff.

33  John Sanford, "Confusion in the Body," *Elijah House Newsletter,* November 1985.

34  Benjamin Warfield, *Counterfeit Miracles* (New York: Charles Scribner's Sons, 1918).

35  *SCP* [Spiritual Counterfeits Project] *Journal,* Vol. 4, No. 1.

**Chapter Four**

1  Michael Scanlan, *Inner Healing* (New York: Paulist Press, 1974). pp. 9-12.

2  *Logos International Bible Commentary, Vol. 1* (Plainfield, NJ: Logos, 1981), p. 55.

3  Don Turner, "Is Inner Healing a Valid Ministry?" *Fulness,* March-April 1986, pp. 17-23.

4  Jim Glennon, *Your Healing Is Within You* (Sydney, Australia: Jim Glennon, 1980), pp. 76-80, 87.

5  David Seamands, *Healing of Memories* (Wheaton, IL: Victor Books, 1985), pp. 62-64.

6  Ibid., pp. 66-68.

7  David Seamands, *Healing for Damaged Emotions* (Wheaton, IL: Victor Books, 1981), p. 51.

8  Francis MacNutt, *Healing,* (Notre Dame, IN: Ave Maria Press, 1974), p. 181.

9  Michael Scanlan, op. cit., p. 71-73.

**Chapter Five**

1  Examples of imagery and symbolism in visions: Gen. 15:1, 20:3, 46:2; Num. 12:6, 24:4, 16; 2 Kings 6:17; 1 Chron. 17:15, 21:16. Examples of visualization as a process or experience: Job 4:16; Ps. 25:15, 119:18; 123:1, 141:8; Isa. 61:1ff, 40:26; Acts 9:12, 11:15; 16:9; 2 Cor. 4:18; Eph. 1:18.

2  Morton Kelsey, *God, Dreams and Revelation* (Minneapolis, MN: Augsburg Publishing, 1969), p. 20.

3  Ibid., p. 21.

4  Ibid., p. 81-86.

5  Walker, *History of the Christian Church*, p. 127.

6  Anthony Mottola, *The Spiritual Exercises of St. Ignatius* (Garden City, NY: Image Books, 1964).

**Chapter Six**
1 Don Turner, "Is Inner Healing a Valid Ministry?" *Fulness* magazine, March-April 1986.
2 Hugh Missildine, *Your Inner Child of the Past* (New York: Simon & Schuster, 1982).

**Chapter Seven**
1 Don Gossett, *What You Say Is What You Get* (Springdale, PA: Whitaker House, 1976).
2 Ibid., back cover.
3 Hunt & McMahon, *The Seduction of Christianity* (Eugene, OR: Harvest House, 1985), p. 100.
4 Don Gossett, op. cit., p. 36.
5 Ibid., p. 182.
6 Gerhard Kittell, *Theological Dictionary of the New Testament* (Grand Rapids, MI: Eerdmans, 1964), 1:361 (section 3).
7 Ibid., p. 362.
8 A.T. Robertson, *Word Pictures in the New Testament* (Grand Rapids, MI: Baker, 1982), 6:39.
9 F. deSassure, "Course in General Linguistics" (translated from French) 1959, p. 69.
10 Ibid., p. 71.
11 Ludwib Wittgenstein, *Philosophical Investagations,* third ed., 1968, p. 79.
12 Gerhard Kittel, op. cit., 4:282.
13 Ibid., pp. 113-5b.

**Chapter Nine**
1 Jim Glennon, *How Can I Find Healing?* (South Plainfield, NJ: Bridge Publishing, Inc., 1985), p. 137.
2 Ibid.
3 Tony Lighterness, *Living in the Kingdom Here and Now* (Plainfield, NJ: Logos, 1979), p. 98.
4 Ibid.
5 Joseph Culliton, *Obedience: Gateway to Freedom* (Plainfield, NJ: Logos, 1979), p. 106.
6 Ibid., p. 108.
7 Tony Lighterness, *Living in the Kingdom Here and Now,* p. 67.

**Chapter Ten**

1 David Seamands, *Putting Away Childish Things* (Wheaton, IL: Victor Books, 1982), p. 16.

2 John & Paula Sanford, *Healing the Wounded Spirit* (South Plainfield, NJ: Bridge Publishing, Inc., 1985), p. 181.

3 Agnes Sanford, *Sealed Orders* (Plainfield, NJ: Logos, 1972).

4 Ibid., p. 198.

5 Ibid., p. 117.

6 Agnes Sanford, *Creation Waits* (Plainfield, NJ: Logos, 1977).

7 Agnes Sanford, *Sealed Orders,* p. 99.

8 Ibid., p. 103.

9 Agnes Sanford, *The Healing Light* (St. Paul, MN: MacAlester Park Publishing, 1947), pp. 195-196.

10 Agnes Sanford, *Sealed Orders,* pp. 150-157.

11 Ibid., p. 169.

12 Ibid., p. 148.

13 Ibid., p. 135.

14 Agnes Sanford, *The Healing Light,* p. 116.

# Appendix A
# How God Uses Vision and Image*
## Mark Virkler

The best approach to discovering what God has to say on a subject is to gather all the Scripture from Genesis to Revelation on that subject and then study through it several times, asking God to speak to you and recording the insights you receive. Using the word search option of CompuBIBLE, we have gathered on the following pages verses that deal with dream, vision, seer, look, and eyes, along with occasional contextual verses that give clearer insight.

While asking God to grant you a spirit of revelation (Eph. 1:17, 18) study these verses, allowing God to reveal to you how He desires to use dream and vision in your life.

Index: Vision

Title: *The place of dream and vision in one's spiritual life.*

Range: GENESIS 1:1 to REVELATION 22:21

Subject—
1. dream;    2. vision;    3. seer;    4. look;    5. eyes

NOTE: CompuBIBLE uses parentheses to indicate words that do not appear in the original Greek, words which the King James Version shows in italics.

---

* This concordance study was first published in *Seduction?? A Biblical Response* by Thomas Reid & Mark Virkler.

**Mandates**

**Gen. 3:5** For God doth know that in the day ye eat thereof, then your eyes shall be opened, and ye shall be as gods, knowing good and evil.

**Gen. 3:6** And when the woman saw that the tree (was) good for food, and that it (was) pleasant to the eyes, and a tree to be desired to make (one wise), she took of the fruit thereof, and did eat, and gave also unto her husband with her; and he did eat.

**Gen. 3:7** And the eyes of them both were opened, and they knew that they (were) naked; and they sewed fig leaves together, and made themselves aprons.

**Num. 12:6** And he said, Hear now my words: If there be a prophet among you, I the Lord will make myself known unto him in a vision, (and) will speak unto him in a dream.

**1 Sam. 28:6** And when Saul inquired of the Lord, the Lord answered him not, neither by dreams, nor by Urim, nor by prophets.

**1 Sam. 28:15** And Samuel said to Saul, Why hast thou disquieted me, to bring me up? And Saul answered, I am sore distressed; for the Philistines make war against me, and God is departed from me, and answered me no more, neither by prophets, nor by dreams: therefore I have called thee, that thou mayest make known unto me what I shall do.

**Ps. 89:19** Then thou spakest in vision to thy holy one, and saidst, I have laid help upon (one that is) mighty; I have exalted (one) chosen out of the people.

**Hos. 12:10** I have also spoken by the prophets, and I have multiplied visions, and used similitudes, by the ministry of the prophets.

**Joel 2:28** And it shall come to pass afterward, (that) I will pour out my spirit upon all flesh; and your sons and your daughters shall prophesy, your old men shall dream dreams, your young men shall see visions. . .

**Acts 2:17** And it shall come to pass in the last days, saith God, I will pour out of my Spirit upon all flesh: and your sons and your daughters shall prophesy, and your young men shall see visions, and your old men shall dream dreams. . .

**John 5:19** Then answered Jesus and said unto them, Verily, verily, I say unto you, The Son can do nothing of himself, but what He

202

seeth the Father do: for what things soever He doeth, these also doeth the Son likewise.

**John 5:20** For the Father loveth the Son and showeth him all things that himself doeth: and he will show him greater works than these, that ye may marvel.

**John 8:38** I speak that which I have seen with my Father: and ye do that which ye have seen with your father.

## Opened Eyes

There is a place and a need to have the eyes of our heart opened, so we can see the vision of God. The Scriptures clearly state that not everyone has opened eyes. We must recognize this lack and need, and seek God that He would open the eyes of our hearts.

**Gen. 21:19** And God opened her eyes, and she saw a well of water; and she went, and filled the bottle with water, and gave the lad drink.

**Num. 22:31** Then the Lord opened the eyes of Balaam, and he saw the angel of the Lord standing in the way, and his sword drawn in his hand: and he bowed down his head, and fell flat on his face.

**Num. 24:2** And Balaam lifted up his eyes, and he saw Israel abiding (in his tents) according to their tribes; and the spirit of God came upon him.

**Num. 24:3** And he took up his parable, and said, Balaam the son of Beor hath said, and the man whose eyes are open hath said:

**Num. 24:4** He hath said, which heard the words of God, which saw the vision of the Almighty, falling (into a trance), but having his eyes open. . .

**Num. 24:15** And He took up his parable, and said, Balaam the son of Beor hath said, and the man whose eyes are open hath said:

**Num. 24:16** He hath said, which heard the words of God, and knew the knowledge of the most High, (which) saw the vision of the Almighty, falling (into a trance), but having his eyes open. . .

**Deut. 29:2** And Moses called upon all Israel, and said unto them, Ye have seen all that the Lord did before your eyes in the land of Egypt unto Pharaoh, and unto all his servants, and unto all his land;

**Deut. 29:3** The great temptations which thine eyes have seen, the signs, and those great miracles:

**Deut. 29:4** Yet the Lord hath not given you a heart to perceive, and eyes to see, and ears to hear, unto this day.

**1 Sam. 3:1** And the child Samuel ministered unto the Lord before Eli. And the word of the Lord was precious in those days; (there was) no open vision.

**1 Sam. 3:2** And it came to pass at that time, when Eli (was) laid down in his place, and his eyes began to wax dim, (that) he could not see;

**1 Sam. 3:3** And ere the lamp of God went out in the temple of the Lord, where the ark of God (was), and Samuel was laid down (to sleep);

**1 Sam. 3:4** That the Lord called Samuel: and he answered, Here (am) I.

**1 Sam. 3:5** And he ran unto Eli, and said, Here (am) I; for thou calledst me. And he said, I called not; lie down again. And he went and lay down.

**1 Sam. 3:6** And the Lord called yet again, Samuel. And Samuel arose and went to Eli, and said, Here (am) I; for thou didst call me. And he answered, I called not, my son; lie down again.

**1 Sam. 3:7** Now Samuel did not yet know the Lord, neither was the word of the Lord yet revealed unto him.

**1 Sam. 3:8** And the Lord called Samuel again the third time. And he arose and went to Eli, and said, Here (am) I; for thou didst call me. And Eli perceived that the Lord had called the child.

**1 Sam. 3:9** Therefore Eli said unto Samuel, Go, lie down: and it shall be, if he call thee, that thou shalt say, Speak, Lord; for thy servant heareth. So Samuel went and lay down in his place.

**1 Sam. 3:10** And the Lord came, and stood, and called as at other times, Samuel, Samuel. Then Samuel answered, Speak; for thy servant heareth.

**1 Sam. 3:15** And Samuel lay until the morning, and opened the doors of the house of the Lord. And Samuel feared to shew Eli the vision.

**2 Kings 6:15** And when the servant of the man of of God was risen early, and gone forth, behold, an host compassed the city both with horses and chariots. And his servant said unto him, Alas, my master! how shall we do?

**2 Kings 6:16** And he answered, Fear not: for they that (be) with us (are) more than those that (be) with them.

**2 Kings 6:17** And Elisha prayed, and said, Lord, I pray thee, open his eyes, that he may see. And the Lord opened the eyes of the young man; and he saw: and, behold, the mountain (was) full of horses and chariots of fire round about Elisha.

**Job 33:15** In a dream, in a vision of the night, when deep sleep falleth upon men, in slumberings upon the bed;

**Job 33:16** Then he openeth the ears of men, and sealeth their instruction.

**Ps. 119:18** Open thou mine eyes, that I may behold wondrous things out of thy law.

**Isa. 42:18** Hear, ye deaf; and look, ye blind, that ye may see.

**Isa. 42:19** Who (is) blind, but my servant? or deaf, as my messenger (that) I sent? who (is) blind as (he that is) perfect, and blind and the Lord's servant?

**Isa. 42:20** Seeing many things, but thou observest not; opening the ears, but he heareth not.

**Isa. 44:18** They have not known nor understood: for he hath shut their eyes, that they cannot see; (and) their hearts, that they cannot understand.

**Jer. 5:21** Hear now this, O foolish people, and without understanding; which have eyes, and see not; which have ears, and hear not. . .

**Lam. 2:9** Her gates are sunk into the ground; he hath destroyed and broken her bars: her king and her princes (are) among the Gentiles: the law (is) no (more); her prophets also find no vision from the Lord.

**Matt. 13:15** For this people's heart is waxed gross, and (their) ears are dull of hearing, and their eyes they have closed; lest at any time they should see with (their) eyes, and hear with (their) ears, and should understand with (their) heart, and should be converted, and I should heal them.

**Matt. 13:16** But blessed (are) your eyes, for they see: and your ears, for they hear.

**Mark 8:18** Having eyes, see ye not? and having ears, hear ye not? and do ye not remember?

**John 12:40** He hath blinded their eyes, and hardened their heart; that they should not see with (their) eyes, nor understand with (their) heart, and be converted, and I should heal them.

**Acts 28:27** For the heart of this people is waxed gross, and their ears are dull of hearing, and their eyes have they closed; lest they should see with (their) eyes, and hear with (their) ears, and understand with (their) heart, and should be converted, and I should heal them.

**Rom. 11:8** (According as it is written, God hath given them the spirit of slumber, eyes that should not see, and ears that they should not hear;) unto this day.

**Rom. 11:10** Let their eyes be darkened, that they may not see, and bow down their back alway.

**2 Cor. 4:18** While we look not at the things which are seen, but at the things which are not seen: for the things which are seen (are) temporal; but the things which are not seen (are) eternal.

### Looking to See

Scripture places great emphasis on lifting up our eyes and looking to see.

**Gen. 18:1** And the Lord appeared unto him in the plains of Mamre: and he sat in the tent door in the heat of the day;

**Gen. 18:2** And he lift up his eyes and looked, and, lo, three men stood by him: and when he saw (them), he ran to meet them from the tent door, and bowed himself toward the ground. . .

**Gen. 31:10** And it came to pass at the time that the cattle conceived, that I lifted up mine eyes, and saw in a dream, and, behold, the rams which leaped upon the cattle (were) ringstraked, speckled, and grisled.

**Gen. 31:11** And the angel of God spake unto me in a dream, (saying), Jacob: and I said, Here (am) I.

**Gen. 31:12** And he said, Lift up now thine eyes, and see, all the rams which leap upon the cattle (are) ringstraked, and grisled: for I have seen all that Laban doeth unto thee.

**Exod. 3:1** Now Moses kept the flock of Jethro his father in law, the priest of Midian: and he led the flock to the backside of the desert, and came to the mountain of God, (even) to Horeb.

**Exod. 3:2** And the angel of the Lord appeared unto him in a flame of fire out of the midst of a bush: and he looked, and, behold, the bush burned with fire, and the bush (was) not consumed.

**Exod. 3:3** And Moses said, I will now turn aside, and see this great sight, why the bush is not burnt.

**Exod. 3:4** And when the Lord saw that he turned aside to see, God called upon him out of the midst of the bush, and said, Moses, Moses. And he said, Here (am) I.

**Exod. 3:5** And he said, Draw not nigh hither: put off thy shoes from off thy feet, for the place whereon thou standest (is) holy ground.

**Exod. 3:6** Moreover he said, I (am) the God of thy father, the God of Abraham, the God of Isaac, and the God of Jacob. And Moses hid his face; for he was afraid to look upon God.

**Exod. 16:9** And Moses spake unto Aaron, Say unto all the congregation of the children of Israel, Come near before the Lord: for he hath heard your murmurings.

**Exod. 16:10** And it came to pass, as Aaron spake unto the whole congregation of the children of Israel, that they looked toward the wilderness, and, behold, the glory of the Lord appeared in the cloud.

**Exod. 16:11** And the Lord spake unto Moses saying. . .

**Josh. 5:13** And it came to pass, when Joshua was by Jericho, that he lifted up his eyes and looked, and, behold, there stood a man over against him with his sword drawn in his hand: and Joshua went unto him, and said unto him, (Art) thou for us, or for our adversaries?

**Josh. 5:14** And he said, Nay; but (as) captain of the host of the Lord am I now come. And Joshua fell on his face to the earth, and did worship, and said unto him, What saith my lord unto his servant?

**Josh. 5:15** And the captain of the Lord's host said unto Joshua, Loose thy shoe from off thy foot; for the place whereon thou standest (is) holy. And Joshua did so.

**1 Chron. 21:16** And David lifted up his eyes, and saw the angel of the Lord stand between the earth and the heaven, having a drawn sword in his hand stretched out over Jerusalem. Then David and the elders (of Israel, who were) clothed in sackcloth, fell upon their faces.

**Dan. 10:1** In the third year of Cyrus king of Persia, a thing was revealed unto Daniel, whose name was called Belteshazzar; and the thing (was) true, but the time appointed (was) long: and he understood the thing, and had understanding of the vision.

**Dan. 10:5** Then I lifted up mine eyes, and looked, and behold a certain man clothed in linen, whose loins (were) girded with fine gold of Uphaz:

**Dan. 10:6** His body also (was) like the beryl, and his face as the appearance of lightning, and his eyes as lamps of fire, and his arms and his feet like in colour to polished brass, and the voice of his words like the voice of a multitude.

**Dan. 10:7** And I Daniel alone saw the vision: for the men that were with me saw not the vision; but a great quaking fell upon them, so that they fled to hide themselves.

**Dan. 10:8** Therefore I was left alone, and saw this great vision, and there remained no strength in me: for my comeliness was turned in me into corruption, and I retained no strength.

**Dan. 10:9** Yet heard I the voice of his words: and when I heard the voice of his words, then I was in a deep sleep on my face, and my face toward the ground.

**Dan. 10:10** And, behold, a hand touched me, which set me upon my knees and (upon) the palms of my hands.

**Dan. 10:11** And he said unto me, O Daniel, a man greatly beloved, understand the words that I speak unto thee, and stand upright: for unto thee am I now sent. And when he had spoken this word unto me, I stood trembling.

**Dan. 10:12** Then said he unto me, Fear not, Daniel: for from the first day that thou didst set thine heart to understand, and to chasten thyself before thy God, thy words were heard, and I am come for thy words.

**Dan. 10:13** But the prince of the kingdom of Persia withstood me one and twenty days; but, lo, Michael, one of the chief princes came to help me; and I remained there with the kings of Persia.

**Dan. 10:14** Now I am come to make thee understand what shall befall thy people in the latter days: for yet the vision (is) for (many) days.

**Dan. 10:15** And when he had spoken such words unto me, I set my face toward the ground, and I became dumb.

**Dan. 10:16** And, behold, (one) like the similitude of the sons of men touched my lips: then I opened my mouth, and spake, and said unto him that stood before me, O my lord, by the vision my sorrows are turned upon me, and I have retained no strength.

**Ps. 5:3** My voice shalt thou hear in the morning, O Lord; in the morning will I direct (my prayer) unto thee, and will look up.

**Ps. 25:15** Mine eyes (are) ever toward the Lord; for he shall pluck my feet out of the net.

**Ps. 123:1** Unto thee lift I up mine eyes, O thou that dwellest in the heavens.

**Ps. 123:2** Behold, as the eyes of servants (look) unto the hand of their masters, (and) as the eyes of a maiden unto the hand of her mistress; so our eyes (wait) upon the Lord our God, until that he have mercy upon us.

**Ps. 141:8** But mine eyes (are) unto thee, O God the Lord: in thee is my trust; leave not my soul destitute.

**Isa. 8:17** And I will wait upon the Lord, that hideth his face from the house of Jacob, and I will look for him.

**Isa. 17:7** At that day shall a man look to his Maker, and his eyes shall have respect to the Holy One of Israel.

**Isa. 17:8** And he shall not look to the altars, the work of his hands, neither shall respect (that) which his fingers have made, either the groves, or the images.

**Isa. 40:26** Lift up your eyes on high, and behold who hath created these (things), that bringeth out their host by number: he calleth them all by names by the greatness of his might, for that (he is) strong in power; not one faileth.

**Ezek. 1:1** Now it came to pass in the thirtieth year, in the fourth (month), in the fifth (day) of the month, as I (was) among the captives by the river of Chebar, (that) the heavens were opened, and I saw visions of God.

**Ezek. 1:4** And I looked, and, behold, a whirlwind came out of the north, a great cloud, and a fire infolding itself, and a brightness (was) about it, and out of the midst thereof as the color of amber, out of the midst of the fire.

**Ezek. 2:9** And when I looked, behold, a hand (was) sent upon me; and, lo, a roll of a book (was) therein. . .

**Ezek. 8:3** And he put forth the form of a hand, and took me by a lock of mine head; and the spirit lifted me up between the earth and the heaven, and brought me in the visions of God to Jerusalem, to the door of the inner gate that looketh toward the north; where (was) the seat of the image of jealousy, which provoketh to jealousy.

**Ezek. 8:4** And, behold, the glory of the God of Israel (was) there, according to the vision that I saw in the plain.

**Ezek. 8:5** Then said he unto me, Son of man, lift up thine eyes now the way toward the north. So I lifted up mine eyes the way toward the north, and behold northward at the gate of the altar this image of jealousy in the entry.

209

**Ezek. 8:7**  And he brought me to the door of the court; and when I looked, behold a hole in the wall.

**Ezek. 10:1**  Then I looked, and, behold, in the firmament that was above the head of the cherubims there appeared over them as it were a sapphire stone, as the appearance of the likeness of a throne.

**Ezek. 10:9**  And when I looked, behind the four wheels by the cherubims, one wheel by one cherub, and another wheel by another cherub: and the appearance of the wheels (was) as the colour of a beryl stone.

**Ezek. 44:1**  Then he brought me back the way of the gate of the outward sanctuary which looketh toward the east; and it (was) shut.

**Ezek. 44:4**  Then brought he me the way of the north gate before the house: and I looked, and, behold, the glory of the Lord filled the house of the Lord: and I fell upon my face.

**Ezek. 44:5**  And the Lord said unto me, Son of man, mark well, and behold with thine eyes, and hear with thine ears all that I say unto thee concerning all the ordinances of the house of the Lord, and all the laws thereof; and mark well the entering in of the house, with every going forth of the sanctuary.

**Dan. 12:5**  Then I Daniel looked, and, behold, there stood other two, the one on this side of the bank of the river, and the other on that side of the bank of the river.

**Zech. 1:18**  Then lifted up mine eyes, and saw, and behold four horns.

**Zech. 2:1**  I lifted up mine eyes again, and looked, and behold a man with a measuring line in his hand.

**Zech. 4:2**  And said unto me, What seest thou? and I said, I have looked, And behold a candlestick all (of) gold, with a bowl upon the top of it, and his seven lamps thereon, and seven pipes to the seven lamps, which (are) upon the top thereof. . .

**Zech. 5:1**  Then I turned, and lifted up mine eyes, and looked, and behold a flying roll.

**Zech. 5:5**  Then the angel that talked with me went forth, and said unto me, Lift up now thine eyes, and see what (is) this that goeth forth.

**Zech. 5:9**  Then lifted I up mine eyes, and looked, and, behold, there came out two women, and the wind (was) in their wings; for they had wings like the wings of a stork: and they lifted up the ephah between the earth and the heaven.

**Zech. 6:1** And I turned, and lifted up mine eyes, and looked, and, behold, there came four chariots out from between two mountains; and the mountains (were) mountains of brass.

**Acts 7:55** But he, being full of the Holy Ghost, looked up steadfastly into the heaven, and saw the glory of God, and Jesus standing on the right hand of God. . .

**Rev. 4:1** After this I looked, and, behold, a door (was) opened in heaven: and the first voice which I heard (was) as it were of a trumpet talking with me; which said, Come up hither, and I will shew thee things which must be hereafter.

**Rev. 6:8** And I looked, and behold a pale horse: and his name that sat on him was Death, and Hell followed with him. And power was given unto them over the fourth part of the earth, to kill with sword, and with hunger, and with death, and with the beasts of the earth.

**Rev. 14:1** And I looked, and, lo, a Lamb stood on the Mount Sion, and with him an hundred forty (and) four thousand, having his Father's name written in their foreheads.

**Rev. 14:14** And I looked, and behold a white cloud, and upon the cloud (one) sat like unto the Son of man, having on his head a golden crown, and in his hand a sharp sickle.

**Rev. 15:5** And after that I looked, and, behold, the temple of the tabernacle of the testimony in heaven was opened. . .

## Seers
Prophets were also called seers.

**2 Sam. 15:27** . . . Zadok . . . a seer . . .
**2 Sam. 24:11** . . . Gad, David's seer . . .
**1 Chron. 25:5** . . . Heman the king's seer . . .
**1 Chron. 29:29** . . . Samuel the seer . . .
**2 Chron. 9:29** . . . Iddo the seer . . .
**2 Chron. 19:2** . . . Hanani the seer . . .
**2 Chron. 29:30** . . . Asaph the seer . . .
**2 Chron. 35:15** . . . Jeduthun the king's seer . . .
**Amos 7:12** . . . Amos . . . thou seer . . .

They were people who saw in the spiritual world the vision of Almighty God. This was a common title and office in Scripture and needs to be restored to the life of the church. We need to again train prophets who are seers. In the New Covenant the veil has been torn, and now we all have access directly before the throne room of Almighty God. We all may prophesy (1 Cor. 14:31).

**1 Sam. 9:9** (Beforetime in Israel, when a man went to inquire of God, thus he spake, Come, and let us go to the seer: for (he that is) now (called) a Prophet was beforetime called a Seer.)

**1 Sam. 9:10** Then said Saul to his servant, Well said; come, let us go. So they went unto the city where the man of God (was).

**1 Sam. 9:11** (And) as they went up the hill to the city, they found young maidens going out to draw water, and said unto them, Is the seer here?

**Responsibilities of Seers**

The responsibilities included consulting and advising kings, exhorting the people, delivering the Word of God to the people, and recording the Word of God.

**2 Sam. 24:11** For when David was up in the morning, the word of the Lord came unto the prophet Gad, David's seer, saying,

**2 Sam. 24:12** Go and say unto David, Thus saith the Lord, I offer thee three (things); choose thee one of them, that I may (do it) unto thee.

**2 Kings 17:13** Yet the Lord testified against Israel, and against Judah, by all the prophets, (and by) all the seers, saying, Turn ye from your evil ways, and keep my commandments (and) my statutes, according to all the law which I commanded your fathers, and which I sent to you by my servant the prophets.

**1 Chron. 9:22** All these (which were) chosen to be porters in the gates (were) two hundred and twelve. These were reckoned by their genealogy in their villages, whom David and Samuel the seer did ordain in their set office.

**1 Chron. 17:3** And it came to pass the same night, that the word of God came to Nathan, saying,

**1 Chron. 17:4** Go and tell David my servant, Thus saith the Lord, Thou shall not build me an house to dwell in. . .

**1 Chron. 17:15** According to all these words, and according to all this vision, so did Nathan speak unto David.

**1 Chron. 21:9** And the Lord spake unto Gad, David's seer, saying,

**1 Chron. 21:10** Go and tell David, saying, Thus saith the Lord, I offer thee three (things): choose thee one of them, that I may do (it) unto thee.

**1 Chron. 26:28** And all that Samuel the seer, and Saul the son of Kish, and Abner the son of Ner, and Joab the son of Zeruiah, had dedicated; (and) whosoever had dedicated (any thing, it was) under the hand of Shelomith, and of his brethren.

**1 Chron. 29:29** Now the acts of David the king, first and last, behold, they (are) written in the book of Samuel the seer, and in the book of Nathan the prophet, and in the book of Gad the seer. . . .

**2 Chron. 9:29** Now the rest of the acts of Solomon, first and last, (are) they not written in the book of Nathan the prophet, and in the prophecy of Ahijah the Shilonite, and in the visions of Iddo the seer against Jeroboam the son of Nebat?

**2 Chron. 12:15** Now the acts of Rehoboam, first and last, (are) they not written in the book of Shemaiah the prophet, and of Iddo the seer concerning genealogies? And (there were) wars between Rehoboam and Jeroboam continually.

**2 Chron. 16:7** And at that time Hanani the seer came to Asa king of Judah, and said unto him, Because thou hast relied on the king of Syria, and not relied on the Lord thy God, therefore is the host of the king of Syria escaped out of thine hand.

**2 Chron. 16:8** Were not the Ethiopians and the Lubims a huge host, with very many chariots and horsemen? yet, because thou didst rely on the Lord, he delivered them into thine hand.

**2 Chron. 16:9** For the eyes of the Lord run to and fro throughout the whole earth, to shew himself strong in the behalf of (them) whose heart (is) perfect toward him. Herein thou hast done foolishly: therefore from henceforth thou shalt have wars.

**2 Chron. 16:10** Then Asa was wroth with the seer, and put him in a prison house; for (he was) in a rage with him because of this (thing). And Asa oppressed (some) of the people the same time.

**2 Chron. 29:25** And he set the Levites in the house of the Lord with cymbals, with psalteries, and with harps, according to the commandment of David, and of Gad the king's seer, and Nathan the prophet: for (so was) the commandment of the Lord by his prophets.

**2 Chron. 32:32** Now the rest of the acts of Hezekiah, and his goodness, behold, they (are) written in the vision of Isaiah the prophet, the son of Amoz, (and) in the book of the kings of Judah and Israel.

**2 Chron. 33:18** Now the rest of the acts of Manasseh, and his prayer unto his God, and the words of the seers that spake to him in the name of the Lord God of Israel, behold, they (are written) in the book of the kings of Israel.

**2 Chron. 33:19** His prayer also, and (how God) was intreated of him, and all his sins, and his trespass, and the places wherein he built high places, and set up groves and graven images, before he was humbled: behold, they (are) written among the sayings of the seers.

**2 Chron. 35:15** And the singers the sons of Asaph (were) in their place, according to the commandment of David, and Asaph, and Heman, and Jeduthun the king's seer; and the porters (waited) at every gate; they might not depart from their service; for their brethren the Levites prepared for them.

**Ezek. 40:2** In the visions of God brought he me into the land of Israel, and set me upon a very high mountain, by which (was) as the frame of a city on the south.

**Ezek. 40:4** And the man said unto me, Son of man, behold with thine eyes, and hear with thine ears, and set thine heart upon all that I shall shew thee; for to the intent that I might shew (them) unto thee (art) thou brought hither: declare all that thou seest to the house of Israel.

**Ezek. 40:6** Then came he unto the gate which looketh toward the east, and went up the stairs thereof, and measured the threshold of the gate, (which was) one reed broad; and the other threshold (of the gate, which was) one reed broad.

**Hab. 2:2** And the Lord answered me, and said, Write the vision, and make (it) plain upon tables, that he may run that readeth it.

**Hab. 2:3** For the vision (is) yet for an appointed time, but at the end it shall speak, and not lie: though it tarry, wait for it; because it will surely come, it will not tarry.

**Rev. 1:10** I was in the Spirit on the Lord's day, and heard behind me a great voice, as of a trumpet. . .

**Rev. 1:11** Saying, I am Alpha and Omega, the first and the last: and, What that sest, write in a book . . . .

**Rev. 1:14** His head and (his) hairs (were) white like wool, as white as snow; and his eyes (were) as a flame of fire. . .

# Appendix B
# Pathfinder for Christian Counseling
# M.L. Huffman

In this pathfinder, the term "Christian counseling" includes both the integration of psychology with Christianity, and the purely biblical counseling approach. This pathfinder is not aimed towards individual, specific problems; rather, it lists resources for looking at the field and process as a whole, primarily those books published in the English language, and primarily in the United States since 1960, because the integration of Christianity and psychology is an aspect of psychology that has only taken off in recent years.

The bibliography includes sources pertinent to the *combination* of the two fields. It excludes most pure psychology sources (except for one or two encyclopedia/dictionary sources), as well as pure Bible study sources. It also excludes the Bible, which is both automatically known and used. The psychology sources are simple enough to be understood by those who do not have a doctorate in psychology, but should be detailed enough to give useful information.

This bibliography does not include call numbers due to the number of locations and cataloging methods in use.

Chapter six identified four perspectives on Christian counseling. This bibliography does not attempt to support any one perspective, but rather to show the sources available to the interested person trying to find a way through the maze.

**Subject headings**
The most helpful subject headings in the library card catalog are:
Christianity—Psychology
Psychology—Pastoral
Pastoral Psychology

217

Pastoral Counseling
Psychology and Religion
Christianity—Bibliography
Psychology—Bibliography
Interpersonal Relations—Religious Aspects—Christianity

There are usually two significantly different understandings of
these headings. One understanding relates to the integration
of psychology and Christianity; the other relates to the psychology *of*
religion, or religious experience, which is a different area entirely.

**Call numbers**
*Library of Congress*

| BR | BF | BV | BL |
|---|---|---|---|
| 110 | 637 | 4012 | 53 |

*Dewey Decimal*
253.5

**Existing bibliographies**
Beit-Hallahmi, B. (1978). *Psychoanalysis and religion: A bibliography.* Norwood, PA: Norwood Editions.
 A selective bibliography of books judged to be "attempts to relate
 religion and psychoanalysis in a meaningful way." Arranged in
 two major sections: (1) a classified subject arrangement under
 thirty-nine subject headings; (2) the same articles in author order.
 Note especially subject section number thirty-nine: "Psychoanalytic
 Influences on Pastoral Counseling."
Berkowitz, M.I. (1967). *Social scientific studies of religion: a
 bibliography.* Pittsburgh: University of Pittsburgh Press.
 A subject guide to books on religion, including psychology-related
 fields. Includes author index. Although not limited to Christianity
 or to counseling, it is a good source book for finding potentially
 helpful books.
Kepple, R.J. (1981). *Reference works for theological research: An
 annotated selective bibliographical guide* (2nd ed.). Lanham, MD:
 University Press of America.
 An excellent annotated bibliography of reference works for
 theological research. Includes one chapter on pastoral psychology
 and counseling. Has index to authors, editors, titles, and
 alternative titles. Extremely helpful guide to literature sources.

*Subject guide to books in print, 1985-1986.* (1985). New York: R.W. Bowker, Co.

This is probably the best source for current books on the whole field of Christian counseling (under Pastoral Counseling or Pastoral Psychology subject headings), given that most university and public libraries include extremely limtied selections in this area.

## Dictionaries

Henry, C.R.H. (1973). *Baker's dictionary of Christian ethics.* Grand Rapids, MI: Baker Book House.

"While this dictionary aims to be authentically evangelical, it does not impose upon readers a partisan view that obscures all differences between, for example, Calvinist and Arminian or pacifist and non-pacifist traditions. In some instances . . . contributors were deliberately chosen for their differing perspective."—Preface. Signed articles, many with bibliographic references added.

Macquarrie, J. (Ed.) (1967). *Dictionary of Christian ethics.* Philadelphia: Westminster Press.

This is a small encyclopedia on specific topics, and represents the thought of many minds, from an interfaith perspective. It includes historical background, analysis, signed articles and brief bibliographical references.

Wolman, B.B. (Ed.) (1973). *Dictionary of behavioral science.* New York: Van Nostrand Reinhold.

An alphabetically arranged dictionary covering all areas of psychology and applied psychology. Prepared for students and interested laymen; it attempts to keep matters as simple as possible. Includes a classification of mental disorders and the "Ethical Standards of Psychologists."

## Encyclopedias

Archer, G.L. (1982). *Encyclopedia of biblical difficulties.* Grand Rapids, MI: Zondervan.

Although not a counseling-oriented tool, it is a good theological source, intended "for all who are troubled by apparent contradictions in the Bible." It is a book-by-book look at difficulties within the Bible and a mixture of "final" or "plausible" solutions to those. Includes person, subject, and Scripture indexes.

Goldenson, R.M. (1970). *The encyclopedia of human behavior; Psychology, psychiatry, and mental health.* (2 Vols.). Garden City, NY: Doubleday.

Intended "to present essential information on . . . man's knowledge of himself . . . in a form that will be readily understood by the student and the interested layman, yet useful to the professional worker." Begins with a "category index" (a classified list of articles) and ends with a selected bibliography and a detailed subject index. Includes more than 1000 articles, some with illustrative cases.

Barrett, D.B. (1982). *World Christian encyclopedia: A comparative study of churches and religions in the modern world, AD 1900-2000.* Oxford: Oxford University Press.

In essence, an encyclopedia atlas of Christianity in the world. It would be helpful to one counseling internationals, primarily for a somewhat up-to-date perspective on Christianity in various cultures. A fascinating look at the world.

Benner, D.G. (Ed.) (1985). *Baker encyclopedia of psychology.* Grand Rapids, MI: Baker Book House.

Contains 1050 entries in one volume. Provides representative treatment of the entire field of psychology, identifying the issues and applications of particular importance from the Christian perspective and suggesting methods of evaluation in light of biblical thinking. Includes signed articles, contributor list and category index.

Corsini, R.J. (1984). *Encyclopedia of psychology* (4 vols.) New York: John Wiley and Sons.

Although not Christian or religious in orientation, it is a reference source both for professionals who practice or do research in human behavior as well as for physicians, lawyers, and ministers. It is useful for basic spot information, summary information, or textbook information. A good, basic source, written for the average intelligent layman.

**Indexes and abstracts**

*Pastoral care and counseling abstracts.* (7 vols.) (1972-78). Richmond, VA: Joint Council on Research.

Maloy, W.V. and Frey, G.H. (1979). *Abstracts of research in pastoral care and counseling.* Annual. Richmond, VA: Joint Council on Research.

These two sources list known published, unpublished and in-progress research for the year, giving abstracts in a classified arrangement. Includes an author index. Abstracts vary in quality and length.

American Theological Library Assocation (1985). *Religion Index one: periodicals (RIO). Vol. 16. Jan. 1983-Dec. 1984.* Edited by P.D. Petersen, Chicago: The Association.

Subtitle: *A subject index to periodical literature including an author index with abstracts and a book review index.* Indexes 381 journal titles—one of the best sources for periodical literature in combined fields. Indexes all periodicals listed in this bibliography.

Association of Christian Librarians (1984). *Christian periodical index.* Houghton, NY: Houghton College Press.

Published quarterly, cumulated annually and every three years, covering sixty-four periodicals and journals, including some not included by *RIO.* Indexes articles back to 1956. A subject and title guide only.

*Comprehensive Dissertation index ten-year cumulation 1973-1982, Vol. 32, philosophy, religion* (1984). Ann Arbor, MI: University Microfilms International.

The Comprehensive Dissertation Index is "the only definitive printed reference to virtually every doctoral dissertation accepted in North America since 1861." As such, the "philosophy and religion" index is a useful (key-word) source for dissertations on the general topic of Christian counseling, as well as for the individual problems. The psychology volumes 17 through 19, and the Social Sciences and Humanities Supplement could also be helpful.

*Psychological abstracts* (1969). Arlington, VA: The American Psychological Association.

A monthly compilation of nonevaluative summaries of the world's literature in psychology and related disciplines. A classified arrangement, with subject and author indexes. Primarily useful topics are Pastoral Counseling, Religious Beliefs, and specific problems. Indexes many of the Christianity and Psychology journals.

**Journals**
*Bibliotheca Sacra* (q.) Dallas, TX: Dallas Theological Seminary. 1843—.

"Coming from a conservative Christian seminary, this quarterly journal, devoted principally to studies of biblical topics, reflects its conservative sponsors in its general view of religious questions and the Bible in particular. . . This is not to suggest that its scholarship is suspect, but that it does have a committed view. The Review section includes articles from other journals as well as books."— *Magazines for Libraries.*

*Christian Scholar's Review* (q) Grand Rapids, MI: Calvin College, 1970—.

A quarterly, thematic journal carrying three to four articles and a number of book reviews in each issue. Its primary objective is "the integration of Christian faith and learning on both the intra- and inter-disciplinary levels" (from *Magazines for Libraries*). It provides not only occasional directly related articles, but also the opportunity to develop all aspects of Christian thought.

*Christianity Today* (20/yr). Carol Stream, IL: Christianity Today, Inc. 1956—.

*Christianity Today* speaks "for the Evangelical side of Protestantism. A very readable magazine, it has a strong biblical flavor that covers some social and political issues as well" (from *Magazines for Libraries*). In these areas, it often includes articles of interest to the field of Christian counseling. "This is certainly one of the best general conservative Protestant religious magazines available" (*Magazines for Libraries*).

*Evangelical Quarterly* (q). Exeter, England: The Paternoster Press Ltd. 1929—.

Called by the editors "a theological review, international in scope and outlook, in defense of the historic Christian faith," it reflects the British scene fairly heavily. Articles are fairly long, written mostly for the specialist. Occasionally includes articles of interest for counselors. Includes book reviews.

*Journal of Religion* (q). Chicago: University of Chicago. 1921—.

"One of the oldest American religious journals directed toward the scholarly public, it is free from polemics or any specific doctrinal position. The articles are mainly in the Christian tradition, but not exclusively, and the editors include articles from disciplines other than theology insofar as they have bearing on the role of religion in our cultural life" (from *Magazines for Libraries.*). Book reviews are excellent.

*Journal of Pastoral Care* (q). Kutztown, PA: Association for Clinical Pastoral Education. 1947—.
Quarterly publication of the Association for Clinical Pastoral Education. Indexed in both *RIO* and *Psychological Abstracts*. Emphasis is primarily for hospital counselors, but is nevertheless a good source for the Christian counselor in other areas.

*Journal of Pastoral Practice* (q). Laverock, PA: Christian Counseling and Educational Foundation.
A quarterly journal published by Jay Adams, with a definite commitment to Adam's nouthetic counseling perspective. As such, the totality of the journal is devoted to counseling.

*Journal for Psychology and Christianity* (q). Farmington Hills, MI: Christian Association for Psychological Studies. 1982).
The quarterly publication of CAPS, this journal is based upon a "genuine commitment to superior scientific enterprise in the theoretical and applied social sciences and theology" (from Encyclopedia of Associations). Indexed in *RIO* and *Psychological Abstracts*.

*Journal of Psychology and Theology* (q). La Mirada, CA: Biola College, 1973—.
A quarterly journal published by Rosemead School of Psychology. Its purpose is to "communicate recent scholarly thinking on the interrelationships of psychological and theological concepts and to consider the application of these concepts to a variety of professional settings." Articles in other journals are reviewed, as well as books. Winter issues include index for previous year. Indexed in *RIO* and *Psychological Abstracts*.

*Leadership: A practical journal for church leaders.* (q). Carol Stream, IL: Christianity Today, Inc. 1980—.
A quarterly publication aimed toward church leaders. As such it occasionally includes articles directly related to the counseling process. Its "To Illustrate" section invariably gives good ways to drive a point home. It also helps counselors handle stress.

*Journal of Religious Ethics* (semiannual). Knoxville, TN: University of Tennessee, 1973).

*Journal of supervision and training in ministry* (annual). Chicago: N. Central Reg, ACPE and Central Reg, AACP. 1978—.

*Journal of the Evangelical Theological Society* (q). Wheaton, IL: Evangelical Theological Society. 1958—.

*Pastoral psychology* (q). New York: Human Sciences Press. 1950—.

## Biographical sources

Bowden, H. (1977). *Dictionary of American religious biography*. Westport, CT: Greenwood Press.

Dictionary arrangements of 425 prominent American religious figures from many theological perspectives, geographical sections, vocational patterns, ethnic identities, and both sexes. Includes appendix with denominational affiliation, and birthplace data.

Fleck, J.R. and Carter, J.D. (Eds.) (1981). *Psychology and Christianity: Integrative readings*. Nashville: Abingdon.

The articles and background data give a good introduction to the bias of many current notables in Christian counseling. Apart from this, the book is a compilation of readings on the integration of psychology and Christianity. Includes index, some references.

*Who's who in religion* (3rd rev.). (1985). Chicago: Marquis Who's Who.

As with the other *Who's Who* publications, this is a biographical listing of people noted in the field, in most cases with the record completed by the subjects themselves.

## Handbooks, directories, manuals, almanacs

Adams, J.E. (1973). *The Christian counselor's manual: The sequel and companion volume to* Competent to Counsel. Grand Rapids, MI: Baker Book House.

A ready reference format, functioning as a sequel *to Competent Counsel* and assuming the principles of that book throughout. It is a "how-to" manual for Adams' nouthetic (from the Greek *noutheto,* meaning "to admonish, warn, instruct"). Includes person, subject, and Scripture indexes and some bibliographic references.

American Association of Pastoral Counselors (1979). *1979-80 Directory*. Washington, D.C.: The Association.

Published at irregular intervals. The main portion of this work is an alphabetical list of members, giving exact name, academic degrees, full address, phone number, relation to the AAPC, and church affiliation of each. Also has a directory of institutional members, a list of affiliate members, and a geographical directory of the U.S. and Canada.

Craddock, J. (1983). *Counselor's desk reference: Counselor training course*. Unpublished manuscript.

A training manual for counselors, not intending to integrate biblical truth with psychology, but developing a "unique counseling system based entirely on the Word of God" (from the Preface). Describes characteristics of a biblical counselor, procedures, legal aspects, techniques, specific problem areas, and tools.

Donaldson, E. (1984). *Neues Leben counselor's manual* (2nd ed.). (Available from Neues Leben International, 10255 N. 32nd Street, Phoenix, AZ 85028).

A biblical counseling manual, in one volume, with a supplement volume of diagrams and other teaching material. An aid to providing "one-on-one exhortation" to others.

Triandis, H.C. and Lambert, W.W. (Eds.) (1980). *Handbook of cross-cultural psychology* (vols. 1-6). Boston: Allyn and Bacon.

This handbook in six volumes is composed of chapters written by different authors covering aspects of cross-cultural psychology. Each chapter concludes with an extensive bibliography. Although written from a secular perspective, it could be quite helpful to a Christian counselor in understanding cultural variations, especially given Christianity's predisposition to worldwide interaction.

## Machine-readable data bases

American Theological Library Association. *ATLA Religion Database* Machine-readable data file. Chicago: The Association.

Available online through BRS and through Lockheed/Dialog. The online database includes *Religion Index One* (RIO) Volumes one through four (1949-59) and twelve (1975—), all of *Religion Index Two: Multi-Author Works* (RIT) (1960—), and all of the *Research in Ministry* abstracts. 250,000 bibliographic items. File 190 for Dialog. Does include a number of non-English publications and articles. $48 per online connect hour, 17¢ per full record printed offline.

The American Psychological Association. *PsychINFO*. Machine-readable data file. Arlington, VA: The Association.

Available from Lockheed/Dialog. $55 per online connect hour, 20¢ per full record printed offline; 35¢ per full record typed or displayed online. File 11. 1967 to present, 493,000 records, monthly updates.

## Associations

American Association of Pastoral Counselors, 9508A Lee Highway, Fairfax, VA 22031. (703) 385-6867. James W. Ewing, PhD., Executive Director.

For all faiths. Aims to set standards and establish criteria for adequate training and practice of pastoral counseling, to provide certification for religious professionals engaged in specialized ministries of counseling, and to approve church-related centers.

Christian Association for Psychological Studies (CAPS), 26705 Farmington Road, Farmington Hills, MI 48018. (313) 477-1350. Dr. J. Harold Ellens, Executive Director.

Aims to help members cooperatively as Christians to explore the fields of social work, psychology, and psychotherapy for a better insight into personality and interpersonal relations and "to articulate and promote the Lordship of Christ in these scientific disciplines."

**Journal article**

McQuilkin, J.R. (1977) The behavioral sciences under the authority of Scripture. *Journal of the Evangelical Theological Society,* 20, 31-43.

Probably the classic article in regard to the integration of psychology and Christianity. "The functional control of Scripture over any discipline will vary in direct proportion to the overlap of that discipline with the substance of biblical revelation. . . . For integration to take place with revelation coming out on top, there must be a commitment to the proposition that Scripture must be in functional control" (from abstract in *RIO*).

**Books**

Adams, J.E. (1970). *Competent to counsel.* Phillipsburg, NJ: Presbyterian and Reformed Publishing.

A reaction to his frustration with secular Freudian and Rogerian techniques, this functions as Adams' polemic and apologetic approach to his form of biblical counseling (called *nouthetic,* from the Greek, "to admonish, warn, instruct"). Includes subject, name, and Scripture indexes.

Carter, J.D. and Narramore, B. (1979). *The integration of psychology and theology:* An introduction. Grand Rapids: Zondervan.

An introduction to the integration of the fields. A precursor to *Psychology and Christianity.* Includes index, annotated bibliography.

Collins, G.R. (1980). *Christian counseling: A comprehensive guide.* Waco: TX: Word Books.

For professionals, lay people, and pastors. Each chapter discusses what the Bible says about problems, causes and effects, counseling techniques, and ways in which particular difficulties can be prevented. Includes index and bibliographic references.

Collins, G.R. (1980). *Helping people grow: Practical approaches to Christian counseling.* Santa Ana, CA: Vision House.

As a collection of perspectives on the field of Christian counseling, this book surveys a wide range of outlooks from authors "who (perhaps with two or three exceptions) assume that the Bible is the Word of God and that the Scriptures must be the basis for our Christian counseling positions." Collins includes a brief introduction to the contributors themselves, causing this work to function as a good biographical source as well as a good analysis of the field. Includes an index and bibliographical references.

Collins, G.R. (1981). *Psychology and theology: Prospects for integration.* Abingdon: Nashville.

Composed primarily of lectures given in 1979 at Fuller Seminary's Ninth Finch Symposium in Psychology and Religion. Sequel, parallel volume to Collins (1979). Responses to Collins' ideas are included in Chapter 4. Includes subject index, name index, and references.

Collins, G.R. (1977). *The rebuilding of psychology: an integration of psychology and Christianity.* Wheaton: Tyndale.

One of the more helpful surveys of basic issues on the integration of psychology and theology. Especially helpful is Collins' nontechnical summary of the underlying presuppositions held by most non-Christian psychologists (empiricism, determinism, naturalism, reductionism) and his evaluation and modification of these assumptions in the light of biblical revelation.

Crabb, L.J. (1975). *Basic principles of biblical counseling.* Grand Rapids: MI: Zondervan.

Crabb, with a Ph.D. in clinical psychology, sets forth here his *preliminary* model for counseling theory and practice which he believes to be consistent with biblical revelation. He attempts to present thoroughly biblical ways to deal with the problems of people rather than solutions relying on the wisdom and power of man.

Crabb, L.J. (1977). *Effective biblical counseling.* Grand Rapids, MI: Zondervan.

Subtitle: *A model for helping caring Christians become capable counselors.* An expansion of his earlier model (Crabb, 1975), this is written for the lay person, and functions as a counseling model which will work as a part of the local church. No index or bibliographic references.

Farnsworth, K.E. (1981). *Integrating psychology and theology: Elbows together but hearts apart.* Washington, D.C.: University Press of America.

From an "all truth is God's truth" perspective, it basically builds a case for the integration of the two disciplines. Chapters cover the psychological, theological, and anthropological bases for integration. Includes bibliographic references, author and subject indexes. Also examines and evaluates different Christian models.

Hoffman, J.C. (1979). *Ethical confrontation in counseling.* Chicago: University of Chicago Press.

Much psychotherapeutic theory emphasizes the need for the counselor to maintain "unconditional positive regard" and avoid ethical confrontations. Hoffman argues that the tension between ethics and psychotherapy is not inevitable and that there can be a legitimate place for moral challenge in a responsible clinical setting.

Hurding, R. (1985). *Roots and shoots: A guide to counseling and psychotherapy.* London: Hodder and Stoughton.

An overview of the history of psychotherapy, and a Christian response to those psychotherapies. Presents theories and practices of Freud, Skinner, Rogers, Laing, etc.; also portrays Lake, Tournier, Oden, Kelsey, Collins, Crabb, and Adams. Written from an integrationist perspective. Includes index.

Jung, C.G. (1938). *Psychology and religion.* New Haven: Yale University Press.

These three compact essays are based on Jung's Terry Lectures delivered at Yale in 1937. They give the reader an overview of Jung's understanding of the religious function as it concerns individual experience. Because of the impact of Jungian psychology on much of Christian counseling, this would be a helpful introduction to his thought. Includes bibliographic references.

Kirwan, W.T. (1984). *Biblical concepts for Christian counseling: A case for integrating psychology and theology.* Grand Rapids, MI: Baker Book House.

Although this is perhaps not "the definitive work on the topic, it is clearly one of the most substantive" (from the Preface). With earned doctorates in Christian ministry and in clinical psychology, Kirwin is at least qualified to work on the issue. Attempts to sort through, define and expand the differing theories present. Includes index and bibliography.

Kelsey, M.T. (1982). *Christo-psychology*. New York: Crossroad.
This book is intended to be a very practical and accessible guide to help people who wish to combine the insights of Jungian depth psychology with those of vital Christianity. Includes bibliographic references for more technical or detailed works.

Koteskey, R.L. (1980). *Psychology from a Christian perspective*. Nashville: Abingdon.
An integrationist perspective on the issue, functioning as a broad overview attempting to bridge the hostility between the two disciplines. It examines major systems, comparative and physiological psychology, human development, sensation and perception, learning and cognitive theories, motivation, personality, theory, adjustment and maladjustment, and social psychology. Includes index and bibliography.

Meier, P.D., Minirith, F.B., and Wichern, F.B. (1982). *Introduction to psychology and counseling: Christian perspectives and applications*. Grand Rapids, MI: Baker Book House.
A good introduction to the integration of the fields, with some helpful information, but not an instruction manual in counseling. Textbook style—extensive bibliography.

Myers, D.G. (1978). *The human puzzle: Psychological research and Christian belief* (A Harper/CAPS Book). San Francisco: Harper and Row.
Part of the Christian Perspectives on Counseling and the Behavioral Sciences series. Correlates the latest (1978) findings of psychology with the historic Hebrew-Christian understanding of human nature. Includes bibliographic references and index.

Vitz, P.C. (1977). *Psychology as religion: The cult and self-worship*. Grand Rapids, MI: Eerdmans.
As a criticism of modern psychology, this functions as a useful balance to the general literature. Includes subject and name indexes as well as bibliographic references.